THOUGHT CONTROL IN PREWAR JAPAN

THOUGHT CONTROL IN PREWAR JAPAN

Richard H. Mitchell

CORNELL UNIVERSITY PRESS ITHACA AND LONDON

First published 1976 by Cornell University Press.
Published in the United Kingdom by Cornell University Press Ltd., 2–4 Brook Street, London W1Y 1AA.

International Standard Book Number 0–8014–1002–9
Library of Congress Catalog Card Number 75–39566
Printed in the United States of America
Librarians: Library of Congress cataloging information appears on the last page of the book.

TO YOSHIKO

Contents

Contents

Tables

Charts

Preface

The modernization of Japan is a phenomenon that has attracted a great deal of attention. Economists in developing nations measure their progress against Japan's mighty leap from the Middle Ages to modern times, and Japanese and American scholars analyze the accomplishments of Japan's modern century. Some scholars view these years as a time of triumph, with Japan held up as the example of successful modernization in Asia. Others, who are concerned with the human costs involved, see not a succession of triumphs but a sad era of governmental repression and exploitation of the people—a tale of harsh laws, violated civil rights, rising militarism, and aggressive imperialism.

The deterministic school of history views the liberalism of the 1920's as shallow and doomed to degenerate into the aggressive imperialism of the 1930's. The Peace Preservation Law of 1925 and the elaborate system of thought control constructed upon it are roundly attacked as part of the framework supporting what some considered "fascism." Not surprisingly, few objective studies on the prewar system of thought control have emerged from this deeply held anger.

There is more than a little irony in the fact that Japanese scholars have paid so little attention to the legal and administrative techniques used to control thought. During the 1930's, critical scholarship on the Peace Preservation Law was forbidden by the authorities, who seized offending publications. After Japan's defeat the scholarly world imposed a kind of self-censorship. The thought-control system was bad, and interwar officials were fascists, so why bother to explain the system from the government's viewpoint?

My purpose here is to investigate this largely untouched subject. A review through the Meiji era (1868–1912) and the Taisho period (1912–1926) of the government's attitude toward subversives is followed by a study of the planning, drafting, enactment, application, revision, and significance of the Peace Preservation Law. The development of special techniques for handling ideological offenders requires detailed analysis, beginning with the first application of the Peace Preservation Law in the arrest of members of the Kyoto Student Association during the winter of 1925–1926 and continuing with the mass arrest of 1,600 suspects on March 15, 1928. Was the Japanese treatment of thought criminals (persons who had thoughts deemed by the government to be criminal) unique, especially the controversial use of *tenkō* (conversion)? Why was it that among the tens of thousands of people arrested for suspected violations of the peace law only one Japanese was ever executed?[1] Are there any similarities with thought-control techniques employed in Nazi Germany, Stalinist Russia, and Maoist China? In exploring the answers to these and other significant questions, this book turns the historical spotlight on a dark corner of Japan's modern history, and re-examines controversial issues on which there has been much speculation (as for example on the repressiveness of the prewar government). It also contributes to our understanding of the limitations of prewar democracy, the rise of a highly authoritarian government during the 1930's, and the deep divisions in postwar politics.

We know much less about interwar bureaucrats than about leading political and military figures. Using official suppression of heresy as a cue, this study reappraises the role of justice officials, police, and others who formulated and then enforced thought-control policies. Hiranuma Kiichirō is one example of an important conservative who has been badly misunderstood and stigmatized with the label "fascist." As a leading figure in the creation of the control apparatus, and as a representative of the conservatives who acted as a primary check against a much more repressive system promoted by civilian and military

1. The single exception was the execution of Ozaki Hotsumi on November 7, 1944. Chalmers Johnson, *An Instance of Treason*, 188–197.

radicals, Hiranuma deserves our attention. Justice officials, especially thought procurators, since they led in the government's antisubversives war, are also brought into the historical spotlight.

Japan's handling of subversives was a great success, as was manipulation of public sentiment. Antiwar and antistate protest was silenced, with nearly everyone strongly supporting the war effort. Naturally, the question arises as to whether this was due to sociocultural reasons or to the effect of enacted law, or to the efforts of police, procurators, judges, education officials, and others within the thought-control bureaucracy. The answer is that both the sociocultural and the administrative mechanisms played important roles, and that one without the other would not have been nearly so successful.

While this book does contain information about the victims of state power, it is concerned chiefly with the authorities who devised the rules and saw to their enforcement. Books on the victims, or by them, are plentiful. As a believer in freedom of expression, I do sympathize with those who were beaten, jailed, or restricted in other ways. Nevertheless, although this book is in no way designed to whitewash or excuse those who suppressed liberal ideas and democratic tendencies, great care has been taken to present official views fairly and objectively. Much criticism of the Japanese thought-control program has proved fatuous, as have the angry self-serving complaints of Marxist scholars who have harshly condemned the entire prewar elite.

The analysis ends on the eve of the Pacific War, with the final revision of the Peace Preservation Law and the launching of the preventive detention system which acted as a capstone for the thought-control structure. Japanese scholars disagree over terms like "prewar" and "wartime." For some the wartime era began with the 1931 takeover of Manchuria, but for others it started when Japan went to war with China in 1937. "Prewar," as used in this book, means prior to the Pacific War (1941–1945), and "interwar" means between the end of World War I and the start of the Pacific War.

Widely ranging secret documents and open sources have been used. Most important are Justice Ministry documents: shorthand records of conferences, instructions, special reports, and others. Among the most valuable is *Shisō Kenkyū Shiryō Tokushū* (Thought Research Materials, Special Number), which is regarded by Professor Watanabe Tōru, Director of the Research Center for Materials on Social Problems at Kyoto University, as "of the highest level of importance."[2] Memoirs of key men like Hiranuma Kiichirō, Suzuki Kisaburō, and Shiono Suehiko are used to supplement these documents. Although there are no autobiographies or biographies of leading thought procurators like Hirata Susumu, Ikeda Katsu, and Tozawa Shigeo, their views on thought control are well articulated in secret documents, books, and postwar interviews. (Tozawa's feelings, for instance, about investigating his former teacher Minobe Tatsukichi, who was accused of writing statements disrespectful to the emperor, are detailed by Miyazawa Toshiyoshi [see Bibliography].) Budget information for the Justice Ministry's Thought Section, if it exists, is hidden someplace away from the eyes of prying scholars.

Documents for the Home Ministry are scarcer. In an effort to destroy documents prior to the arrival of Allied troops, a huge bonfire was fed the secret files of the Metropolitan Police Headquarters for a week in August 1945.[3] Incinerated were the shorthand records of meetings of vice-ministers and bureau chiefs and of the frequent conferences of prefectural police officials.[4] While not as harmful as the burning of books by the First Emperor of the Ch'in dynasty, the loss of these records does leave a gap. Fortunately, most of this information can be pieced together from other sources. Even justice documents are very helpful, since the thought police supplied justice officials with raw information. Among the thought police materials used are *Tokkō Geppō* (Monthly Report of the Special Higher Police), collections of regulations, instruction manuals, the private collection of former Vice-Minister Kobashi Ichita (see *Taisho Kōki Keihokyoku Kankō Shakai Undō Shiryō)*, the report on the March 15, 1928, arrest (in *Gendaishi*

2. Watanabe's comment is in an advertisement promoting a document series published by Tōyō Bunkasha of Kyoto, Shakai Mondai Shiryō Kenkyūkai (ed.), *Shakai Mondai Shiryō Sōsho.*
3. Personal interview with a former officer of the Special Higher Police, Tokyo, August 16, 1966.
4. Personal interview with Professor Satō Seizaburō, Tokyo, July 27, 1972.

Shiryō, XVI), and instructions on the subject of *tenkō*. Documents are supplemented by the semiofficial *Naimushōshi*, which among other things gives former Home Minister Wakatsuki Reijirō's position on the Peace Preservation Law. As in the case of the Justice Ministry, detailed budget information is not available.

Records of House of Representatives and House of Peers committee meetings and floor debates for all peace-law bills, from 1922 to 1941, together with all available Privy Council material are explored. The Privy Council shorthand record for the debate on the Emergency Imperial Ordinance of 1928 has been published for the first time in *Gendaishi Shiryō*, XLV, but, unfortunately, the minutes of the debate on universal suffrage in 1925 remain closed. However, Shinobu Seizaburō, Edward G. Griffin, and others have fully exploited the *Asahi Shimbun's* considerable knowledge of what the councillors discussed. Indeed, according to Griffin, by 1925 "leaks had become institutionalized, and reports such as those appearing in the press were held to be generally reliable."[5]

While this book considers justice and police officials to have played the leading role in creating the mechanism for controlling thought, it does not neglect the importance of education officials. The much feared military police *(kenpei)* receive scant attention, because their real importance for civilian thought control came after 1941.[6]

"Public opinion," as represented by leading newspapers, academic circles, conservative and radical spokesmen, and various pressure groups, has been assembled from many sources. Newspapers were tapped by using books and articles that drew upon them. It is fair to say, therefore, that this study does reflect public opinion.

In the transliteration of Japanese names, the standard form is used, with the family name first. Macrons are used to mark the long vowels. For common words found in collegiate dictionaries, such as Tokyo, Showa, and Taisho, the long vowels are not marked.

I should like to express my gratitude to those who have aided in the

5. Edward G. Griffin, "The Adoption of Universal Manhood Suffrage in Japan," unpublished doctoral dissertation, 167–168, n. 4.

6. A good introduction, by a former *kenpei* officer, is Ōtani Keijirō, *Showa Kenpei Shi*.

publication of this book. I am grateful to the American Philosophical Society for summer grants in 1967 and 1970 and to the University of Missouri for Summer Research Fellowships in 1972 and 1974. I am indebted to Professors Saitō Makoto, Satō Seizaburō, Ishida Takeshi, Hirano Ryūichi, Fujiki Hideo, and Banno Junji. I wish particularly to thank Professor Okudaira Yasuhiro for his assistance. My most heartfelt thanks go to one Japanese scholar to whom I am indebted for the locating and microfilming of documents. This study could not have been completed without him. I would like to thank Doreen Buerck, Jean Westrich, Regis Propst, Maggie Arbini, and Mary Supranowich for typing the various drafts of the manuscript. I owe a special debt to Yoshiko for her double duty as a research assistant and wife.

RICHARD H. MITCHELL

St. Louis, Missouri

THOUGHT CONTROL IN PREWAR JAPAN

CHAPTER 1 The Background

Japan's interwar thought-control system was a product of government fear in the face of an upsurge of ideological crimes. The thought-control system fashioned after 1925 was unique in the Japanese experience, not only for its large-scale repressiveness, but also for its system of rehabilitation. Even though the thought-control apparatus of the Showa era (1926————) was unlike anything envisioned by Meiji bureaucrats, it is best understood by first looking at the period after the Meiji Restoration of 1868, since the interwar response was conditioned by earlier social attitudes, administrative techniques, and laws.

The basic problem of the new Meiji regime (1868–1912) was the creation of unity in order to promote rapid modernization. Loyal supporters could be created, the leaders felt, by establishing national goals and by using the new emperor system, rescripts, laws, institutions, and family and group pressures to regulate society. Meiji leaders early concluded that socialization for nationalistic ends was best promoted by strengthening the ancient emperor symbol, since the emperor was an easily understood link between the past and the future, a link that gave the people a feeling of identity and security.[1] During the two decades following the Meiji Restoration, the position of the emperor underwent a startling transformation; by 1890, the emperor was no longer merely the repository of divine authority—that authority was becoming part of his own person.[2] The imperial system was further

1. John W. Hall, "A Monarch for Modern Japan," in Robert E. Ward (ed.), *Political Development in Modern Japan,* 63.
2. Wilbur M. Fridell, "Government Ethics Textbooks in Late Meiji Japan," *The Journal of Asian Studies,* XXIX (August, 1970), 824.

reinforced by anachronistic concepts embodied in the term *kokutai,* referring to the development of a distinct pattern of national unity around the emperor.[3] A new Western-style legal code, harnessed to the emperor system, was exploited as part of these efforts to create unity.

The ruling elite protected their position and the new ideological framework which supported rapid modernization by enhancing and protecting the imperial figurehead by all possible means. While criticism of the government was permitted under the Meiji Constitution, any attack upon the new emperor system, even a symbolic one, brought forth a strong and emotional response, and any ideological dissemination that did not complement the established political framework caused an immediate allergic reaction.[4]

Meiji leaders were authoritarian. Many of them felt that conflicts of loyalty must not be permitted, and they reacted in a harsh manner to their political foes, not only to protect their own political positions, but also to maintain the integrative force that was carrying the nation into the modern world. The more radical champions of early Meiji civil-rights movements were suppressed—by raw police power or by more subtle methods. Tight government controls were not strongly

3. Kawahara Hiroshi observes that the concept of *kokutai* is not easy to analyze with modern thought. Kawahara, " 'Chian Ijihō' no Suishinshatachi," *Shakai Kagaku Tōkyū,* XXXVIII (August, 1968), 18. Richard H. Minear, in *Japanese Tradition and Western Law,* sees at least five separate usages for *kokutai.* The first is "national prestige or face" and the second, a concept equivalent to the term "ship of state." Much more common is the third usage which "refers in a relatively specific manner to the unique essence of Japanese society." Caught up in this usage are the ancient emperor system, with its divine origins and long unbroken line of rulers, "the 'national character' as embodied in those moral virtues which were considered indispensable to social unity and order," and the family system. The fourth and fifth usages, both modern, were defined by professors of constitutional law, Hozumi Yatsuka and Minobe Tatsukichi. For Hozumi, it identified the locus of sovereignty—"the emperor is the state." Minobe, while agreeing that *kokutai* was useful in describing Japan's historical development and ethics, denied its legal meaning. In its broader traditional sense *kokutai* has parallels in phrases like "the American way of life." This comparison is particularly good when the user is engaged in polemics and denounces ideas considered antithetical or inimical to the *kokutai.* In this sense *kokutai's* similarity to "un-American" is obvious. Minear (57, 65–68) feels that *kokutai* is best left untranslated, saying that "the forewarned reader will understand that its meaning varies with its user."

4. Maruyama Masao, *Thought and Behavior in Modern Japanese Politics,* 77.

resented by most of the common people, because along with the leadership they shared a view of a basically hierarchically ordered society in which the individual could best express himself by serving the collective body. Rapid urbanization and concomitant social change began to alter traditional views, rapidly politicizing large numbers of formerly passive citizens. Government leaders, positive that unless the new groups entering the political arena were accommodated they would become alienated and disruptive, were forced to make concessions, such as agreeing to the adoption of a parliamentary system.[5]

Central to the government's plans for economic expansion was the improvement of the people's spiritual health by the promotion of proper thinking and the suppression of injurious ideas. In this area, however, the Japanese faced one of their most challenging problems, that is, how to integrate only helpful alien ideology into the indigenous thought system. Bureaucrats in government agencies labored to mobilize material and spiritual support behind the government. They were certain that Japan, too, would be inevitably subjected to the social problems that accompanied industrialization in the West, including, among other problems, the destruction of the peasant village, class hostilities, and labor unrest. At the same time, they thought that by learning lessons from the Western experience, and by taking the proper preventative steps, they could guide Japan through this dangerous period with a minimum of social chaos.[6] Nevertheless, despite their shrewd planning, heterodox Western ideas flowed in along with capitalistic industrial development, ideas such as anarchism, socialism, and other radical notions that clashed with the values of the new economic and political structure. Thus, the urbanization process, which was so vital for successful modernization, undermined traditional harmony among the people, with the development measures initiated by the government inevitably producing a sociological and psychological threat, not only to the rural sector, but also to the modernizing elite itself. This conflict helps explain the overly sensitive attitude of the

5. Kenneth B. Pyle, "The Technology of Japanese Nationalism: the Local Improvement Movement, 1900–1918," *The Journal of Asian Studies*, XXXIII (November, 1973), 56.

6. *Ibid.*, 57.

government toward anarchists, socialists, and other political opponents; authorities were worried about further disturbing the already precariously balanced national harmony.[7]

Suppression of Radicalism

Precedent established in the Tokugawa era (1600–1867) encouraged the new Meiji government to curb civil liberties. This tendency was reinforced by Western advisers who "were . . . warning the Meiji government of the need for press controls, while opposition intellectuals, politicians and students were bolstering their demands for a more untrammelled press than the government would allow, with quotations from Western thinkers and reference to Western experience."[8] Foreign advice to censor the press and to regulate public expression accorded so well with what Japanese leaders were thinking and doing that it was like a sermon to those already converted.[9] Therefore, in spite of the new Meiji government's promise to lay great emphasis upon public discussion (as embodied in the Charter Oath, April 6, 1868) the government immediately passed ordinances to censor the press and to control other literature. In 1875, more systematic legislation was promulgated which located the seat of censorship in the Police Bureau of the Home Ministry. Any book regarded as harmful to public peace might be seized, and its printing press might be destroyed. The method used to control newspapers was changed from one of direct censorship (prepublication) to indirect (postpublication); heavy penalties were imposed upon writers and editors who displeased the censors.[10] Article 13 of the 1875 Newspaper Ordinance provided that "any person who publishes any article in which the writer argues for the change of the Government or destroying the State, or which is inclined to provoke social disorder, shall be subject to imprisonment from one to three years." Moreover, if after publication a social disorder erupted, the

7. Ishida Takeshi, "Urbanization and Its Impact on Japanese Politics—A Case of a Late and Rapidly Developed Country," *Annals of the Institute of Social Science*, Number 8 (March, 1967), 2–3.

8. Albert A. Altman, "A Recently Discovered Document on Early Meiji Press Censorship Legislation," *Gazette*, XVII (Number 4, 1971), 220.

9. *Ibid.*, 217–218.

10. Okudaira Yasuhiro, *Political Censorship in Japan from 1931 to 1945*, 3–4.

writer would be held responsible for the crime. [11] The following year the penalty was stiffened by authorizing the home minister to prohibit or suspend publication of any newspaper or periodical. This resulted in the suspension of numerous newspapers and periodicals for publishing material judged "harmful to the peace of the State." [12]

Further amendments to the press laws tightened government control. Under the provisions of Articles 19 and 22 of the Newspaper Law (1887) and Article 16 of the Publications Law (1887) powers of censorship were held by various government agencies (for example, by the Home and Foreign Ministries and the military ministries). While the authorities were unable to enforce prepublication censorship, because of the large volume of material published, censorship laws were held over the heads of publishing firms, with objectionable material placed under ban without trial. Appeals to courts were not allowed—the administrative decision was final. [13]

By the turn of the century, other laws were in force to govern acts of violence and terror against citizens, to protect the imperial family, and to regulate political associations. One of the most important was the Public Peace Police Law (Chian Keisatsuhō) of 1900, designed by the statesman Yamagata Aritomo. This law, while it restricted organized labor, was aimed primarily at antigovernment political groups: they were required to register their programs with police and needed special permission to meet; police could dissolve their meetings and disband their organizations; joining a secret organization was forbidden, with violations of this law punishable by fines and up to one year in prison. [14]

11. *Ibid.*, 4.
12. *Ibid.*, 5.
13. W. W. McLaren, "Government Documents, First Half of the Meiji Era," *Transactions, Asiatic Society of Japan*, XLII, Part I (1914), 547, 553. Later amendment further tightened government control. Harry E. Wildes, "Press Freedom in Japan," *The American Journal of Sociology*, XXXII (January, 1927), 611.
14. Japan, Kōchi Ken Tokubetsu Kōtōka, *Tokubetsu Kōtō Keisatsu Kankei Hōki Kaigi Shūroku*, 19, 83–86. The 1900 peace law was a direct descendant of the Peace Preservation Ordinance (Hoan Jōrei) of December 26, 1887, which Home Minister Yamagata created to still antigovernment political agitators who were swarming to the capital, attracted by the hot issue of treaty revision. Yamagata, who was already aware that the government was in danger (a situation signaled by local revolts and popular rights demonstrations demanding freedom of speech, press, and assembly), ordered Police

The Home Ministry's Police Bureau was the primary agency for suppressing radicals and controlling protest movements. Unlike the case in some Western nations, in Japan violations of the law involving political organizations and publications were primarily regulated, not by the courts through trials, but in an administrative fashion by the police, using prohibition orders. Thus, from the early Meiji period, the government tended to rely on administrative management rather than on criminal trials in order to maintain public tranquillity. This point is important in understanding the state's approach to the "thought problem" after 1925.

Secret police reports, such as "The Development of the Socialists," illustrate that so-called "socialists" were under close watch. Volume one of this document, which ends at July 1908, identified four hundred and sixty resident Japanese socialists, with ninety-eight considered as active propagandists. Individual files were kept on members of the smaller group, including an analysis of their character and their past.[15] Volume three, published during the summer of 1911, indicates a better-organized police network and a growing sophistication: "Among those we have been calling socialists are some who are anarchists, communists, socialists, and people who are calling for a redistribution of land. . . . Since there is the possibility of making errors if we con-

---

Bureau head Kiyoura Keigo to draft a tough law to stop the political agitation centered in Tokyo. Among others, Itō Miyoji, who was helping Itō Hirobumi draft the constitution, was one of the 1887 law's authors. Roger F. Hackett, *Yamagata Aritomo in the Rise of Modern Japan*, 103–105. Evidence indicates that the 1887 law was a copy of Bismarck's method of dealing with leftists, and that the intent of the 1900 peace law was the same. The German Socialist Law (1878) prohibited all activities which might undermine the government or social order: police could forbid or halt any meeting or demonstration; socialist agitators could be jailed and refused residence in specified areas. For details see William H. Dawson, *The German Empire*, I, 466–467. The 1887 Peace Preservation Ordinance bears the mark of the participation of Albert Mosse (a disciple of Rudolph Gneist), a man Yamagata invited to Japan as an adviser in 1886. Kurt Steiner, *Local Government in Japan*, 35. The idea of exiling political foes, however, may have come from a similar Tokugawa era practice of "expulsion from Edo" (Edobarai). Dan F. Henderson, "Law and Political Modernization in Japan," in Robert E. Ward (ed.), *Political Development in Modern Japan*, 419. Edo was the Tokugawa period's name for Tokyo and it was the seat of Tokugawa political power.

15. Nihon Kindai Shiryō Kenkyūkai (ed.), *Taisho Kōki Keihokyoku Kankō Shakai Undō Shiryō* (hereafter TKKKSUS), 4.

tinue to simply class them as socialists, we have decided to call all of them *tokubetsu yō shisatsunin* (people under special surveillance)."[16] Faced with an upsurge of leftist radicals, the government created a Higher Police (Kōtō Keisatsu) unit in 1904. By 1911, authorities had made a second unit, the Special Higher Police (Tokubetsu Kōtō Keisatsu), to reinforce the efforts of the first. The following year Special Higher Police sections within the Metropolitan Police Headquarters and the Osaka Prefectural Police Headquarters became independent of the Higher Police.[17] The main mission of the Special Higher Police, the so-called "thought police," was to investigate and control social movements, and to suppress radicals spreading dangerous foreign ideologies. Detailed reports were regularly sent to the Home Ministry.[18]

It appears that the thought police were organized in 1911 because of the high-treason case of the previous year, on which occasion the authorities, after arresting a lumbermill worker for manufacturing and transporting explosives, carried out a nationwide arrest of several hundred anarchists and socialists, including the leading anarchist Kōtoku Shūsui.[19] This dramatic event, together with the urging of the powerful politician Yamagata, accelerated Home Ministry plans to create a special unit to deal with leftist extremists. After the arrest of Kōtoku Shūsui and other radicals, Yamagata spent the summer of 1910

16. Quoted in *ibid.*, 4–5. These secret reports are the ancestors of a very detailed series compiled beginning in 1929 under the title *Shōwa . . . Nenjū ni Okeru Shakai Undō no Jōkyō* (Conditions of the Social Movement during the Year. . . .)

17. TKKKSUS, 1–2. See Appendix I, Chart 1.

18. The wholesale introduction of Western ideas, together with the rapid process of industrialization, produced serious economic and political dislocations and stimulated a reaction among intellectuals, farmers, laborers, and others. Politically motivated groups formed, whose activities were called "social movements" *(shakai undō)*. George O. Totten, *The Social Democratic Movement in Prewar Japan*, 4.

19. Eleven others were hanged with Kōtoku for planning to assassinate the emperor. See Totten (31) for the views of those who feel that the trial of Kōtoku was "a conscious frame-up by the Katsura government." F. G. Notehelfer, *Kōtoku Shūsui*, 175, however, holds that Kōtoku did take an active role in the plot, in the form of discussion, and that people under his influence acted on his suggestions. While the Supreme Court accepted the defense contention that Kōtoku's involvement was only theoretical, it ruled that "discussions in which Kōtoku openly revealed his approval of [plans] to assassinate the emperor irrevocably linked him to the crime contemplated by the others." Nihon Bengoshi Rengōkai (ed.), *Nihon Bengoshi Enkakushi*, 98–99.

studying the thought and activities of leftist radicals and writing out his plan for controlling them and their ideas: increased police power and stricter legislation were the solution. His views were circulated among top officials.[20]

Besides special laws and police, other means were employed to discourage radicalism and promote public support. Not long before the Russo-Japanese War (1904–1905) the Home Ministry launched the Local Improvement Movement, considered to be "the first organized and sustained effort . . . to deal with social problems created by industrialism and imperialism." This movement "was to overcome the disintegrative effects of industrialization, to create national loyalties among all classes of people at the local level, and thus to promote further economic development."[21] In 1906, the government began a nationwide shrine merger movement as a means of strengthening local administration and fostering nationalism.[22] Education bureaucrats sought to achieve the same goals by strengthening moral education. A conservative ethics textbook was published in 1910 which stressed traditional family relations, the importance of Ise Shrine, the founding of the nation, and the *kokutai*.[23] Military leaders, disturbed by antiwar activities and the apparent decline in national spirit, spearheaded a successful drive to create a veterans' association through which they planned to promote loyalty. Thus, when the new Imperial Military Reserve Association held its opening ceremony on November 3, 1910 (the emperor's birthday), military bureaucrats planned first to indoctrinate its members with patriotism and then to influence the entire nation.[24] Justice bureaucrats, too, were sensitive to the potential danger of imported radical thought and were acutely aware of the world-wide flow of socialism. Part of their response was to dispatch officials like

20. Notehelfer, 187.

21. Pyle, 52.

22. Wilbur M. Fridell, *Japanese Shrine Mergers, 1906–1912*, vii.

23. Fridell, "Government Ethics Textbooks," 828–833.

24. For Yamagata's feelings about "radicalism" see Hackett, *Yamagata Aritomo in the Rise of Modern Japan*, 238, and Hackett, "The Meiji Leaders and Modernization: The Case of Yamagata Aritomo," in Marius B. Jansen (ed.), *Changing Japanese Attitudes Toward Modernization*, 272. In connection with the Imperial Military Reserve Association see Inoue Kiyoshi (ed.), *Taishoki no Seiji to Shakai*, 376, and Richard J. Smethurst, *A Social Basis for Prewar Japanese Militarism*, 14–19, 23–25.

Hiranuma Kiichirō and Suzuki Kisaburō to Europe for a firsthand look
at measures being taken to control anarchism, socialism, and strikes.[25]

Party Government Response

Japanese society changed rapidly during the late Meiji and Taisho
eras (1912–1926). Long-festering economic, social, and political
problems burst open during the inflationary years of World War I in the
form of an unprecedented series of strikes and the explosive Rice Riots
of 1918. Simultaneously, discontented intellectuals and students joined
farmers and laborers in pressing for economic, political, and social
reforms. It was against this background that the first party cabinet was
appointed on September 29, 1918. Prime Minister Hara Kei, who had
been a powerful figure in the political world for over a decade,
represented the Seiyūkai party political machine in particular and the
new breed of party politicians in general. Hara and his followers had
struggled against and compromised with the powerful clique from
western Japan, the former fiefs of Satsuma-Chōshū, which dominated
the government from the Meiji Restoration until after the turn of the
century. During his fight to reach the political pinnacle, Hara became
excessively concerned with acquiring power, willing to make nearly
any compromise to achieve it. Central to his character were the
"profound psychological frustrations inherited from his youthful days
as an outsider" from northeastern Japan, an area described as the home
of traitors by the loyalists who restored the emperor in 1868.[26] The
challenge for Hara, then, was to prove the loyalty of himself and other
outsiders, and to achieve power for himself.

Once in power, Hara did much to liberalize the political atmosphere,
but he was blind to needed social reform and insensitive to civil
liberties. Perhaps this was because he believed, like the statesmen Itō
Hirobumi and Yamagata Aritomo, in an orderly government and
society.[27] Distrust of anything that appeared radical stemmed from this

25. Hiranuma (a bureau chief) and Suzuki (a Supreme Court judge) visited courts,
prisons, and police stations. Notehelfer, n. 1, 160.; Hiranuma Kiichirō Kaikoroku Hensan
Iinkai, *Hiranuma Kiichirō Kaikoroku*, 122, 190, 195; and Suzuki Kisaburō Sensei Denki
Hensankai, *Suzuki Kisaburō*, 36, 47–63.

26. Najita Tetsuo, *Hara Kei in the Politics of Compromise*, 13, 24.

27. *Ibid.*, 11.

desire for order, and from his lifelong wish to show that he was as loyal a supporter of the throne as anyone. Hara, therefore, treated leftist radicals and other social protesters in a manner reminiscent of Meiji leaders.

Hara and his successor Takahashi Korekiyo equated the developing suffrage movement with dangerous thought, replied to labor demands with suppression, distrusted intellectuals and foreign ideas, and disapproved of student activism.[28] Shortly before his death on November 4, 1921, Hara wrote in his diary that "there was need for more stringent regulations to supplement existing laws" for the control of radicals.[29] Hara's antipathy toward leftist radicals was reinforced by his need to cultivate conservatives like Yamagata. Since the universities were viewed as the seedbeds of radicalism, the Hara Cabinet (1918–1921) used an imperial ordinance to order them to pay more attention to "the training of character and the cultivation of national thought."[30] Moreover, education officials ordered students not to join suffrage-movement demonstrations.[31] Hara's stubborn refusal to repeal the antilabor provisions of the 1900 peace law illustrates his deep mistrust of labor organizations.[32] Among his positive acts to promote industrial peace was an attempt to win over moderate labor leaders to the government camp by the formation in December 1919 of the Kyōchōkai (Harmonization Society) to encourage harmony between business and labor, and the sponsorship of the Dai Nihon Kokusuikai (Great Japan National Essence Society), which had as part of its mission the extinction of disputes between labor and business.[33]

28. Inoue, 136, 172, 199; Shinobu Seizaburō, *Taisho Seijishi*, 900–901; and Peter Duus, *Party Rivalry and Political Change in Taishō Japan*, 139–142.

29. Duus, 204. For Hara's strong attack upon extremist thought entering Japan, see his speech at the opening of the Forty-Second Imperial Diet on December 26, 1919. Maezawa Hiroaki (ed.), *Nihon Kokkai Nanajūnen Shi*, 523–525. Takahashi's views on bad alien thought and the proper countermeasures were given to the Forty-Fifth Imperial Diet on December 26, 1921 (Hara was killed on November 4). *Ibid.*, 585–587.

30. Quoted in Miyaji Masato, "Morito Tatsuo Jiken," in Wagatsuma Sakae (ed.), *Nihon Seiji Saiban Shiroku, Taisho* (hereafter NSSST), 229–230.

31. Inoue, 172.

32. *Ibid.*, 217.

33. Robert A. Scalapino, *Democracy and the Party Movement in Prewar Japan*, n. 6, 353; and Stephen S. Large, *The Rise of Labor in Japan*, 159, 165, 173–174.

While something like the Kyōchōkai had been discussed by the preceding Terauchi Masatake Cabinet (1916–1918), there was a direct connection between the violence of 1918 and the creation of this organization in 1919. After the disturbance, the Home Ministry sent an official of the Police Bureau on a nationwide inspection tour. His report concluded that it was urgent to do something to calm the strife between capitalists and laborers. Kawamura Takeji, chief of the bureau, realized the significance of the report and sent it to Home Minister Tokonami Takejirō who was inspired to take action.[34]

Bureaucrats under Hara expanded police work; in order to keep up with the social protest movement more factual data on individuals, more reports at more frequent intervals, and more research concentrating squarely on organizations were required.[35] The 1919 issue of *People under Special Surveillance* was voluminous, containing details on over 500 suspects. Since authorities were especially concerned over the importation of radicalism, special attention was paid to 118 people who had contacted foreign ideologists, had themselves lived abroad, or had communicated with people living outside the country.[36]

Beginning in 1921, the Police Bureau produced *Shakaishugi Undō Geppō* (Monthly Report on the Socialism Movement) and *Shisō Dantai Jōkyō* (The Condition of Thought Groups). The latter document reflected increased concern with over one hundred potentially subversive groups. Labor developments, as well, were covered more frequently in *Hompō Rōdō Undō Geppō* (A Monthly Report on the Labor Movement in Our Country).[37]

At the center of the Special Higher Police network was its Book Section. This organ's peaceful-sounding title masked its real function, the censorship of newspapers and magazines. According to Horikiri Zenjirō, its chief in 1917 and 1918: "We prohibited things which were against public order and good morals." Generally he relied upon his own judgment.[38] Under the Hara and Takahashi regimes, the Book

34. Kimbara Samon, *Taishoki no Seitō to Kokumin*, 164.
35. TKKKSUS, 9–10.
36. *Ibid.*, 6–7.
37. *Ibid.*, 8–11.
38. *Ibid.*, 13.

Section began to publish a summary of leftist publications, on what may have been a monthly basis. The government, too, utilized this agency to gather information and compile numerous reports on the suffrage movement.[39]

A Time of Crisis

The late Meiji and early Taisho periods were not only a time of victories and national expansion (the Russo-Japanese War, the annexation of Korea, participation in World War I), but also a period of growing uneasiness plagued by riots and strikes. The political world became increasingly fragmented, as the old-line leadership was replaced by a new more-numerous elite; and increasingly after 1900 conservatives heard the voices of those who rejected the emperor system in favor of Western-style radicalism. It seemed to some people that they were in the midst of a general breakdown of traditional morals and a denigration of the spirit of self-sacrifice. Also frightening to conservatives were the associations springing up to put into practice democratic and leftist radical ideas. The sometimes violent suffrage demonstrations, coupled with the discovery that teachers and students were joining the communist movement, had a profound impact. Besides the general rise of radicalism, conservatives were also worried about the refusal of the younger generation to think in terms of service to the nation. Too many young people appeared to be lost in a world of irresponsibility and self-centered existence. So-called *mobo* and *moga* (modern boys and modern girls) dressed in Western clothes appeared, shocking many people. Much like today's hippies, the typical *mobo* wore long hair and sometimes a beard and bell-bottomed pants. Coffee shops, dance halls, and other Western imports caused concern over the nation's future.[40]

Informed people in and out of government were exceedingly anxious about the rapid changes taking place in the world of ideas, and a main topic of conversation was what could be done to suppress "dangerous thought" (*kiken shisō*).[41] The term dangerous thought, which was not

39. *Ibid.*, 8, 10–12.
40. Bamba Nobuya, *Japanese Diplomacy in a Dilemma*, 53.
41. The elder statesman Egi Senshi said that in 1917 officials and concerned citizens were very worried about radical ideas and how to stop their spread. Itō Takashi,

an official or legal phrase, meant ideas which might be dangerous to the *kokutai* or might be in some manner un-Japanese. Although dangerous thought was a vague term, in most instances it was linked to ideas imported from abroad, ideas which seemed to some Japanese to threaten national solidarity. Thus, "the central notion seems to be a fear of certain foreign ideas which have made their way into the minds of certain groups in Japan. These ideas are at variance with the national ideology."[42] Mounting concern over the increase in "abnormal alien thought" was reflected in an imperial message issued in November 1923, in which people were ordered to shun all radical thought and to lessen their social criticism.[43]

Despite the government's laws, the police, and social policies, some people continued to promote anarchist, socialist, and communist ideas. Bureaucrats, who shared the politicians' increased concern over radical activities, must have considered what would happen if angry mobs of rice rioters were taken over by politically motivated radicals. Led by such people, the social protest movement would become an extension of the revolutionary storm breaking over Europe.

In July 1922, a small band of Japanese formed a branch of the communist party, accepting Russian aid and money. Government restrictions were circumvented by organizing in secret and operating

---

Showa Shoki Seijishi Kenkyū, 391. Den Kenjirō, a minister in the Terauchi Cabinet, wrote in his diary on August 17, 1918, that since the Chinese and Russian Revolutions dangerous democratic and communist thought had been eating into the brains of the lower classes. He saw a direct link between the Rice Riots of 1918 and the harmful ideas coming into Japan. Other officials strongly suspected that the riots could not have spread so rapidly without some sort of unified control. Kimbara, 20. Hiranuma and others suggested to the Cabinet in 1917 that the public be informed of the limits on speech and research, that publishers be encouraged to print good books, and that publications be strictly controlled. Itō, 391–392. For Suzuki's views see *Suzuki Kisaburō,* 118–119.

42. John P. Reed, *Kokutai,* 64.

43. Yamada Yoshio, *Kokumin Seishin Sakkō ni Kansuru Shōsho Gikai,* 1, 10. The Cabinet utilized a gubernatorial conference held in mid-November to stress the seriousness of the deterioration of thought. Prime Minister Yamamoto Gonnohyōe called for a renewal of the national spirit based upon education in traditional morals. Home Minister Gotō Shimpei deplored the dangerous thought current, and suggested a plan to counter it: a revival of the national spirit by clarification of its origins, an investigation of the reasons why people absorbed dangerous thought, and more government attention to social problems. *Ibid.,* 51, 53–54.

underground. The new party's official platform demanded that the emperor, the army, the thought police, and the military police be abolished; that large estates and other selected property be confiscated and given to poor farmers; that Japanese military forces be withdrawn from China and other areas; and that the Soviet Union be recognized.[44] This program hit at the heart of the ideological structure supporting the state. Moreover, the government viewed the organization's relationship with the Soviet Union as extremely dangerous. Actually, the tiny fifty-member party posed no physical danger, but the symbolic threat was quite real, since the loyalty of all citizens was so important to the government. Especially since the party appeared in the midst of a political, economic, and social crisis, the ruling elite perceived it as a greater menace than it actually was.

In September 1923, a terrible earthquake struck the capital area. A good portion of the city of Tokyo was gutted by vast fires and about 100,000 people were killed. It is understandable why a shocked public, aware of the financial and political scandals of the period, interpreted the earthquake "as a kind of supernatural punishment for the frivolity and individualism of the times."[45] Many people felt that the nation in its forced march toward prosperity and international recognition had somehow strayed from the proper path.

By the early 1920's many Japanese saw signs of institutional decay. Because of growing economic and social problems, plus the feuds and corruption rampant in parliamentary politics, people were inclined to turn their backs on the emerging political system in favor of a return to the stability they imagined had existed earlier. In other terms, Japan was suffering from a too rapid modernization which had led to a state of social disorganization, or anomie, in which large numbers of individuals felt that stable institutional patterns were crumbling and that their own personal stability was in jeopardy:[46] "An increase in anomie may be the consequence of almost any change in the social situation which upsets previous established definitions of the situation. . . . There

44. George M. Beckmann and Okubo Genji, *The Japanese Communist Party, 1922–1945.* 64–66, 279–282.
    45. Richard Storry, *The Double Patriots,* 25.
    46. Talcott Parsons, *Politics and Social Structure,* 83–84.

is a limit to the extent and rapidity of change which can take place without engendering anomie on a large scale."[47] Moreover, anomie can reach serious proportions if enough individuals are disturbed, even in a society, like prewar Japan, in which the collectivist ethic is still strong and in which the social cement remains comparatively firm. It appears that the perception of large numbers of Japanese became distorted; social problems were magnified, and faith in the emerging parliamentary system was lost. For a majority, a strong reaffirmation of harmony and unity was the normal method of escaping psychological stress induced by rapid modernization.

By the end of the Taisho era, a growing sense of national frustration and crisis had created a mood within the government and among the concerned public for new methods to control radical thought. It was obvious that the old methods were becoming less effective, particularly in the face of a rapidly rising level of ideological and political sophistication among the general populace. One scholar has neatly summed up the attitude of the establishment: "The rulers who faced the new conditions after World War One . . . had a strong sense of crisis, and this strong sense of crisis again drove the rulers in the direction of controlling the thoughts of the people."[48]

The Central Role of the Justice Ministry

After World War I all parts of the plural elite were concerned over the rise of social unrest and radical ideology. Yet, while the elder statesmen, military men, party politicians, court nobles, and business leaders discussed these problems, the imperial bureaucracy created institutions to solve them. Thus, we must turn our attention to the activities of the interwar bureaucracy, a faceless crowd about whom much less is known than about the leading political and military figures. And most important were the justice officials who led the bureaucratic attack upon subversives.

Like other parts of the bureaucracy, the Justice Ministry was subject to interdepartmental and intersectional conflicts. Increase in size, the creation of new bureaus, and the complicated problems involved in

47. *Ibid.*, 85.
48. Itō, 358.

attacking subversive ideology all acted as centrifugal forces. The justice minister and his deputies strove to counter this decentralization process by creating conferences and other special devices to promote unity. It is difficult to pinpoint the exact locus of power because of the nature of bureaucracies in general and the Japanese system in particular. Naturally, it shifted with changing social conditions, new ministers, and each political case under consideration. Nevertheless, when a strong-willed career minister was in charge, most of the ministry's personnel were his troops to command. During the interwar years, a period when "Cabinet ministers became more heterogeneous" in other ministries,[49] the Justice Ministry had an unusually high percentage of career-service ministers who had served only in justice. During the 1920's some "heterogeneous" outsiders were in office, but career men like Hiranuma Kiichirō and Suzuki Kisaburō were there as well. As for the second half of the period, all Cabinets were served by career men, and the majority were in the Hiranuma Kiichirō clique. Thus, most of the time the Justice Ministry was run by a career bureaucrat who had deep roots in the justice field. With an experienced man at the top, one who had the personal bonds with subordinates needed to obtain cooperation, this ministry suffered less than others from weak transient ministers, thus giving the ministry an edge in its dealings with others in officialdom.

Justice bureaucrats were generally in a better position to present a united front than other ministries. Most of them, due to their functional specialization or high degree of professionalization, did not transfer out of the justice field. Justice officials, therefore, were unlike multipurpose Home Ministry personnel who were able to enter and exit with comparative ease.[50] Because of this, and the fact that the Justice Ministry was much smaller than the huge Home Ministry, it was more homogeneous and more easily dominated by its chief officers. The comparative solidarity of justice officials proved to be highly desirable when the Justice Ministry challenged the Home Ministry.

49. Robert M. Spaulding, Jr., "The Bureaucracy as a Political Force, 1920–1945," in James W. Morley (ed.), *Dilemmas of Growth in Prewar Japan,* 43.

50. Kubota Akira, *Higher Civil Servants in Postwar Japan,* 103, 104–106.

Officials within the ministry were divided into three groups: administrators, judges, and procurators. The first group was directly under the thumb of the central headquarters. Judges, while they enjoyed judicial independence and were in theory free from outside pressure, were subject to manipulation by other justice officials, especially by those in Tokyo. The chief flaw in the court system's independence was that it was under the control of central administrators who could pressure recalcitrant judges in various ways, including demoting them to less desirable benches.[51] An ambitious young judge would be inclined to make decisions with one eye cocked toward the minister. One specialist on Japanese law acknowledges this situation but claims that "there is little evidence of interference in specific cases."[52] While it is doubtful that a judge was ever ordered by the minister to "throw" a case, it is clear that pressure was exerted upon the bench in a number of important political trials.[53] In this sense, the judicial independence so highly valued by the courts was breached again and again. However, few judges were able to stand rock-firm in the nationalistic flood that swept Japan.

Procurators were in a strong position. From the Meiji period, procurators dressed like judges, sat on the same level at trials, and identified themselves closely with the bench. Procurators dominated the police and the preliminary examination judges. Often they gave advice to police in the drafting of documents and handling of cases, and they usurped the most important duties of preliminary judges. Indeed, preliminary judges eventually became little more than "rubber stamps" for procurators, who evaluated each case and marked it guilty before sending it on to the judges. The Preliminary Examination Record, which was the only document considered legal proof at a trial, was usually done by a procurator, and the preliminary judge did little to modify it. This key document went into the formal trial where it was

51. Ushiomi Toshitaka (ed.), *Gendai no Hōritsuka*, 12, 15.
52. Dan F. Henderson, 426.
53. For details see "Kanketsu ni Atatte (Zadankai)," in Wagatsuma Sakae (ed.), *Nihon Seiji Saiban Shiroku, Showakō*, 568–569, 576, 583 (hereafter Zadankai); and Amamiya Shōichi, "Ketsumeidan Jiken," in Wagatsuma Sakae (ed.), *Nihon Seiji Saiban Shiroku, Showazen*, 400–461.

generally accepted as an accurate account of what had occurred. Truly, it was often a case of trial and conviction by procurators.[54]

A special characteristic of the procurators' wide-ranging power was the system of *ryūho shobun* (charges withheld). The suspect was neither released nor prosecuted, but was held in a suspended state under the control of the procurator. It was easy in political or thought cases for this power to be abused. This fact plus the enormous powers they gathered to control thought naturally promoted the politicization of procurators.[55]

There were, of course, stresses and strains within the procuratorial camp. Nevertheless, they were a tightly controlled, disciplined, strongly motivated, and highly integrated organization. As one scholar puts it, "when the top gave an order the bottom obeyed."[56]

Neither the development of the Justice Ministry nor its role in fighting dangerous ideology can be properly understood without considering the career of Hiranuma Kiichirō. Together with loyal supporters like Suzuki Kisaburō, he exerted a strong influence upon the justice field and the wider political world.[57] Hiranuma continued to dominate the Justice Ministry even after he entered the Privy Council. This was possible because of the personal following he built up during his record nine-year tenure as procurator-general (1912–1921).

Hiranuma was born one year before the Meiji Restoration. Like the sons of other samurai, his early education stressed the primacy of loyalty and duty. In 1888, he graduated from Tokyo Imperial University with a degree in English law. Exposure to Western ideas only reinforced Hiranuma's feeling that Japan's *kokutai* was unique and that Japan's educational system was placing too much emphasis upon alien ideas—which were corrupting.[58] Thus, when he entered the Justice Ministry in 1888, he saw himself as a reformer dedicated to the promotion of traditional morality. Over the years Hiranuma assembled a loyal following and then carried out a campaign to remove bad officials.

54. Zadankai, 580–581, 583.
55. *Ibid.*, 583.
56. *Ibid.*, 584.
57. Ushiomi, 10–11; *Suzuki Kisaburō*, 76; and Richard Yasko, "Hiranuma Kiichirō and Conservative Politics in Pre-war Japan" (unpublished doctoral dissertation), 13, 37.
58. *Hiranuma Kiichirō Kaikoroku*, 26; and Yasko, 10.

During his long term as procurator-general, he enlarged the power of that office and of its procurators. The political world was shocked at the vigorous prosecution which the formerly complacent Justice Ministry carried out in obtaining convictions of politicians in bribery cases,[59] and by 1915 the Hiranuma clique was a significant factor in national politics.

Therefore, when the surge of leftist ideology hit Japan, the procuracy had already been molded into a vigorous and efficient tool by Hiranuma. The new danger confronting the state presented Hiranuma and his followers a further opportunity to expand their power, this time throughout the entire society, as they sought to stamp out "dangerous thought." Armed now with a two-edged sword, they could cut corrupt politicians with one side and ideological heretics with the other. Moreover, the clear threat presented by radical leftists enabled Hiranuma to renew his cry for expelling superfluous foreign ideas and returning to the pure state of an earlier age.

Justice Minister Hiranuma in 1922 and 1923 had tight control of the bureaucratic domain which he had entered nearly forty years earlier; and as vice-president of the Privy Council (1926–1936), he continued to influence Justice Ministry decisions. In 1926, for instance, he secretly called justice officials to his office and reprimanded them for mishandling certain important cases, and a year later he influenced Prime Minister Tanaka Giichi to appoint Hara Yoshimichi, an old friend, as justice minister.[60] Furthermore, between 1931 and 1940, four out of six justice ministers were Hiranuma clique members (e.g., Suzuki, Koyama Matsukichi, Shiono Suehiko, and Miyagi Chōgorō).[61] Thus, Hiranuma was so influential that it would not be far off the mark to suggest that it was not a case of "the Justice Ministry's Hiranuma" but of "Hiranuma's Justice Ministry."

Throughout his career Hiranuma sought to preserve essential Japanese political and social values. He "was determined to safeguard what he considered to be the internally coherent qualities of the Japanese political system. Chief among these qualities was the

59. Yasko, 46.

60. *Ibid.*, 70–76.

61. The two justice ministers who were considered anti-Hiranuma were Ohara Naoshi and Hayashi Raisaburō. Kawahara, 6–7.

fundamental principle that imperial rule was to be administered by a bureaucracy that combined legal expertise and moral rectitude."[62] In his middle years, he became highly critical of new thought currents. As the procurator handling the high-treason incident, Hiranuma expressed his concern over the fact that intellectuals were neglecting to study Japan's past. Kōtoku's education was badly flawed, he felt, because it distorted the meaning of the *kokutai* and the history upon which it was based.[63] Throughout his long public career Hiranuma's zeal to raise the prestige of the emperor and the *kokutai* matched that of Yamagata Aritomo. Indeed, a desire to protect the *kokutai* brought the two together, and they quickly established a mutual accord on the proper treatment of the imperial institution.[64]

Hiranuma was a conservative reformer whose motives were higher than those of most of his contemporaries. Early in his career he cleansed the Justice Ministry of corruption and inefficiency and in his fifties he called for a second restoration. The term "Showa Restoration" is linked to him, but it might well be called a "Taisho Restoration," since he first suggested the needed reform then. The reformist zeal he had applied first to the Justice Ministry, and then to other parts of the bureaucracy, was to be extended to the entire nation. Restoration would cleanse the state of the corruption that had accumulated since 1868. Just as a house sometimes needed repair, he said, so did the state.[65]

62. Yasko, 3–4.
63. *Hiranuma Kiichirō Kaikoroku,* 26, 61, 63.
64. *Ibid.,* 26, 34.
65. *Ibid.,* 282–286.

CHAPTER 2 The Peace Preservation Law

During the early 1920's, Japanese were shocked by the spread of communist and anarchist ideas, the establishment of an illegal communist party, and an attempt to kill the prince regent. These events stimulated officials to consider new methods of controlling leftists and startled the common people sufficiently to put them into a receptive state of mind for considering the passage of stricter laws. Then, in 1925, the government enacted the Peace Preservation Law which established ideological limits for organizations and individuals.

Many politicians and bureaucrats were supportive of harsher laws to control leftist radicals, but the real promoters of the Peace Preservation Law, the key figures in the planning and drafting over several years, were the bureaucrats Hiranuma and Suzuki. Of course, politicians like Wakatsuki Reijirō of the moderately liberal Kenseikai party and Tokonami Takejirō of the conservative Seiyūkai party, and Home Ministry bureaucrats like Kawasaki Takukichi played roles as active supporters of the peace law. The main driving force behind the peace-law bill, however, was the missionary zeal of the Hiranuma-Suzuki clique.[1]

A Milestone on the Way

Our point of departure on the road leading to enactment of the Peace Preservation Law is the trial of Morito Tatsuo, a junior professor of

1. Kawahara Hiroshi, "'Chian Ijihō' no Suishinshatachi," *Shakai Kagaku Tōkyū*, XXXVIII (August, 1968), 6–7, 10. For an earlier version of the material in this chapter see Richard H. Mitchell, "Japan's Peace Preservation Law of 1925: Its Origins and Significance," *Monumenta Nipponica*, XXVIII (Autumn, 1973), 317–345.

economics at Tokyo Imperial University. The precipitating incident was the publication in January 1920 of Morito's article, "Kuropotokin no Shakai Shisō no Kenkyū" (Research on the Social Thought of Kropotkin), in the first issue of *Keizaigaku Kenkyū* (Research in Economics). His essay, in which Yamagata and Procurator-General Hiranuma must have seen the spirit of Kōtoku whom they exorcised in 1911, became the target of campus rightists and finally the basis of a political trial.

This trial had a great impact upon the scholarly world, involving as it did the issues of academic freedom and free speech. Moreover, disclosures at the trial set justice officials to thinking about measures to stop the flow of harmful ideologies into Japan. And, further, the case prompted Hiranuma and other bureaucrats to establish private organizations to combat subversion and reform the national spirit.

Morito was prosecuted not only because of the supposedly illegal nature of his article, but because of the timing of its publication. The government was at that point in a mood to set an example in order to reinforce the national moral tone. Prime Minister Hara Kei was eager for a chance to express his displeasure over the activities of radical university professors, some of whom, he felt, strove for publicity by expressing radical, dangerous views.[2] He was strongly supported by Hiranuma and Yamagata. The former had been brooding for some time over the corrupting influences of alien ideology and had, in 1917, urged the government to tighten controls on publications. The latter charged that scholars like Morito were "acting against the fundamental great spirit of our empire." Professors at the most prestigious universities, he said, were attracted by new intellectual currents like socialism and anarchism because they hoped to become famous.[3] Thus the Cabinet decided on January 13 to prosecute Professors Morito and Ōuchi Hyōe, the editor of the journal.

Morito's article defined the ideal society and summarized the anarchistic communism of Kropotkin, whose social ideal, Morito concluded, had a rational basis and was not merely a beautiful fantasy. "Therefore, even if I do not discuss whether anarchistic communism

2. Miyaji Masato, "Morito Tatsuo Jiken," in NSSST, 238; and Shinobu Seizaburō, *Taisho Seijishi,* 900.

3. Miyaji, in NSSST, 239.

can be put into practice immediately, I do think it has now been clarified as to why [Kropotkin's thought] can become a social ideal which should be realized." At the same time, Morito sounded a note of caution by criticizing flaws in Kropotkin's theory, pointing out the difficulty of putting theory into practice. Ending on a moderate tone, he repudiated violent means, suggesting that the masses should be politically awakened through legal channels.[4]

Criticism by Professor Uesugi Shinkichi and his rightist student group, the Kōkoku Dōshikai (Society for the Preservation of the State), brought the article to the attention of government and university authorities.[5] The university sought to solve the Morito problem by withdrawing the offending publication and urging the professor to sign a statement repudiating anarchistic communism. After Morito refused either to resign or to sign the document, he was forced to retire.[6]

The lawyer Takeuchi Kakuji, a close associate of Hiranuma, published an article in the *Legal Newspaper (Hōritsu Shimbun)* entitled "A Study of the Morito Problem" (Morito Mondai no Kenkyū). In view of Takeuchi's deep involvement with the Hiranuma-Suzuki clique, we can assume that he was expressing their opinions as well. Because of their positions of great trust, he wrote, scholars had a duty to protect the nation. Professors should sift all foreign ideas, importing only those which were capable of being assimilated. "In other words, Tokyo Imperial University should become the quarantine office for imported [ideologies]. . . . If a thought is harmful, it should be treated as a harmful thought. For an ideology which is both harmful and harmless, the university should remove the harmful portion, and import the profitable part." Unfortunately, said Takeuchi, "Mr. Morito has not only forgotten about the duty of the quarantiner, but has himself become the importer of a harmful germ." Not only did Morito, and scholars like him, endanger the state, but they were also guilty of the terrible crime of radicalizing their students.[7]

4. *Ibid.*, 232–233.
5. *Ibid.*, 233. Uesugi was Hozumi Yatsuka's disciple and an avid supporter of the orthodox view that the emperor was the state. He strongly opposed Minobe Tatsukichi's contention that legally Japan was like European constitutional monarchies, where the emperor was one of the state's organs.
6. *Ibid.*, 235–236, 239.
7. Quoted in *ibid.*, 239.

The closed trial began on January 30. Morito and Ōuchi were charged with violating Article 42 of the Newspaper Law (one clause made it treasonable to act in defiance of the constitution). The defendants were represented by a distinguished group of lawyers and intellectuals. In explaining why he decided to support the defendants, Sasaki Sōichi, a professor of constitutional law at Kyoto Imperial University, spoke, no doubt, for other intellectuals. He felt that the trial, the first such incident, would be bound to heavily influence future government actions.[8]

Professor Sasaki interpreted Article 42's high-treason clause "as meaning that the contents of the [essay] itself must be in defiance of the constitution. . . . If you punish a person for writing something that might precipitate an action in defiance of the constitution, you are entering a hazy area where the law can never be precise." Defiance of the constitution meant acting in such a manner as to endanger the "basic structure of national life." Professor Morito had given only a value judgment about an ideal system, and had intended neither to destroy the social structure nor to defy the constitution. Sasaki maintained, therefore, that Morito's essay did not endanger the basic structure of national life or contain any illegal material as defined under Article 42.[9]

The court ruled on March 3 that Morito had not violated Article 42, but instead had violated Article 41 which covered crimes disturbing the public peace. The judge explained that Morito's essay would cause its readers "to have doubts about our nation's sovereignty, or it will cause them to have contempt for private property. Furthermore, there is a danger that his thesis might disturb the [kokutai]." Morito was sentenced to prison for two months, and Ōuchi was fined twenty yen.[10]

The prosecution appealed the case, and the original judgment was reversed. Interpreting the term "sedition" broadly, the court held that Morito had violated Article 42 and sentenced him to three months in jail and fined him seventy yen. Ōuchi was fined twenty yen and sentenced to one month in prison and one year on probation.[11]

The defendants appealed to the Supreme Court, where the debate centered on the meaning of the term "high treason." Morito argued that

8. *Ibid.*, 239, 243–245.
9. Quoted in *ibid.*, 244–246.
10. Quoted in *ibid.*, 246–247.
11. *Ibid.*, 248–249.

his essay had not endangered the state or the public peace. In fact, he had cautioned his readers to be wary of accepting all of Kropotkin's argument, since it contained "many exaggerations, misunderstandings, and mistakes." Morito went on to say that he had "emphasized the point of slow and legal change."[12] The court conceded that the defendant appeared to advocate peaceful change, but "as long as the ideology he maintains has aspects which endanger the existence of our nation . . . his thesis falls under the purview of Article 42 of the Newspaper Law." The judges added: "The reason for the original sentence was because the court recognized that throughout the entire article the suspect [Morito] Tatsuo was engaged in the action of propagandizing dangerous thought." Morito entered prison on November 4.[13]

By prosecuting Morito, the state proclaimed new boundaries for speech and publication—a preliminary announcement that was to be followed by a stronger statement in 1925. At the same time, the trial informed the general public that steps were being taken to promote traditional morals. In one sense, the Morito case was a preview of the political trials of the following decade, in some of which the Meiji Constitution and the concept of *kokutai* became the issues instead of the facts of criminal law involved in each case. Though the Morito case only skirted these issues, they were involved in the decision. One scholar regards this decision as a weakening of the frail reed of judicial independence of which judges were so proud; it exemplified judicial complicity in the Cabinet's plan to restrict the range of free expression.[14] And in view of the court's central position, as perhaps the most important interpreter of the emperor system and the concept of *kokutai*, the court's decision to support the government in this case was crucial.

By the end of the Morito case, conservatives had closed ranks in their determination to dam the individualistic ethic and other dangerous thought seeping out of the universities. Hiranuma, for example, began to fashion an organization to stamp out subversive thought and reform national life. Sounding a call for restoration of the ideals of the Meiji

12. Quoted in *ibid.*, 249–250.
13. Quoted in *ibid.*, 251, 271.
14. Zadankai, 595.

era, Hiranuma, and men under his influence, founded semiofficial groups like the Suiyōkai (Wednesday Association), a gathering of men of distinction, and the Getsuyōkai (Monday Association), a group of middle-level bureaucrats. By 1921, Hiranuma had established another group called the Shin'yūkai,[15] whose nucleus consisted of a mixture of civil and military bureaucrats like Ugaki Kazushige, Shiono Suehiko, Hiramatsu Ichizō, Tōjō Hideki, Horikiri Zenjirō, Katō Kanji, and Tanabe Harumichi. By June 10, 1922, the membership numbered fifty-seven. Former General Araki Sadao recalled that the group's meetings were a kind of continuing round-table discussion with Hiranuma in the center. The main topic of conversation, he said, was how to deal with the rising communist party.[16]

Thus, the Morito case not only tightened the bond between Hiranuma's faction and the rightists at Tokyo Imperial University, but it also stimulated already concerned bureaucrats to take concrete action. Officials began to look outside their own departments to discover what other officials were doing to cope with the rising left wing.[17] Alarmed by fears similar to Hiranuma's, they joined groups with which he maintained contact. At meetings in Hiranuma's home, or elsewhere, bureaucrats and others discussed the danger facing the state. It was Hiranuma and Suzuki who brought them together, defined the danger for them, and set them thinking about a counterplan.

Hiranuma's and Suzuki's Antiradical Bill

Some time after Morito's conviction, politicians and bureaucrats began to consider new antisubversive legislation. In July 1921, Hara wrote in his diary that he and Yamagata agreed that stronger laws were

15. Shin'yū is one of the names in the Chinese sexagenary cycle. For instance, 901 and every sixtieth year thereafter, including 1921, is a Shin'yū year. Since according to Chinese theory revolutions occurred during Shin'yū, the Japanese began during the Heian period (794–1185) to change the era name whenever Shin'yū came round. It seems that Hiranuma picked this name in order to suggest the need for reform during a period of confusion and danger. It is interesting to note that 1861 was the last time that the government had changed an era name in a Shin'yū year. This illustrates Hiranuma's traditionalism.

16. Itō Takashi, *Showa Shoki Seijishi Kenkyū*, 355–356.

17. *Ibid.*

needed to control radicals.[18] Hiranuma and Vice-Minister Suzuki Kisaburō were also discussing the need for a new law.[19] It took the discovery of Kondō Eizō's dramatic activities, however, to prod them into translating their thought into the drafting of a special bill to control leftist radicals.

Kondō, who had met in May with Comintern agents in Shanghai, was arrested upon his return to Japan. Police were certain that he planned subversive activities (he carried a large amount of money and a coded message), but there was no law with which to punish him; the 1900 peace law covered cases in which people organized a secret society or joined one. Nothing could be done to a person who carried money for propaganda purposes, but who had not begun to propagandize. Kondō's first arrest spotlighted this legal loophole. After his release, Kondō attempted to organize a communist party, and he distributed propaganda posters. When apprehended a second time, seized documents enabled authorities to use the Publications Law and Public Peace Police Law against him, and by late November Kondō's group was crushed.

Following Kondō's arrest, Hiranuma and Suzuki, supported by Hara and Yamagata, supervised the drafting of antisubversive legislation. The extent of cooperation between justice and police bureaucrats is unclear, but it is known that justice officials reviewed foreign laws and legal theories dealing with sedition. Suzuki Kisaburō (who replaced Hiranuma as procurator-general on October 5, 1921) cites two English antisubversive laws as of special interest to the drafters of the Japanese bill.[20]

The proposed bill, entitled "Law to Control Radical Social Movements" (Kageki Shakai Undō Torishimarihō), was introduced into a committee of the House of Peers on February 21, 1922, by Justice Minister Ōki Enkichi and Home Minister Tokonami Takejirō. Although the bill was jointly supported by both ministries, it was primarily justice officials who presented the government's case to the legislators.

18. Hara Keiichirō (ed.), *Hara Kei Nikki*, IX, 387.
19. Suzuki Kisaburō Sensei Denki Hensankai, *Suzuki Kisaburō*, 255.
20. *Ibid.*, 254–255. Itō, 226. Shinobu, 900. Cecil H. Uyehara, *Leftwing Social Movements in Japan*, 381. Shibata Yoshihiko, *Shisō Torishimari Kankei Hōrei Hanrei Gakusetsu Sōran*, 4.

The provisions of the bill were:

Art. 1. Anyone who propagandizes, or attempts to propagandize, in order to subvert the laws of the state in matters connected with anarchism, communism, and others shall be liable to imprisonment with or without hard labor for a term not exceeding seven years.

Anyone who persuades others, or anyone who responds to such persuasion, to execute the above matters will receive the same punishment mentioned above.

Art. 2. Anyone who organizes a society, or organizes a meeting, or engages in a mass movement with the purpose of executing or propagandizing the matters specified in Article One shall be liable to imprisonment with or without hard labor for a term not exceeding ten years.

Art. 3. Anyone who propagandizes, or attempts to propagandize, in order to revolutionize the foundation of the social structure by means of a riot, violence, intimidation, or in other illegal ways, shall be liable to imprisonment with or without hard labor for a term not exceeding five years.

Article Four covered people who supported the above actions with money or gifts, and Article Five extended the carrot to radicals by offering a reduction in punishment, or freedom, for those who informed the authorities. The final article stipulated that Articles One through Four of the proposed law applied also to Japanese who violated its provisions while outside of Japan.[21]

In view of Kondō's activities, it is not surprising that the proposed law was intended to stem the flow of radical propaganda entering Japan and to prevent Japanese from working in concert with foreign radicals.[22] At the first meeting of the committee, on February 25, Justice Vice-Minister Yamanouchi Kakusaburō clearly outlined the bill's scope. Existing laws such as the Public Peace Police Law of 1900, the Newspaper Law, the Publications Law, and the Criminal Code were inadequate, he said, to control Japanese who were in contact with foreign radicals, especially anarchists and communists. Yamanouchi carefully pointed out that the proposed law would strike only at radicals who were engaged in propagandizing, soliciting, or organizing illegal groups, and would not be used to threaten the scholarly world; people doing serious research on radical ideologies would not fall within the law's provisions.[23]

21. Okudaira Yasuhiro (ed.), *Gendaishi Shiryō* (hereafter GS, XLV), XLV, 3–4.

22. Shinobu, 927. Shakai Bunko (ed.), *Taishoki Shisōdan Shisatsunin Hōkoku*, II, 161.

23. Okudaira, GS, XLV, 5–6.

At a later meeting, Chief of the Criminal Affairs Bureau Hayashi Raisaburō presented a summary of recent radical activities. He illustrated that, while it was true that the Criminal Code could be directed at those plotting a rebellion, it could not always be employed against those who "injected dangerous ideas into the hearts of the people." Subversives such as these, because they often employed nonviolent methods, were outside the reach of current laws. Kondō Eizō, for example, was free to spread his ideas for months before he could be prosecuted. Even when current laws were applicable, maximum prison sentences were too lenient; a person who organized a secret society to promote a radical ideology could only be given a maximum punishment of one year in prison.[24]

Justice Secretary Miyagi Chōgorō, who also appeared before the committee, supported Hayashi's argument. It was difficult, in the first place, to attach specific illegal acts to activities of the new type of criminal. Secondly, even when they could be charged with a specific violation, say, for instance, Article Sixteen of the Public Peace Police Law of 1900 (which prohibited the spreading of propaganda that disturbed public peace), the maximum jail term was only one month. And, if they obeyed police orders to stop speaking, they could not be prosecuted. The Newspaper Law, too, was obsolete. True, the Home Minister could issue a prohibition order, but generally those who obeyed were not punished, and those who did not were subject to a maximum sentence of only six months. Moreover, violators of Article 42 of the Newspaper Law (which made it treasonable to act in defiance of the constitution—Morito, for instance, was caught by this law) risked only a maximum two-year sentence. Furthermore, the Newspaper Law was usually applied to publishers and editors and not to writers of subversive articles.[25]

A majority of the committee agreed, and accepted the government's pledge that the law would only be used to cut out the cancer of leftist radicalism. However, the phrasing of the bill displeased nearly everyone. This was not surprising, since Cabinet ministers had had a lively debate on the wording. Some had objected to the title because it lacked precision, suggesting instead *chian torishimari* (controlling

24. *Ibid.*, 7–8.
25. *Ibid.*, 8–10.

public peace). It was decided, however, that this had too broad an application, and the original title was kept. Committee members reflected the Cabinet's dissatisfaction by asking for a "calmer" title so as not to cause commotion in the minds of the people. They preferred to use *chian ijihō* (peace preservation law), *chian hogohō* (peace protection law), or *shakai undō torishimarihō* (law to control social movements). They solved the dilemma by dropping the title and calling the bill by number.[26]

More complicated to deal with was the bill's phrasing. Since key words had various possible interpretations, the committee was concerned lest they be misinterpreted. Unclear were phrases like Article One's "anyone who attempts to propagandize" (*senden sento shitaru mono*) and "subvert the laws of the state" (*chōken o binran suru*). The words "anarchism, communism, and others," especially "and others," were nearly impossible to define. Therefore, they were deleted. In a further effort to clarify the law's scope, they dropped the idea of "attempting to propagandize" while retaining "propagandizes." "Subvert the laws of the state" was grudgingly kept, since they could think of nothing better. Article One emerged from the committee as: "Anyone who has contact with foreigners, or any other persons who are located in an area outside this law's jurisdiction, and then who propagandizes in order to subvert the laws of the state, shall be liable to imprisonment with or without hard labor for a term not exceeding three years." The committee felt that the new version was more precise.[27]

By the time the Peers had completed their scissors-and-paste job, the original six articles had been lengthened to eight. Yet the thrust of the bill and its vocabulary remained little altered. Words were taken from one article and put in another, or similar words were substituted. For example, the "attempts to propagandize," removed from Article One, were incorporated into the new version of Article Four, dressed up as *misuizai* (an attempted crime). The phrase "outside this law's jurisdiction" (*hompō shikō kuiki gai*) was lifted from Article Six and placed in new Article One.[28] Article Three's "foundation of the social

26. *Ibid.*, 11–12. Shinobu, 924.
27. Okudaira, GS, XLV, 3, 12–13.
28. *Ibid.*, 4, 13.

structure" (*shakai no konpon soshiki*) caused committee members some pain. Even though they labored to devise a more exact phrase, in the end they failed. The chairman spoke for the majority when he noted that without the phrase "this article will become a body without bones." On March 14, a majority of the committee voted to pass the bill.[29]

During the floor debate, the bill received some harsh criticism. One strong critic was Izawa Takio, a former prefectural governor and Metropolitan Police Superintendent. Izawa, a committee member, pointed out that the law's provisions were unclear. The concept of "subverting the laws of the state," for example, remained unclear even to scholars of constitutional law. The courts, too, could not agree on this term, even though it had been in use since 1882. The trial of Professor Morito was one example. Passing a law with such vague provisions, Izawa argued, was a serious mistake. It seemed to him that the law was written in such a manner as to make its scope much greater than the government was willing to admit. The government proposed in this law to protect the state from preparatory activities for a rebellion. Yet, the committee, far from limiting the range of the bill, had increased it, with the government happily accepting their modifications. He feared that such a law would be used to stifle scholarship.[30] Why not modify existing laws to control a few radicals? Izawa ridiculed those who thought that Kondō Eizō and a few other subversives, subsidized with only a few thousand yen, would be able to disturb the traditional polity.[31]

Why was Izawa, who was a foe of dangerous alien ideology, against this bill? Besides his liberal tendencies, his Kenseikai political connections and his Home Ministry background placed him automatically in opposition to a Seiyūkai-sponsored bill, a bill from which justice bureaucrats would gain ground at the expense of police officials. Indeed, he accused justice bureaucrats of favoring the bill's vague terminology because it would increase their power.[32] "Above all," it was reported, "one point of his argument, that, in restraining dangerous thoughts, there is no need for new laws, since the full use of

29. *Ibid.*, 13–15.
30. *Ibid.*, 16, 18–19.
31. *Ibid.*, 18, 22–23.
32. *Ibid.*, 19–20.

the established laws can check them, seems to be based on his belief
that this domain of law should be left to the Ministry of Home Affairs
(the Special Higher Police) as before."[33]

The proposed law generated considerable opposition in academic
circles and in the press. Well-known Tokyo Imperial University
professors like Suehiro Izutarō (law) and Fukuda Tokuzō (economics)
attacked the bill on several counts: the government had not
demonstrated a compelling need for such a law and its vocabulary was
extremely ambiguous.[34] "Propaganda" (*senden*), for instance, wrote
Suehiro, was a relatively new term in Japanese. Indeed, not too many
years earlier military and Foreign Ministry bureaucrats had disagreed on
terms to express this idea. Therefore, not many people would have a
correct understanding of the word. Basing a harsh law on such vague
terminology, argued Suehiro, would inevitably result in the suppression
of speech.[35]

Editorials in the Tokyo edition of the *Asahi Shimbun* saw the basic
fault as the government's mistaken notion that force could be used to
suppress thought. Moreover, to shut off new ideas would be a serious
error, since nations develop and change like individuals, and new ideas
were important for this process of change. Existing laws should be used
to suppress truly illegal movements. Finally, said the newspaper, it was
clear that the government had presented a poorly prepared bill.[36]

Despite such criticism, the bill passed the House of Peers near the end
of March, but the Cabinet did not try to push it through the House of
Representatives for fear it would disturb more pressing legislation.[37] It
is noteworthy that neither *kokutai* nor *seitai* (the form of government),
terms which were to generate debate in 1925, were included in this
1922 bill. In spite of this, and other minor differences, it was clearly the
precursor of the Peace Preservation Law of 1925.

33. Okudaira Yasuhiro, "Some Preparatory Notes for the Study of the Peace
Preservation Law in Pre-war Japan," *Annals of the Institute of Social Science,* Number 14
(1973), 60.

34. Okudaira, GS, XLV, 26, 42.

35. *Ibid.,* 27–28. Kazahaya Yasoji points out that it was mainly liberals in the
scholarly, newspaper, and political worlds who promoted the antibill movement—with
little help from labor. The reason for this, he feels, is that labor was preoccupied with the
suffrage movement. Kazahaya, *Seiji Hanzai no Shomondai,* 15.

36. Shinobu, 931–935.

37. Peter Duus, *Party Rivalry and Political Change in Taishō Japan,* 204.

Preparing a New Peace-Law Bill

Failure of the 1922 bill did not deter the Hiranuma-Suzuki clique, which continued to advocate an antiradical law. A series of shocking developments during 1923 highlighted the need for such legislation and served to rally support behind their cause.

On June 5, 1923, suspected communists were arrested throughout Japan and Korea. Twenty-nine were charged with violations of Article 28 of the Public Peace Police Law of 1900.[38] In the midst of the preliminary examination of the suspects, police arrested Pak Yol (Boku Retsu), who had a close relationship with the anarchist Ōsugi Sakae. It was said that Pak had plotted to kill the emperor and prince regent. An even more sensational incident took place on the morning of December 27, as the regent was on his way to open the new Diet session. Namba Daisuke, whose father was in the House of Representatives, fired a shot into the regent's automobile. Although the prince was unhurt, this assassination attempt was regarded by some as the most ominous and shocking incident in the nation's modern history. The new government of Prime Minister Yamamoto Gonnohyōe resigned in atonement, and other officials followed its example.[39]

The trial of the Japanese Communist Party stretched out into a three-year legal battle, during which the prosecution was forced to use the 1900 peace law, even though the Peace Preservation Law was enacted during the trial. Moreover, suspect Takase Kiyoshi's shrewd decision to omit any written mention of the party's antiemperor stance deprived authorities of legal grounds for charging the suspects with high treason.[40]

At first the suspects refused to discuss the party with the preliminary examination judge. Then party member Tokuda Kyūichi pointed out

38. Article 28 provided a penalty of from six months to one year in prison for those who organized or joined a secret society.

39. Tanaka Tokihiko, "Toranomon Jiken," in NSSST, 439, 459–460. Japan, Naimushō, Keihokyoku, *Dai 50-kai Teikoku Gikai Chian Ijihō ni Kansuru Sokkiroku* (hereafter Dai 50-kai), 85. Imai Seiichi, *Nihon no Rekishi*, XXIII, 413.

40. Although the daring demand for the abolition of the emperor was regarded as a key objective, it was never included in any public statement of policy. Sakai Toshihiko and others were concerned about making the demand public, since the government could then charge them with high treason. Therefore, Takase who was secretary for the meeting recorded none of the debate on the emperor. Odanaka Toshiki, "Daiichiji Kyōsantō Jiken," in NSSST, 352–353.

that it was not profitable to remain silent, since this was bound to prolong the trial, and in the end the suspects would spend more time waiting for a decision than the maximum one-year sentence. Defendant Nosaka Sanzō urged that the suspects propagandize the party's platform during the trial. Others suggested that since the authorities appeared to have little concrete evidence, it would be best to deny everything. Finally, the suspects decided to reply to the preliminary judge's questions, in order to quicken the process, and then to deny everything at the trial.[41]

These tactics substantially aided the prosecution. The defendants' actions make more sense, however, if we recall that their personal danger was slight (the extreme penalty was one year in jail) and that the party was very young, with slogans and principles which were not well established. Nevertheless, defense attorney Fuse Tatsuji felt that the tactics adopted by his clients were regrettable, since their statements informed authorities about the contents of the revolutionary movement, and this forced the government to re-examine the existing legal machinery.[42]

During the trial, which opened in April 1925 at the Tokyo District Court, the prosecution employed handwriting experts to link party leaders to party documents. On August 20, twenty-three defendants were found guilty and sentenced to terms of eight to ten months. Defense lawyers said that the trial was being utilized by the government to demonstrate the urgent need for the recently enacted Peace Preservation Law. They were, no doubt, correct, since the court in passing sentence did mention the new peace law, quickly adding that it could not be applied to the present case.[43]

Generally ignorant about communists until this episode, many people had regarded them as less dangerous than anarchists who were inclined toward dramatic assassinations. As a result of the investigation and trial, however, the fear of communism eclipsed that of anarchism.[44] Certainly, frank confessions at the preliminary trial spurred justice authorities to renew their drive to obtain a new peace law.

41. *Ibid.*, 362–363.
42. *Ibid.*, 364.
43. *Ibid.*, 357, 361, 372–373.
44. Shinobu, 924, 927, 931.

In the case of the Korean, Pak, authorities saw the double threat of the growing Korean nationalist movement and the likelihood of cooperation between domestic radicals and those in the peninsula. Concerned about developments, for example, after the great earthquake, Home Ministry officials authorized a radio broadcast warning that it was Japanese and Korean anarchists who were doing the murdering and pillaging. Also, the Ministry sent a directive throughout Japan, blaming Korean radicals for starting fires and carrying bombs, and advocating that strong measures be taken to stop them.[45]

Because of the grave nature of the Namba Daisuke case, justice officials carefully investigated his motives. Supreme Court Chief Justice Yokota Hideo conducted the preliminary examination, while Procurator-General Suzuki kept close watch on the proceedings. After months of investigation, they announced that it was a senseless act committed because of the defendant's ill health. Namba thought otherwise, stoutly insisting that he had acted to avenge the death of Kōtoku and because of his strong belief in communism.[46]

The trial record tends to support Namba's view. Until he was about twenty-one years old, he had no sympathy for radicals. Then, beginning in 1919, he attended political lectures, and early in 1920 he demonstrated to support the suffrage movement. The attitude of Prime Minister Hara caused him to become angry at politicians, more critical of his father's political role, and certain that some kind of direct action would force the government into giving concessions.[47] Namba's reading of leftist literature and old newspaper accounts of the 1910 high-treason incident involving Kōtoku Shūsui increased his indignation at the government. An article by the distinguished Professor Kawakami Hajime on the Russian Revolution convinced him that the revolution had succeeded because of the sacrifices made by dedicated terrorists. Finally, angered by the brutal slaying of Japanese anarchists and the killing of Koreans during the earthquake-induced panic, he decided that the time had come for a terrorist act.[48]

45. Richard H. Mitchell, *The Korean Minority in Japan,* 34–35, 39.

46. Tanaka, in NSSST, 456–457, 459, 461–465, 469, 470–471, 477. Professors at Tokyo Imperial University Medical School examined Namba and pronounced him sane.

47. *Ibid.,* 443–444.

48. *Ibid.,* 456–457.

Even this fragmentary record makes the preliminary court's conclusion of ill health or insanity unlikely. Government documents do not explain why justice officials chose to present this conclusion to the public, but one may hypothesize that the traumatic events of 1923 made the government eager to calm the nerves of the people. Since most Japanese could not conceive of a rational person attacking the emperor, they were conditioned to accept this reasoning. However, comments made later by Justice Minister Ogawa Heikichi show that, secretly, justice officials held the view that Namba had acted rationally, after having been converted by anarchist and communist propaganda.

Namba's act caused authorities to increase their estimate of the danger presented by the first Japanese Communist Party. Indeed, in 1925, when Justice Minister Ogawa was urging a Diet committee to pass the new peace-law bill, he cited Namba's case as a compelling reason.[49] In Namba's trial record, the government had a dramatic example of a loyal supporter being radicalized by leftist propaganda. This case gave justice bureaucrats the example they required in order to bring party politicians and others into line. The need for adequate protection of the emperor and the *kokutai* was a subject on which no debate was allowed. Except for extreme leftist radicals, all elements of society agreed upon this point.

One of Justice Minister Hiranuma's conditions for entering the second Yamamoto Cabinet (in September 1923) was the enactment of a new law to suppress communists.[50] He was, therefore, deeply chagrined by Namba's deed and was convinced that antistate forces were nearly out of control.[51] After the fall of the Cabinet, Hiranuma held almost daily discussions on how to prevent another such incident. The participants agreed that their main purpose was to enlighten the nation about the "frightening foreign ideologies." Hiranuma decided to pull together conservatives and ultranationalists with whom he had contact in a new organization called the Kokuhonsha (National Foundation Society).[52] The Kokuhonsha combined a broad cross section of highly placed civil and military bureaucrats with a body of

49. *Dai 50-kai*, 85.
50. Okudaira, "Some Preparatory Notes," 61.
51. Takeuchi Kakuji Den Kankōkai, *Takeuchi Kakuji Den*, 75.
52. Itō, 353, 356, 358–359.

justice officials who exerted the guiding force. Of the just-over 300 association officers in late 1926, nearly one-half were connected with the Justice Ministry. Much of their attention was devoted to the extirpation of dangerous thought, especially communist ideology.[53]

The dramatic events of 1923 stimulated justice officials to redouble their efforts to draft a new peace-law bill. Suzuki was motivated primarily by his past support for such a law. Recent developments, however, such as new information about the communist party coming out of the preliminary examination, or even the closed trial of Namba Daisuke, surely influenced his thinking about the draft's contents. It is probable that the communist party network caused Suzuki more concern than the actions of highly individualistic anarchists or communist loners like Namba.

As Justice Minister in the brief Kiyoura Cabinet (January–May 1924), Suzuki ordered another antisubversives bill prepared. Kiyoura supported these efforts.[54] Suzuki's Chief of the Criminal Affairs Bureau Yamaoka Mannosuke prepared draft legislation.[55] Assisting him were Motoji Shinguma, head of the Penal Administration Bureau, and other officials who had knowledge of this subject, especially of foreign antisubversives laws.[56] They planned, at first, to reuse old terms from the 1922 bill such as *chōken binran,* or slightly modified ones such as *annei chitsujo binran* (act in defiance of public peace and order). After much discussion, it was concluded that these unclear terms were bound again to generate criticism, and it would be best to substitute words like *kokutai, seitai* (form of government), and *shiyū zaisan* (private property).[57] The short life of the Kiyoura Cabinet, however, prevented Suzuki from introducing the draft into a Diet committee.

Not unexpectedly, Home Ministry officials claim to have played a major role in preparation of the bill. A recent history of that ministry states that terms like *kokutai, seitai,* and *shiyū zaisan,* were suggested by Home Minister Wakatsuki Reijirō (in the Katō Takaaki Cabinet, 1924–1926) and his assistants. According to Wakatsuki's recollection,

53. *Ibid.,* 353–356.
54. Kawahara, 9; Maezawa Hiroaki (ed.), *Nihon Kokkai Nanajūnenshi,* 643.
55. Ushiomi Toshitaka, *Gendai no Hōritsuka,* 15. *Suzuki Kisaburō,* 259.
56. Okudaira, "Some Preparatory Notes," 62.
57. *Suzuki Kisaburō,* 260.

terms like *chōken binran* were discarded because they lacked clarity and because they generated fear in the publishing world.[58] Wakatsuki was unhappy with the terminology in the 1922 bill, and with the 1924 draft drawn up by his ministry and the Justice Ministry. This jointly produced draft aimed the law at those who advocated "the denial of the state, alteration of the national structure [*kokutai*], and so forth, which illegally revolutionizes the system established by the constitution" and at those who sought "the illegal revolutionizing of the laws and discipline of society."[59] In order to make the language more specific, Wakatsuki "revised it to apply to those who advocated revolutionary changes in the national structure (*kokutai*) or the political system (*seitai*) and those who denied the system."[60]

In spite of this claim, most evidence points to justice officials as the ones who were the main driving force behind the planning, drafting, and submitting of a peace-law bill. At any rate, in January 1925, both ministries sent draft bills to the board of legislation where a compromise bill was worked out for submission to the House of Representatives.[61] Comments made during the committee hearings on the bill support other evidence that the Hiranuma-Suzuki group was primarily responsible for the 1925 peace-law bill.[62]

Passage of the 1925 Peace Law

By 1924, it was obvious that the three transcendental Cabinets (nonparty Cabinets, 1922–1924) which had followed the Hara-Takahashi regime (1918–1922) had been unable to cure Japan's political instability. Thus, after the Kenseikai party and its allies won control of the House of Representatives in the 1924 election, the nation's political power brokers, realizing that another neutral Cabinet would not be tolerated by the public or parties, advised the emperor to give the mandate to Katō Takaaki. Among party politicians, Katō had been the most faithful to the concept of constitutional government, and he had

58. Ōkasumikai (ed.), *Naimushōshi*, I, 367.

59. Quoted in Duus, 205.

60. *Ibid.*

61. Eun Sik Yang, "Katō Kōmei (1860–1926)" (unpublished doctoral dissertation), 266.

62. Okudaira, "Some Preparatory Notes," 61.

consistently refused to compromise his principles.[63] Katō discovered, however, that it was much easier to maintain his political principles as a leader of the opposition than as prime minister. As the leader of a coalition government, Katō was forced to distribute some Cabinet positions to supporters in the Seiyūkai party: Yokota Sennosuke to head the Justice Ministry, Takahashi Korekiyo to run agriculture and commerce, and Inukai Tsuyoshi as minister of transportation.

Meanwhile, Suzuki's draft for a peace law was completed. The timing was propitious, since information about the preliminary examinations of communist party members and of Namba Daisuke were providing bureaucrats and Diet members with an intimate view of a communist organization and the thinking of a terrorist; this must have shocked them into an awareness of the potential danger, and must have given justice officials extra leverage in their arguments for the need of a new peace law.

Katō's biographer says that although "there is little information as to what extent Katō influenced this legislation," he may have "recognized the need to appease conservative elements who advocated" the law. Katō, he said, concentrated upon what he thought to be more important programs and allowed his ministers to deal with this problem.[64] This statement rings true, since the Katō Cabinet was built upon an unstable coalition, of which the strong Seiyūkai party element was well known for its antileftist bias. In addition to this, it should be recognized that while Katō had a reputation as a liberal and a moderate, he leaned heavily toward duty, cooperation, and protecting the *kokutai*. And the general Kenseikai party leadership, in spite of the efforts of liberals such as Nagai Ryūtarō, harbored a fear of the awakening lower classes and their intellectual supporters. Moreover, the sixty-five-year-old Katō became more conservative after coming to power.[65]

It is noteworthy that the Katō Cabinet regarded the Peace Preservation Law as but one law in a series designed to stem the radical tide. The Cabinet moved first to defuse explosive conditions in rural areas by reintroducing a 1920 Seiyūkai party bill designed to control

63. Yang, 241.
64. *Ibid.*, 267–268.
65. *Ibid.*, 262.

tenant disputes. On the surface the Tenant Dispute Arbitration Law of
December 1, 1924, appeared to support tenants, but it was used to
dampen conflict and to save landlords.[66] On the labor front, another
Seiyūkai bill was reintroduced as the Labor Union Law. This antilabor
bill's real purpose was to control unions. It failed to pass, because
capitalists were deeply suspicious of any union legislation, and labor
disliked its obvious antilabor provisions.[67] Simultaneously, the Diet
was also considering a compulsory mediation law designed to protect
big business.[68] Probably the support for these bills did not come as
much from Katō as from Seiyūkai party members of the coalition
government. Katō, who was in ill health, and whose reform legislation
was sharply opposed by the House of Peers and Privy Council, was
forced to make concessions.[69]

While support for a new peace law had been building for several
years, new reasons for such a law were advanced after Katō took office.
The restoration of diplomatic relations with Russia (occurring on
February 26, 1925) was expected to stimulate an increase in the amount
of radical thought entering Japan.[70] Furthermore, the Privy Council and
House of Peers were lobbying for a law to counter the excesses they
feared would result from the extension of suffrage.[71] The electorate was
sharply restricted by a property qualification. The passage of the
Universal Manhood Suffrage Act (May 1925) increased the size of the
electorate from three million to thirteen.

Katō's biographer sees the enactment of the Peace Preservation Law
as the "passport for passage of universal suffrage." This view that a
deal was made between the Cabinet and the Privy Council first appeared
in the midst of the debate on the peace law, when Kiyose Ichirō and
Hoshijima Jirō interpellated Home Minister Wakatsuki. Had the Privy
Council forced the government to introduce the peace-law bill as a

66. Shinobu, 1155, 1164–1167.
67. *Ibid.*, 1172–1176, 1213–1221.
68. *Ibid.*, 1221–1222.
69. Yang, 244.
70. Matsuo Hiroya, "Kyoto Gakuren Jiken," in Wagatsuma Sakae (ed.), *Nihon Seiji Saiban Shiroku, Showazen,* 69. Duus, 276, n. 38. The convention restoring relations is cited in George A. Lensen, *Japanese Recognition of the U.S.S.R.,* 177–183.
71. Shinobu, 1181.

precondition for acceptance of the expansion of suffrage?[72] Wakatsuki replied: "The government's trying to establish the Peace Preservation Law has no connection whatsoever with the putting into practice of manhood suffrage. The government presented the . . . bill because of the necessity of maintaining public order."[73] Despite Wakatsuki's strong denial, the possibility of a deal between the Cabinet and the Privy Council has strongly influenced scholarship on the Katō Cabinet, with a common feeling being that a quid pro quo was reached with the Privy Council.[74]

Circumstantial evidence supports this "plot" thesis. Although both the suffrage and peace-law bills were long-pending pieces of legislation aimed at solving different problems, they did touch each other. This fact was established in the House of Representatives in 1922, when politicians heatedly debated the merits of a Kenseikai party bill to increase the number of voters. Those in favor argued that since agitation for economic, social, and political reforms had reached a boiling point, the logical solution was to give the masses the vote. Then, the government would gain support from the people, and would reverse the tendency toward radicalism.[75] Those opposed, mainly Seiyūkai party members, insisted that passage would only stimulate radicals and promote revolution. Universal suffrage, said Hatoyama Ichirō, was "the fuse for dangerous thought."[76] It was logical for Seiyūkai politicians in Katō's Cabinet to maintain this position. Indeed, because of events during 1923 they had undoubtedly become more concerned about excesses that might result from an enlargement of the voting public. The Privy Council also felt strongly on this issue, and in a report to the throne, councillors asked for a control law to counterbalance universal suffrage.[77] In addition, the passage of Katō's reform program (which was generating stubborn opposition in the House of Peers and

72. Kawahara, 9. Shinobu, 1181.

73. *Dai 50-Kai*, 46.

74. Shinobu, 1181.

75. *Ibid.*, 915–917.

76. *Ibid.*, 918–920. For a good study on the origins and politics of the suffrage bill see Edward G. Griffin, "The Universal Suffrage Issue in Japanese Politics, 1918–25," *The Journal of Asian Studies*, XXXI (February, 1972), 275–290.

77. *Dai 50-Kai*, 46.

Privy Council) forced the Cabinet to compromise. Katō's speech to his party in late October illustrated his willingness to negotiate with the Privy Council: "The accomplishment of universal suffrage has been the most urgent policy of our party for years. Nonetheless, many obstructions have prevented us from achieving this. Now we aspire to see this accomplished *at any price*."[78] Finally, it should be noted that Katō must have realized that passage of a harsh peace law would pacify critics in the House of Peers and Privy Council.

The role of the Privy Council is often misunderstood. It was completely independent from the executive and legislative parts of the government, with a direct responsibility to the emperor. As the highest constitutional consultant of the throne, the Privy Council had the duty to give opinions on drafts of laws supplementary to the constitution, treaties, and certain imperial ordinances. However, the categories of legislation subject to Privy Council review were not sharply defined, and the Cabinet enjoyed some discretion in deciding which bills and ordinances to submit.[79] What about the two draft laws in question? Universal suffrage, because it was an amendment to the election law, was legislation supplementary to the constitution, and the government was clearly obligated to submit it for Privy Council scrutiny. But the peace-law bills of 1922 and 1925 were not subject to Council inspection, and were sent directly to the Diet. This was true of the 1928 revision bill as well, which was turned over to the Privy Council for enactment as an imperial ordinance only after the Diet shelved it due to adjournment.

A comparison of the order of events in drafting and approving the suffrage bill and the peace bill will shed some light on the connection, if any, between the passage of these laws.

In November 1924, the Justice Ministry was studying plans for a peace law. A meeting with Home Ministry officials, on January 7, failed to reach a compromise on the wording of the draft bill. Therefore,

78. Quoted in Yang, 257.

79. Emergency Imperial Ordinance (No. 403) of September 7, 1923 issued following the great earthquake was considered valid even though not submitted to the Privy Council. For details about the Council see Kenneth Colegrove, "The Japanese Privy Council," *The American Political Science Review*, XXV (August, 1931), 589–614 and (November, 1931), 881–905.

on January 16, both ministries submitted bills to the board of legislation for consideration. A new draft was completed by the board of legislation on February 1; was presented by Home Minister Wakatsuki to representatives from Katō's coalition government on February 12; and reached the House of Representatives on February 18.[80] As for the suffrage bill, it went before a Privy Council committee on December 27. Subsequently, if we can believe information leaked to the press, it was debated on January 8, 15, 17, and on February 3 and 13. At the January 8 meeting, the government was asked what was being done to stop the leftward trend; it replied that the Peace Preservation Law bill was under consideration. The last meeting produced a compromise between the views of the government and the Council; the final bill disqualified only a small number of the adult males.[81]

Edward Griffin, who has made a close study of the passage of the suffrage bill, feels that the sequence of events indicates no "explicit agreement" between the Privy Council and the Cabinet to exchange one law for the other. "The government announced the final text of its Peace Preservation Law bill on the morning of February 12, and it was on the afternoon of that day, that the Privy Council's committee of inquiry returned its recommendations on the suffrage law— recommendations which were not acceptable to the government."[82] This action indicates that the government's announcement of the bill was not sufficient to sway the councillors. It would seem that a "deal" would have produced a more harmonious outcome. Furthermore, it should be noted that when an agreement was reached by Katō and Hamao Arata (head of the Privy Council) on February 13, to be formalized by the full committee the next day, the government had done nothing more to guarantee passage of the peace-law bill.[83]

Others support this persuasive argument. Kawasaki Takukichi, who was head of the Police Bureau of the Home Ministry, accompanied Wakatsuki to meetings of the Privy Council. The government made no

---

80. Edward G. Griffin, "The Adoption of Universal Manhood Suffrage in Japan" (unpublished doctoral dissertation), 173–176.

81. *Ibid.*, 165–172.

82. *Ibid.*, 176.

83. *Ibid.*, 176–177.

deal with the Council, and the peace law was not payment for the passage of the suffrage bill. The peace-law bill, Kawasaki insisted, was aimed at suppression of leftist thought movements, and it dated back to the ministry of Tokonami Takejirō (under Hara and Takahashi).[84] And, of course, Wakatsuki denied any connection, pointing out that the Home Ministry had been working on such a bill for a long time.[85]

What was it that gave the impression of a package deal involving the two bills? One thing was the fact that they went into the legislative mill together. Another item was the mystery surrounding the secret debates of the old men sitting on the Privy Council. For instance, when Wakatsuki was asked about such a deal, he replied that there was none, and that he could say no more because Council minutes were secret.[86] This sort of reply was bound to create suspicion. Then, the fact that the Council had asked about measures being taken to combat radicals, and had mentioned the need for such a law in its report to the throne, supplied more fuel for the fires of suspicion.[87] Finally, and not least important, there is a determined effort by present-day Japanese historians of the Marxist-Leninist faction to blacken the image of the interwar government elite. They cannot imagine the passage of these bills without an explicit agreement, because to do otherwise would run counter to their general theories about prewar politics.

In summary, even if there was no outright deal between the Cabinet and the Privy Council, there was, because of the legislation's timing, some connection between the two bills. Council members were aware of the government's plan to introduce a peace-law bill—which must have pacified them. As for the Cabinet, since it planned to pass the peace law anyway, its intention may have been to hurry the draft bill into the Diet where it might influence conservative councillors to release the suffrage bill. A connection existed, then, but one much less direct than critics have charged.

On the matter of the introduction of the bill to the Diet, Kawasaki Takukichi shed some interesting light. There was a group of Home

---

84. Kawasaki Takukichi Denki Hensankai, *Kawasaki Takukichi,* 277–278, 286.
85. Kawahara, 10.
86. *Ibid.*
87. Kawasaki, 277. *Dai 50-Kai,* 46.

Ministry advisers clustered around Vice-Minister Yuasa Kurahei who were against joining the Justice Ministry in presenting the peace-law bill to the legislators, and who urged that the Justice Ministry be given sole responsibility.[88] Yuasa's opposition to the bill did not end here, but continued during the committee of inquiry held by the House of Representatives. At the March 6 meeting, for instance, he attacked the bill, arguing that police and judges would misuse its wide powers.[89] In contrast to this serious split in the Home Ministry, the Justice Ministry's attitude was very different and very positive; the bill was a good one and was sorely needed. Justice officials were, no doubt, reflecting the feelings of Hiranuma and Suzuki, and this episode underscores their influence in the justice field and the prime importance of the Justice Ministry in the promotion of the peace law. In spite of Yuasa's misgivings, Wakatsuki decided to cooperate with Justice Minister Ogawa Heikichi (Yokota had died). Wakatsuki pointed out that his ministry had to cooperate in presenting this bill, because the peace law would not be the exclusive possession of either one. The Home Ministry was intimately involved, since the law would apply to organizations and publications.[90] The bill was introduced to the lower house committee on February 19, 1925. Its provisions were:

Art. 1. Anyone who has organized an association with the objective of altering the *kokutai* or the form of government or denying the system of private property, and anyone who has joined such an association with full knowledge of its object, shall be liable to imprisonment with or without hard labor for a term not exceeding ten years.

Any attempt to commit the crime in the preceding clause will [also] be punished.

Art. 2. Anyone who has discussed the execution of matters specified in Paragraph One of Article One with the object mentioned therein shall be liable to imprisonment with or without hard labor for a term not exceeding seven years.

Art. 3. Anyone who has instigated the execution of the matters specified in Paragraph One of Article One with the object mentioned therein shall be liable to imprisonment with or without hard labor for a term not exceeding seven years.

88. Kawasaki, 288–289.
89. *Dai 50-Kai,* 176.
90. Okudaira, GS, XLV, 76.

Other provisions specified sentences of up to ten years for agitators who instigate others to engage in violence or damage to life and property for the purpose of committing those crimes described in Article One, Paragraph One; sentences of up to five years for supporting such crimes with money or gifts, or for knowingly receiving money or gifts for such a purpose (amnesty or reduction of punishment were offered to violators of the preceding articles if they surrendered). The final article stipulated that the law's provision applied even to those outside its jurisdiction.[91]

The committee was receptive to the idea of a new law, but there was considerable discussion about the bill's terminology. Justice Minister Ogawa explained that anarchism and communism were not used because they were difficult to define. Instead the phrase "altering the *kokutai* or the *seitai*," which had a wider meaning, was chosen. As a practical example of the difficulty in distinguishing between an anarchist and a communist, he cited the Namba case.[92] When one committee member pointed out that not even constitutional scholars could agree on the meaning of *kokutai*, Wakatsuki replied that by this word the government meant the "imperial nation combined with the emperor above." Thus, he was saying that *kokutai* meant the "imperial system" (*tenno sei*) and corresponded to the term "constitution" (*chōken*), which was used in the 1922 bill.[93] According to Wakatsuki, the committee worried that the bill, which was aimed at communism and anarchism, might also be used to suppress freedom of speech, to which the Home Minister replied, "Let's change it," pulling a paper and pen out of his pocket. But after a painstaking review of each article, the committee could not devise more precise terms.[94]

Ogawa pointed out the dire need for such a law, reviewing in detail the development of the Japanese Communist Party and the increasing contacts with Russia. "These agitators are people greatly to be feared, since we cannot give them the proper punishment for this kind of terrible crime. . . . Under present conditions, there is no law to properly

91. Okudaira, GS, XLV, 51.
92. *Dai 50-Kai*, 85–86.
93. Shinobu, 1200–1201.
94. Ōkasumikai, 367.

punish this kind of dangerous action.'' Communists planned not only to divide property equally, but also to create a government controlled by laborers and farmers. The only way to stop them was to pass this law.[95] When asked to define anarchism and communism, however, the bill's sponsors admitted that they could not produce exact definitions. Moreover, Wakatsuki confessed that they were unable to distinguish socialism from the other terms as well. Government representatives also had difficulty explaining the meaning of private property and the word ''instigation'' (*sendo*) which appeared in Article Three. Despite these problems, the committee accepted the government's contention that the law was directed only against extreme leftist radicals, and voted in favor, with the provision that *seitai* be deleted.[96]

During committee debates it was pointed out that the law would greatly strengthen the police who might misuse its wide powers.[97] In 1925 public criticism was weaker than in 1922, with mainly the Tokyo and Osaka *Asahi Shimbun,* some labor unions, and liberal elements in the scholarly and political worlds opposed. Tokyo Imperial University professors kept strangely silent, and the *Chūō Kōron* (*Central Review*) carried fewer antibill articles than in 1922.[98] Perhaps the shocking events of 1923 had muted some critics.

On March 7, 1925, committee chairman Maeda Yonezō gave his report to the House of Representatives. Supported by Home Minister Wakatsuki and Justice Minister Ogawa, Maeda announced that the law was not intended to block free speech and scholarly research. Scholars and students would be permitted to research leftist ideology, and would be free to publish their conclusions. However, anyone who acted on radical leftist ideas, by becoming involved in creating organizations, agitation, and meetings, would fall within the law's scope. The bill

95. *Dai 50-Kai,* 46–48, 86.

96. Shinobu, 1204, 1207–1208, 1212–1213.

97. *Dai 50-Kai,* 65.

98. Shinobu, 1182, 1186, 1188, 1190–1191. Comment by Professor Okudaira Yasuhiro, panel on ''Thought Control in Interwar Japan,'' Association for Asian Studies, April 1, 1974. Details of labor activities against the peace-law bill are difficult to find. Kazahaya thinks that the labor response was much greater than in 1922, and mentions several demonstrations, 18–19. Aoki Kōji, *Nihon Rōdō Undō Shi Nempyō* (533–534), mentions several demonstrations. Unfortunately, the eleven-volume *Nihon Rōdō Undō Shiryō,* edited by Rōdō Undō Shiryō Iinkai, is incomplete for the period in question.

passed with overwhelming support on March 7. The House of Peers gave its assent on March 19, and the bill became law on May 11.[99]

There was no great public outcry against the new law. The Tokyo *Asahi Shimbun* accused the government of disregarding the needs of the people, by representing only big business and big landholders.[100] One legal association questioned the law's value, wondering if it might not stimulate antigovernment activity instead of reducing it.[101] It appears, however, that the Diet's strong support in passing the law reflected a deeply felt need among the populace. In the spring of 1925, it is unlikely that a majority of politically sensitive Japanese saw the fundamental contradiction between the law's passage and the maintenance of free speech and free association. Indeed, as they saw it, the creation of a special law was a logical solution to the era's disturbances.

Conclusion

There were two main currents of constitutional interpretation after the promulgation of the Meiji Constitution in 1889. One emphasized traditional attitudes toward the divinity of the emperor and assumed that ethics and law were nearly identical. Professor Hozumi Yatsuka was one of its chief spokesmen. The other current, represented by the legal theorist Minobe Tatsukichi, emphasized a secular view of the emperor and state and borrowed from the modern West its concept that ethics and law were completely distinct. In his rational view of the state, Minobe superimposed upon the *kokutai* theory a German theory that described the emperor as the highest organ of the state, which was a legal person, with the power to carry out executive functions of the state. For Minobe the emperor was less than the state and subordinate to its laws. For Hozumi the throne represented an ethical imperative. "Implicit in the symbol was a commitment to a parochialism which ran directly counter to many of the political, ethical, and legal ideas which entered Japan from the West."[102]

The enactment of the Peace Preservation Law proved to be of great

99. *Dai 50-Kai,* 162, 176. Shinobu, 1211–1212.
100. Shinobu, 1209–1210.
101. Nihon Bengoshi Rengōkai (ed.), *Nihon Bengoshi Enkakushi,* 120.
102. Minear, Richard H., *Japanese Tradition and Western Law,* 12.

significance. Few Japanese in 1925 could have suspected the wide influence this law would have during the following two decades. The Diet, by converting *kokutai* into a legal term, signaled its support of Hozumi Yatsuka's theory of state and partially repudiated Minobe Tatsukichi's liberal, democratic construction of the Meiji Constitution. In effect, the government announced that it had decided to maintain the comforting Japanese tradition in which politics and ethics were intertwined. Furthermore, by passing a peace law with the phrase "altering the *kokutai*," instead of something more concrete like *chōken o binran suru* (subvert the laws of the state), the Diet unwittingly helped create a legal Hydra.

"The main criticism that can be made of the Peace Preservation Law," writes one scholar, "was that it was superfluous and that it was liable to be interpreted with excessive zeal by the police; like most repressive legislation, the main danger lay less in how it was worded than in how it was applied."[103] The point about enforcement is, of course, well taken, but the idea that it was an unnecessary law is mistaken. Faced with serious political, economic, and social problems, the government used the new peace law as more than a weapon against leftist thought criminals; certainly this law was intended as both criminal legislation and as a strong reaffirmation of the nation's basic unity and harmony. Thus, the law had a political purpose (to suppress thought criminals) and an ethical one (to soothe society and pull it toward integration).

Moreover, the use of *kokutai* in the law was highly significant. In choosing *kokutai*, the Hiranuma-Suzuki clique picked a term that aroused a strong emotional response in the emperor's subjects; *kokutai* symbolized everything worth protecting. They could not have devised a better one. The use of the enigmatic and highly emotional term *kokutai* reflected a continuation of the government drive to indoctrinate its subjects in the way of reverence for the emperor. While not yet a legal term, *kokutai* had been used for nationalistic purposes for several decades. The Imperial Rescript on Education (1890) had dressed Confucian ethical precepts in the garb of modern nationalism.[104] The

103. Duus, 206.
104. Besides the use of *kokutai* in the Imperial Rescript on Education, Article I of the

drafters of the Rescript, by employing the term *kokutai,* had turned their backs on Westernization and sought refuge in the purity of "Japanism." Therefore, the use of *kokutai* in the Peace Preservation Law was a logical extension of this ongoing reaction to modernization and Westernization. By using this phrase, the government informed all the emperor's subjects of its intention to preserve the Japanese way of life in the face of rapid change.

Meiji Constitution proclaimed the imperial line as unbroken for ages eternal. As Robert N. Bellah notes: "No clearer assertion of Japanese particularism was possible." Bellah, "Japan's Cultural Identity," *The Journal of Asian Studies,* XXIV (August, 1965), 575.

3 Applying the New Peace Law

The Peace Preservation Law was used by justice officials before the end of 1925. Since they had taken the lead in planning and drafting this law, they could be expected to test it. That its first use was directed at student radicals is hardly surprising, since their antigovernment activities made them highly visible targets.

During the debate preceding enactment of the peace law, academic freedom and the limits of student research and protest were discussed by the Diet. It is interesting to note that Home Minister Wakatsuki and Justice Minister Ogawa held different views on student rights. Teachers and students, said Wakatsuki, should be free to study any subject, provided they did not attempt to carry out the aims of a subversive ideology. Justice Minister Ogawa, however, when asked about the rights of scholars and students, differentiated between mature scholars and students when defining academic freedom. Since many examples were available of students being radicalized by reading improper books and hearing inflammatory lectures, students should be prevented, Ogawa said, from organizing groups to study radical ideas. The business of students was to study, and not to pay attention to unhealthy thought.

Shinobu Seizaburō, writing in 1968, felt that Ogawa's reply illustrated that the government's promise of academic freedom for research and thought had not been fully guaranteed by the new law. The authorities had shifted, Shinobu argued, from a position promising total freedom to one providing only limited freedom: they had ended up, he maintained, by denying what they said they were going to do.[1]

1. Shinobu Seizaburō, *Taisho Seijishi,* 1194–1195, 1199–1200.

It appears that Shinobu has slipped into the error of regarding Ogawa's views as identical with those of other officials. Certainly, there were those who shared Ogawa's opinions, but, nonetheless, his views were not necessarily the same as those of Wakatsuki, who declared that the new law guaranteed academic and student freedom.[2] Moreover, Ogawa, a former Director of the Census Bureau and a Seiyūkai politician, did not fully reflect the views of justice bureaucrats. The law's provisions naturally meant different things to different people, but it is mistaken to view the crackdown on student associations as part of a great conspiracy to constrict civil rights that was being formulated even before the law's passage.

First Use of the Law

The activities of radical students had concerned the government for some time. Prior to 1925, however, the authorities seldom interfered in campus activities, and even when students were caught in illegal off-campus activities the police were usually understanding. This feeling of toleration underwent a marked change, however, as students organized nationwide and became more vocal in their antigovernment protests. By 1925, student associations, which had before been only mildly objectionable, had become intolerable. To many conservatives they were so many festering splinters which had to be extracted.

The most visible target for the conservatives' wrath was the Marxist-oriented Student Federation of Social Science (Gakusei Shakai Kagaku Rengōkai), or Gakuren. From a tiny study association created in 1922, Gakuren quickly expanded throughout the country. This strong, tightly organized student federation got its start in debating clubs at Tokyo Imperial University and at Waseda, a private university in the metropolis. At first, students interested in Gakuren followed the lead of the off-campus left, supporting them in street demonstrations and campus rallies. Soon, however, Gakuren leaders altered the nature of their role and began to initiate campus-related radicalism. The new thrust of Gakuren's movement is reflected in two incidents in 1923. Waseda University officials planned to reorganize a student equestrian club into a Military Study Group, to be run with the aid of army

2. Peter Duus, *Party Rivalry and Political Change in Taishō Japan*, 206.

officers. Agitators dispatched by Gakuren disrupted the founding ceremonies. Dignitaries, including the army vice-minister, were jeered into silence. The second variant of this new emphasis upon the university itself also occurred at Waseda. On this occasion a police search for communist party documents on the morning of June 5 triggered a strong student protest. Gakuren was greatly strengthened by both these incidents, for they presented the student movement with an opportunity to take a clear political position on two important campus-related issues: military education and academic freedom. For the first time the organization gained wide public attention.[3]

The newly inspired students rapidly expanded their organization. Gakuren built not only a country-wide horizontal organization, but also a vertical structure embracing the nation's leading provincial higher schools. Thus, higher school graduating classes provided the universities with fresh and highly motivated recruits. On September 14, 1924, Gakuren held its First Congress at Tokyo Imperial University. The organization, which claimed 1,600 members on forty-nine campuses, had become a united, nationwide student federation. By the end of that year, it had established branches at nearly every higher school and university in the country, as well as in other schools. Mainly, the students agitated on campus-related problems, but a few of them, impatient with the slow pace of social and political reforms, joined the communist party and adopted its more radical demands. The entire Gakuren organization became more radicalized in the eyes of authorities, in the spring of 1925, when its affiliation with the labor movement began to change. When a schism in the labor movement resulted in the creation of the Japan Labor Union Council (Nihon Rōdō Kumiai Hyōgikai), or Hyōgikai, Gakuren chose to support labor's new radical wing. Moreover, students became intensely involved in strikes, organizing activities, and propagandizing to create a new breed of revolutionary labor leaders.[4] The organization's Second Congress secretly accepted a platform which declared that ''the student movement must hereafter act as one wing . . . of the proletarian movement with Marxism-Leninism as its guiding principle.''[5]

3. Henry Smith, *Japan's First Student Radicals*, 100–110.
4. *Ibid.*, 112–113.
5. Quoted in *Ibid.*, 124.

Following the conference, students under Gakuren became deeply involved in the activities of Hyōgikai and, by doing so, they unwittingly provided authorities with evidence for their indictment under the terms of the new peace law.

In late November 1925, when antimilitary education posters appeared on the campus of Dōshisha University in Kyoto, police authorities saw the handiwork of the illegal Japanese Communist Party, working through Gakuren.[6] The head of Kyoto's thought police, Kubota Shun, was especially sensitive to the activities of Gakuren, because it had held a convention there in July, and because Kubota had been involved in the arrest of communists just two years earlier.[7] According to Vice-Minister Kawasaki Takukichi (prior to September he had been head of the Police Bureau of the Home Ministry), Kubota contacted Tokyo and asked what was to be done about the posters and Gakuren. The Home Ministry was inclined to go easy on the students and told Kubota to wait. However, the procurator at the Kyoto District Court was insistent that arrests be made. Kawasaki and other high officials then ordered the police to carry out the arrests.[8]

On December 1, raids were carried out on dormitories, boarding houses, and private homes, as the police searched for incriminating documents. Thirty-seven students were charged with passing out antimilitary printed material, but because of insufficient evidence they were released. Probably much to the surprise of Kubota and his men the arrests triggered huge student rallies and severe criticism in the press. Public reaction to the raids, plus inability to obtain indictments, must have galled the police. Stung by failure, they prepared for another try, since there was growing confidence that some of the documents seized earlier might be covered by the Peace Preservation Law.[9] Meanwhile, in Tokyo, on December 16, justice and police officials from across the nation attended a meeting at the Justice Ministry. Vice-Minister of Justice Hayashi Raisaburō, Procurator-General Koyama Matsukichi, procurators from the most important courts, and thought police chiefs from each prefecture were present. The decision

6. Kawasaki Takukichi Denki Hensankai, *Kawasaki Takukichi*, 304.
7. Smith, 191.
8. Kawasaki, 304–305.
9. Smith, 191–192. Kikukawa Tadao, *Gakusei Shakai Undōshi*, 432.

was made to destroy Gakuren.[10] The second round of arrests began in mid-January and lasted for four months; any book that looked as though it might have the slightest connection with radicalism was seized, including those by Marx, Engels, and Lenin which had been legally imported and were being openly sold. Private homes of well-known professors such as Kawakami Hajime were invaded, and research materials, books, private mail, and diaries were seized. Finally, thirty-eight students, of whom twenty were from Kyoto Imperial University, were charged with violating the Peace Preservation and Publication Laws.[11]

"The precise aims of the officials who masterminded the Kyoto Gakuren arrests have never been made clear; perhaps a precedent for the use of the Peace Preservation Law was desired, or perhaps Kubota's inordinate ambition was the deciding factor,"[12] writes one student of this affair. This view seems off the mark, given the previous aggressiveness of justice officials in creating the peace law; it was natural for them to follow up by making use of the law. Besides this, we have Vice-Minister Kawasaki's statement that it was the procurator in Kyoto who spurred Kubota into action, and, further, the record of decisions made at the conference held at the Justice Ministry on December 16.

This first application of the Peace Preservation Law was significant for several reasons. Under the new law the courts upheld the prosecution's argument that conspiracy to overthrow the existing political, social, and economic structure was a criminal act under the 1925 law, thus setting a legal precedent that applied the law not only to those directly engaged in revolution, but also to those who were involved in antistate discussions, meetings, distributing leaflets, and other propaganda activities. In enforcing the new law justice officials, especially procurators at the Kyoto District Court and the Osaka Court of Appeals, played the leading role, thus establishing their predominance in the area of thought control. By making use of Article 19 of the Newspaper Law to impose a news blackout on this case, a

10. Kikukawa, 439.
11. Matsuo Hiroya, "Kyoto Gakuren Jiken," in Wagatsuma Sakae (ed.), *Nihon Seiji Saiban Shiroku, Showazen*, 71–72. Kikukawa, 439.
12. Smith, 193.

precedent was established for later thought cases when it became the practice to prohibit newspapers from reporting anything until the preliminary investigation was completed.[13]

That the Justice Ministry saw this as an important case is obvious from the top talent assembled in Kyoto. A special team of procurators was sent: Ikeda Katsu, Hirata Susumu, and Kurokawa Wataru from Tokyo, and Yoshimura Takeo from the Osaka District Court. For Ikeda and Hirata, who were already engaged in careers as thought specialists, this case was an important training exercise.

Preparing the case was a strain, for the procurators knew little about communist ideology. However, they learned by reading books seized as evidence, and by interrogating students who were delighted to engage in theoretical debates. During these arguments the students thoroughly attacked Japanese society and unwittingly educated the procurators in the esoteric doctrines of communism. In so doing, the students helped build the government's case. The procurators were struck by the fact that the defendants were eager to engage in verbal battle on all subjects except the imperial system.[14] At a later time, this weak spot was to be fully exploited.

The thirty-eight defendants were on trial at the Kyoto District Court between April 4 and May 30, 1927. All of them were charged with crimes against the Peace Preservation Law: they had joined organizations which had ratified the subversive policies adopted by Gakuren; they believed in Marxist-Leninist doctrine and had plotted to overthrow the state and form a communist regime; they had drafted a statement of purpose and had discussed ways to carry out their plan to overturn capitalism and introduce communism.[15] Seven of the defendants were in addition charged with violations of the Publication Law. They had, said the prosecution, published writings and drawings which debased the dignity of the imperial family, or which advocated changing the form of government, or they had written things in defiance

13. Okudaira Yasuhiro, "Some Preparatory Notes for the Study of the Peace Preservation Law in Pre-war Japan," *Annals of the Institute of Social Science,* Number 14 (1973), 63.

14. Japan, Shihōshō, Keijikyoku, *Shisō Kenkyū Shiryō Tokushū* (hereafter SKST), XII, May, 1934, 211–213.

15. Matsuo, 75.

of the constitution. Finally, one was also charged with lese majesty for comments he made while giving a lecture at Kyoto University Christian Youth Hall (this charge was dropped because of a political amnesty after the death of the Taisho emperor).[16]

The main argument of the team of defense lawyers was that the activities of their clients were well within the acceptable limits of academic freedom, and that the Peace Preservation Law should not be used to punish the development of thought and educational activities. Support came from outside the courtroom as well, by well-known intellectuals like Yoshino Sakuzō, Yamakawa Hitoshi, and Ōuchi Hyōe who wrote that the students were inexperienced youths who had been merely playacting at social change and who were not a serious danger to the government.[17] Professor Sasaki Sōichi spoke out forcefully, as he had done at the Morito trial, and said that the 1925 peace law did not cover this case.[18]

There are indications that the matter of "intention" was weighed by the courts. Judge Arai Misao, of the Kyoto District Court, rejected the prosecution's request for a stiff three-year sentence. Since the factor of intent versus action is at the heart of this case, we can surmise that Judge Arai must have deeply pondered this subject. Yet, technically, they had conspired, which was a violation. Nonetheless, Arai's verdict appears to be a compromise in favor of the defendants, of whom four were sentenced to one year and the others were given either eight or ten months. Nearly one-half of the defendants were put on probation for the following two years. After pronouncing the verdict, the judge said that the court regarded the defendants as men with a promising future, and he urged them to try to understand that freedom of research could not be permitted to go beyond legal bounds. Finally, he admonished them to obey their parents and to be good sons.[19] Reflecting this tolerant attitude, Yamada Shōzō, chairman of the Department of Law at Kyoto Imperial University, said that school officials would take no further action.[20]

16. *Ibid.*
17. Kikukawa, 450. Matsuo, 73, 77.
18. Kikukawa, 445.
19. Matsuo, 76–77.
20. *Ibid.*, 77–78.

Next the case moved to the Osaka Court of Appeals where it was scheduled to begin the following April. However, since nearly half of those on trial were also implicated in another incident, one occurring on March 15, 1928 (and described below), the appeal action was delayed. The trial began, finally, on September 24, 1929. At its conclusion, twenty-one defendants received a prison sentence; the longest was seven years and the shortest was one year and six months.[21] The court, in passing sentence, cited specific meetings, discussions, and other actions in which each defendant committed an illegal act. For instance, Gotō Toshio and Shimizu Heikurō had in June 1925, at the headquarters of Tokyo Imperial University's social science research association, prepared the draft which was secretly adopted by Gakuren at its second national conference. Moreover, they had with others formed a committee to debate in detail each plank of the draft platform. (It should be recalled that the Kyoto District Court declared that Gakuren's platform called for the overthrow of the state and the formation of a communist regime.) In July, at the headquarters of Kyoto Imperial University's social science research association, students had been told by their leaders that the driving spirit behind Gakuren was Marxist-Leninist ideology, and that Gakuren's purpose was to change Japanese society from capitalism to communism. Gakuren had wanted its supporters to create a revolutionary vanguard among students, so that they might lead the workers. Students, at that meeting, were urged to carry out this policy and to pull in new members. Off-campus they were to enlighten the working class. Interestingly, Shimizu had also been at this meeting. The court was given proof that some of those at the Kyoto meeting later discussed this matter and put the plan into action. Here, said the court, they had moved beyond the stage of theory and personally held opinion, and were illegally agitating for the overthrow of Japan's "social structure."[22]

Some recent scholarship on this case strongly attacks the use of the Peace Preservation Law. An American scholar makes this interesting observation: "The case rests on the evidence of specific acts which involve the individual defendants as organization members, but the

21. *Ibid.*, 78–79.
22. Okudaira, GS, XLV, 540–541.

major summary statement slides over the distinction between members and group to consider the thoughts and thought-generated activities of the defendants directly. Moreover, the whole case concerns ideas, plans, and intentions, rather than any real implementation of the revolutionary changes delineated.''[23] A Japanese scholar writes: ''In this case, the Peace Preservation Law was applied to a group of students which was not engaged in a direct, actual revolutionary movement . . . and its activities were no more than distributing leaflets, holding meetings for the purpose of enlightening the working class.''[24] From the court's viewpoint, however, the students were more than ''playacting,'' when they noisily argued for revolutionary change and propagandized among students and workers by handing out subversive material. These activities, however slight the danger to the government and society, were a step beyond scholarly discussion and research. In 1925, Maeda Yonezō had emphasized to the Diet that ''when thought becomes involved in creating organizations, agitation, and meetings, then, for the first time it will be punished.''[25] Therefore, the defendants, with their work to support Gakuren's illegal activities, their propaganda meetings to spread subversive ideas, and their passing out leaflets with revolutionary contents, fell within the law's scope.

The Justice Ministry's Thought Section

The Justice Ministry informally created a Thought Section in 1926 and formalized this action with a special budget in 1927. Information on the first months of operation is meager, but publications which began to appear in January 1927 indicate that a special Thought Section was at work. According to Egi Tasuku's biography, justice officials were working to establish the new unit in late 1925. Egi, who replaced Ogawa, was concerned over the apparent rapid growth of radicalism and social problems, and he felt that the Justice Ministry must lead the way in formulating a detailed antiradical counterplan. Therefore, he gathered reference materials on the ''thought problem'' (*shisō mondai*)

23. Patricia G. Steinhoff, ''Tenkō: Ideology and Social Integration in Prewar Japan'' (unpublished doctoral dissertation), 49.

24. Okudaira, ''Some Preparatory Notes,'' 63.

25. Japan, Naimushō, Keihokyoku, *Dai 50-Kai Oyobi Dai 56-Kai Teikoku Gikai Chian Ijihō ni Kansuru Sokkiroku*, 162. Also see Matsuo, 74–75.

from the Home Ministry, had them reproduced, and circulated them throughout the Justice Ministry headquarters. Furthermore, he requested special funds in the 1927 budget for the establishment of a Thought Section in the Criminal Affairs Bureau. Subsequently, thirty-five people were placed in the new organ.[26]

Beyond this, a two-part Justice Research Committee was created on April 20, 1926. One section of the Committee promoted Conferences of Administrators; judges and procurators were to consider ideological problems at its meetings. Their speeches, discussions, and other materials were to be circulated in a new publication entitled *Shihō Kenkyū* (Justice Research). The Committee's other section was to bring procurators and judges together in Tokyo for research and discussion on ideological problems. Their reports were also issued under the title *Shihō Kenkyū*, but in a different series.[27] These activities, plus the creation of a Thought Section, represented the beginning of a coordinated effort to identify and prosecute ideological offenders.

In June, the first section held a meeting in Tokyo, at which thirty-two judges and procurators studied procedures in connection with criminal administration. Between early August and December, eleven judges and seven procurators gathered at the Justice Ministry to initiate the second section's program. A major research theme was the relationship between the social movements and criminal offenses.[28] In addition, subjects such as "Criminal Disposition for Anarchists and Communists," "Crimes Caused by Social Development," "Organizational Crimes," and political crimes from after the Meiji Restoration were explored.[29]

Shisō Buhō (Thought Section Report), the section's first report published on January 1, 1927, contained a summary of rightist and leftist activities up to the end of 1925, material on communism in China and Europe, an outline of Japanese proletarian parties, and an article on plans for investigating thought offenses.[30] The second through the sixth

26. Egi Tasuku Kun Denki Hensankai, *Egi Tasuku Den*, 365.

27. Japan, Shihōshō, *Shihō Enkakushi*, 397. Omori Megumu (ed.), *Teikoku Kenpōka ni Okeru Shakai: Shisō Kankei Shiryō*, 3. See Appendix II, Chart 1.

28. Cecil H. Uyehara, *Leftwing Social Movements in Japan*, 384.

29. Omori, 26.

30. *Ibid.*

numbers were published under the title *Shisō Chōsa* (Thought Investigation). The March, April, September, and November issues focused on anarchists, the Suihei movement,[31] proletarian political parties, the student movement, translations of articles by Russian leftists, the connection between leftists in China and Japan, the urban and rural labor movements, and "Condition of the Thought Movement."[32] Since justice bureaucrats were anxious to define a thought crime, issue number six also summarized such crimes between January 1922 and December 1926. The list of 261 illustrative offenses occurred in connection with the labor movement, tenant disputes, Suihei activities, the rise of the Japanese Communist Party, right-wing movements, and the Kyoto Student Association case. Each example included a synopsis of the preliminary examination, the verdict, and the people involved. The authors confessed that it was difficult to "subjectively give a general view of thought crimes."[33]

The Conference of Administrators held in late May 1927 discussed the difficulty of prosecuting ideological offenders. How should the courts maintain their dignity and carry on trials in the face of such abuses as defendants refusing to stand and using the courtrooms as a forum for propagandizing? A solution, it was concluded, would be to limit the speech of defendants, to hear cases rapidly and in secret, and to be strict.[34] Besides these tactics, thought criminals must be squarely confronted on the issue of ideology in order to learn why they committed an ideological offense. It was agreed that a deeper understanding of thought-criminal motivation was important.[35]

The Justice Ministry was criticized for inadequate logistical support, and was urged to disseminate information on thought crimes and control techniques. Reference materials such as name lists, cases handled at

31. For centuries a pariah class had performed "unclean" tasks connected with blood, death, and other forms of ritual uncleanliness. Even after 1871, when such discrimination was legally removed, the "special class" people continued to live outside the mainstream of society. Some of them created the Suiheisha (Equality Society), during the upsurge of social protest in the 1920's.

32. Omori, 26.

33. Quoted in Uyehara, 390.

34. Japan, Shihōshō, Chōsaka, *Shihō Kenkyū* (hereafter SK), IV, May, 1927, 6–7, 23–24, 80. This series began in December, 1926.

35. *Ibid.*, 13.

each court, other statistical data, and copies of reports compiled by the headquarters, it was said, would all be helpful. Also, in order to standardize each court's approach, a uniform plan of action was necessary. Finally, some urged the appointment of special procurators to investigate thought crimes.[36]

Shortly after this conference, the Justice Ministry prepared the Tokyo District Court for ideological cases. Procurator Shiono Suehiko, who was appointed to this task, was one of Hiranuma Kiichirō's closest followers. His first act as head of the procuratorial bureau of the Tokyo District Court was to appoint Matsuzaka Hiromasa his deputy. Together they purged incompetent personnel and divided the bureau into four general sections, with a special fifth section to deal exclusively with thought offenses. Hirata Susumu who had worked on the Kyoto Student Association case was its head. Hirata was assisted by Kameyama Shin'ichirō and Oka Gorō. This was the first district court bureau to create a special section for thought crimes.[37]

The forty-eight-year-old Shiono was an excellent choice, for he was an innovative reformer. Shiono's new position was one to which he had aspired for years; chief of the Tokyo bureau was a job near the pyramid's top. The position was one of great responsibility, since the actions of the Tokyo bureau set the pace for other bureaus. After taking office, Shiono began a zealous prosecution not only of thought cases, but also of those involving graft and corruption.[38] Shiono felt strongly that procurators had a special mission to protect the nation from harm. He ordered his subordinates, therefore, to strive mightily to maintain *seigi* (righteousness or justice) in order to protect the nation (*kokka*) and people (*kokumin*). As dedicated men, they were to have the spiritual strength needed to forge ahead against all odds and even be willing to resign rather than to compromise their convictions. Superior and perfect work was required from his bureau, he said, because public criticism over mistakes might cause the entire procuratorial system to crumble.[39]

36. *Ibid.*, 23–24.
37. Shiono Suehiko Kaikoroku Kankōkai, *Shiono Suehiko Kaikoroku*, 246–247.
38. *Ibid.*, 242, 249.
39. *Ibid.*

Prelude to the Mass Arrests

Conservatives like Ogawa Heikichi considered the Wakatsuki Cabinet (1926–1927) too soft on leftists and were not unhappy when it resigned over a financial crisis.[40] Hiranuma, who had rallied the Privy Council to attack Wakatsuki, was rewarded by the new Tanaka Giichi government. Hiranuma's close friend Hara Yoshimichi was appointed justice minister and his loyal supporter Suzuki Kisaburō was made home minister.[41] Thus, at the start of Tanaka's Seiyūkai party regime (1927–1929) a unique situation arose, with justice officials and their supporters in control of both ministries. Suzuki, who was the first former justice minister to run the Home Ministry, brought in Yamaoka Mannosuke (former head of justice's Bureau of Criminal Affairs) as Chief of the Police Bureau. These developments, together with Tanaka's strong hatred of leftists, explain his government's tough line toward radicals.

The Justice Ministry and its thought procurators led the government forces in the mass arrest of March 15, 1928. Shiono's Tokyo District Court bureau and a few justice bureaucrats planned the arrest, supervised it, and prepared for the trial held in Tokyo. Only a few police leaders helped in the planning, and they functioned strictly under the orders of justice officials. This was a significant development, since prior to this time Tokyo police had acted without consulting procurators. Now the Special Higher Police had become a subsidiary organ of the prosecution.[42]

The mass arrest of 1928 was triggered by the renewed activities of the Japanese Communist Party. Spies and other sources provided authorities with information on Comintern orders to re-establish the party and an important leadership conference held at Goshiki Spa in December 1926.[43] In early 1928, the hitherto clandestine party emerged

40. Ogawa Heikichi Bunsho Kenkyūkai Hen. *Ogawa Heikichi Kankei Bunsho*, I, 619.

41. Richard Yasko, "Hiranuma Kiichirō and Conservative Politics in Pre-war Japan" (unpublished doctoral dissertation), 70.

42. *Shiono Suehiko Kaikoroku*, 248. Okudaira, "Some Preparatory Notes," 64.

43. George M. Beckmann and Okubo Genji, *The Japanese Communist Party*, 94. Yamabe Kentarō (ed.)., *Gendaishi Shiryō* (hereafter GS), XVI, xii. Itō Miyoji, "Himitsu Kessha Nihon Kyōsantō Jiken no Gaiyō, in *ibid.*, 1. Matsuzaka Hiromasa, "San'ichigo, Yon'ichiroku Jiken Kaiko," in *ibid.*, 45.

from the shadows to aid proletarian parties in the first national election held under the new suffrage law. Before this time, party orders, plans and other materials had filtered into police hands, but the party's name was not on them. During the spirited election campaign, however, communists engaged in a flurry of propagandizing, with the first issue of *Red Flag* calling upon laborers and farmers to wage an all-out struggle. Also, highly subversive handbills bearing the party's name were scattered nationwide.[44] The election of February 20 resulted in a near defeat for Tanaka's Seiyūkai party (219 seats), with the Kenseikai party achieving 217. The leftist parties, in spite of strong police pressure, won eight seats, an occurrence which alarmed conservative politicians who saw that the near balance between the major parties favored the radicals.

Shiono's bureau was the government's nerve center for watching communists. But, unfortunately, they knew little about communism and were often unable to recognize the party line when it appeared in a legal publication. Indeed, it was nearly impossible to draw a precise line between illegal party activities and legal ones by the labor movement. And spies were not fully reliable. For example, while details about the Goshiki Spa meeting remained unknown until after the March 15 arrest, the spies had noted and reported on the upsurge of communist activities after the meeting. "Thus, we realize that they [communists] were at work," recalled Matsuzaka, "but we could not obtain enough evidence. . . . We had to wait for them to somehow expose themselves."[45] Although communist election activities did expose the party, procurators still did not have sufficient direct evidence for prosecution. The Justice Ministry decided, therefore, to gamble on a nationwide sweep in order to capture the required solid evidence.

Yamabe Kentarō, a prewar communist party member and a postwar scholar of the party's history, argues that the authorities planned to build their legal case upon confessions obtained by torture, and not upon seized documents.[46] Secret government records, however, contradict him. While Yamabe is correct in pointing out the importance

44. Itō Miyoji, 5–6. Matsuzaka, 44. Beckmann and Okubo, 139–143.
45. Matsuzaka, 42, 44–46.
46. Yamabe (ed.), GS, XVI, xv–xvi.

of confessions, whether "forced" or voluntary, he is mistaken in assuming that the authorities planned to prove their case by squeezing out confessions. The procurators in command planned to obtain legal proof by seizing documents in a well-coordinated blitzkrieg. Matsuzaka helps clear up this point. The authorities, he reported, expected a difficult case, since information gained from spies could not be used in court. Besides, "when we considered our experience in arresting the first communist party, we could guess that they would not easily confess. . . . We could be sure, since the prison term could be up to ten years, that they would not want to talk." Consequently, he said, the procurators could not plan to build a case based on confessions. "We had to obtain the evidence by searching their homes. If they had letters or party organization papers in their possession, these could be used as powerful evidence against them."[47]

The mass roundup was prepared and executed with extreme secrecy. Procurator-General Koyama and several of his deputies were cognizant, but at the Tokyo bureau only Shiono, Matsuzaka, and Hirata knew. Assistant procurators and others were not informed until two days ahead of time. Only a few in the Special Higher Police knew.[48] While close contact and cooperation between those privy to the plan was crucial, this had to be accomplished without creating suspicion that something unusual was happening. In order to escape detection, justice officials did much of their planning over private telephones and at meetings held at the homes of relatives. Even then there were a few anxious moments. On March 10, for instance, a final session was held at the home of one of Matsuzaka's relatives in the Ginza area. The next day Matsuzaka was shocked when a newspaperman explained that he had recognized the procurator's automobile and wondered why they had met. Matsuzaka replied that it was nothing more than a common courtesy call.[49]

Care was exercised to prepare the case in a proper manner. Doubtlessly, the procurators were more concerned about technical flaws when they prosecuted than about the civil rights of those arrested. Nevertheless, written arrest warrants and domiciliary search orders

47. Matsuzaka, 49.
48. *Ibid.*, 46. Okudaira, "Some Preparatory Notes," 64.
49. Matsuzaka, 51.

were obtained. In Tokyo fifteen suspects were named on warrants, but
elsewhere local officials used their own judgment. Those selected in
Tokyo appeared to be active communists. Named on the Tokyo warrants
were: Fukumoto Kazuo, Sano Fumio, Watanabe Masanosuke, Nakao
Katsuo, Matsuo Naoyoshi, Katayama Mineto, Hikabe Chiyoichi,
Kadoya Hiroshi, Kokuryō Goichirō, Saitō Hisao, Nakano Tsuneo,
Nabeyama Sadachika, Shindō Kyūzō, Kawada Kenji, and Minami
Kiichi. Writing the warrants was exceedingly difficult, as few details
were known about the Goshiki Spa meeting, including whether or not
all the suspects were party members. The inclusion of Minami Kiichi,
who was in Hamamatsu Prison during the Goshiki meeting, indicates
their confusion. Conversely, others from the Tokyo area who attended
the meeting were not on the list.[50]

Since authorities lacked important details about party membership
and activities, arrest warrants were written in an abstract manner:

Facts About the Suspect

The objective of the suspect and others is to overthrow the present
organization of our country, and by a proletarian dictatorship to realize a
communist society. Around the end of 1926, the suspect and others organized a
secret organization in Tokyo City, the Japanese Communist Party, which has the
above objective. Since that time they have had secret meetings in Tokyo and
other places, have infiltrated into the various kinds of labor and farmer groups to
recruit new members for the party, and have broadcast handbills with
imflammatory contents. The suspect and others are engaged in propagandizing
their principles and in carrying them out.[51]

In addition, one secretary was secretly at Shiono's official residence
writing other documents for use by local procurators. To explain his
three-day absence, his colleagues were told that he was ill. Procurators
masked such activities by acting as though business was routine. They
even held a news conference at the official residence while the secretary
was still at work.[52]

The next step was to distribute documents to local authorities. Here,
the matter of timing was crucial, since an early arrival might precipitate

50. *Ibid.,* 49. Yamabe (ed.), GS, XVI, xvi. Beckmann and Okubo, 112, note.
51. Matsuzaka, 49.
52. *Ibid.,* 52.

a flurry of activity at a local procurator's office, and this might alert local newspaper reporters. It was decided, therefore, to have legal documents arrive in each area the night before the arrest. The March 15 date was picked in order to mask any signs of unusual activity, for at that particular time the Justice Ministry was in the midst of investigating election irregularities, with officials traveling throughout the country investigating incidents and arresting election violators. Thus, the confusion of the postelection period was utilized as camouflage. Another ruse was to send some of the legal papers by registered mail and deliver others by hand. For instance, one justice official, who was scheduled to depart for western Japan on the evening train of March 13, was given sealed orders to deliver to Nagoya, Kyoto, Osaka, and Kobe. Simultaneously, the Tokyo bureau announced to newspapers that procurators were being dispatched to investigate election irregularities.[53]

Shiono's bureau prepared a detailed list of things to be seized and places to be searched. Police were to seize: all documents connected with the organization of the Japanese Communist Party (e.g., party platforms, regulations, and minutes of each meeting); party orders and propaganda materials (e.g., written appeals, handbills, pamphlets, and leaflets); letters, diaries, and notes, in order to prove the connection between individuals and the party; and communist publications. Such material would be used to connect party leaders with the illegal organization. The places to be raided were the more active left-wing political party headquarters, labor-union headquarters, newspaper and publishing firms, and the homes of selected individuals.[54]

March 15

At precisely 5:00 A.M., several thousand government agents began a series of raids ranging from the far north in Hokkaido to the extreme south in Kyushu, investigating over one hundred and twenty places. In the capital city, thirty-two places were carefully searched. Special teams led by preliminary judges and procurators visited the most important locations. One team, headed by Senior Preliminary Judge

53. *Ibid.*, 51–52.
54. *Ibid.*, 50–51.

Tsukada Shōzō and Procurator Nakajima, investigated the headquarters of the Nihon Rōdō Kumiai Hyōgikai (Japan Labor Union Council). Other teams investigated the *Musansha Newspaper*, the headquarters of the Labor-Farmer Party, the Kanto Women's League, the League of Tokyo Reporters, and the home of Ōyama Ikuo. Among other places searched were the residences of Yamamoto Kenzō and Nosaka Sanzō.[55]

The Japanese Communist Party was not yet mortally wounded, but the raid was a tremendous success. About 1,600 suspects were arrested, and others were apprehended during the next several months. Of those arrested, approximately 500 were ultimately prosecuted. The authorities seized thousands of valuable documents, including a coded list of party members which was deciphered within several days. Before finding the name list, party strength was estimated at about one hundred people. Thus 409 registered members and 500 candidates for membership came as a shock.[56]

On March 30, Shiono sent instructions, information about the recent arrests, and a copy of the seized name list to procurators wherever arrests had been made. Procurators were ordered to have police arrest anyone on the list who was within their jurisdiction. They were told that after the arrests were completed "we will tie everything together and have an open trial at the [Tokyo District Court]." Information about the growth of the party, social background of its members, the establishment of factory cells, all knowledge gained since the arrest, was included. Shiono closed his cover letter by saying: "I would like you to report to my office promptly [information] about the suspects' addresses, names, occupations, ages, and an outline of the facts involving them in the cases."[57]

55. *Ibid.*, 35–36, 50–51. For a communist viewpoint see Kobayashi Takiji's novel: *The Fifteenth of March, 1928*, recent printing of which is in *Senkyūhyakunijūhachinen Sangatsu Jūgonichi, Kanikōsen, Tō Seikatsusha*. A less emotional account of the mass arrest is in Watanabe Sōzō, *Hokkaido Shakai Undō Shi*, 262–267.

56. Nabeyama Sadachika, *Watakushi wa Kyōsantō o Suteta*, 121. Matsuzaka, 53–54. Odanaka Toshiki, "San'ichigo, Yon'ichiroku Jiken," in Wagatsuma Sakae (ed.), *Nihon Seiji Saiban Shiroku, Showazen*, 130.

57. "Nihon Kyōsantō Jiken ni Kanshi, Shiono Kenjisei Yori Chihō Kenjisei e no Tsūchō (Fu, Angō Tōin Meibo) in Yamabe (ed.), GS, XVI, 56–64.

Discovery of the name list encouraged investigators, but the over 300 suspects in Toyko, the uncertainties about party organization, and the lack of skilled interrogators, slowed the work considerably. According to Matsuzaka, the procurators were not even certain which ones were members and which ones were organizers. Hirata, their only real "expert" on thought crimes, was assisted by Kameyama and Oka, each of whom had only two months of special training (it appears that Matsuzaka's experience was equally limited). Most of the procurators "did not know about thought" and "did not know what the communist party was." To correct this deficiency, Hirata and his small staff instructed their colleagues about communism and the correct treatment of thought offenders. In addition, of course, they learned as they processed communist suspects. It was a difficult and tense time for both the procurators and the suspects, with many sleepless nights.[58]

Naturally, suspects were not eager to aid the authorities. A typical exchange between a procurator and a suspect went like this: Procurator: "You joined the communist party, didn't you?" Suspect: "What is the communist party? Is there such a thing in Japan?" Procurator: "These are the documents of the communist party." Suspect: "That must be scribbling." Eventually, however, a crack appeared in the suspects' solid front, when one of them admitted joining the communist party and made a confession. The prosecution now had the critical proof it needed.[59]

New Measures to Control Radicals

On April 10, the front page of the Tokyo *Asahi Shimbun* was filled with the mass-arrest story, and the public first learned about it.[60] The next day Prime Minister Tanaka announced new measures to suppress radicalism. Anyone who attacked the imperial family or the *kokutai* would be crushed without mercy. We will be firm, he emphasized, in "correcting terrible thought." At the same time, the government would become more deeply involved in helping students and youth who might

58. Matsuzaka, 53–54.
59. *Ibid*, Itō, 4.
60. Asahi Jānaru (ed.), *Showashi no Shunkan*, I, 43.

be influenced by radicalism. He also appealed to citizens to respect the *kokutai* and constitution.[61]

Police units quickly enforced Tanaka's harsh policy by banning the Labor-Farmer Party, the All-Japan Proletarian Youth League, and the Council of Japanese Labor Unions. This action was justified by explaining that the organizations were controlled by communists and used communist election slogans.[62] These organizations were dissolved under the provisions of Article Eight, Item Two, of the 1900 Public Peace Police Law,[63] which gave the home minister wide powers. In order to maintain public peace, the minister could disband any organization he felt endangered society. Thus, the freedom of all political groups depended upon the minister's discretion. Home Minister Suzuki Kisaburō signed the disbandment order.

Tanaka's strong action is hardly surprising. As a firm opponent of leftists, he took action consistent with his own ideological beliefs. Moreover, Tanaka had good cause for disliking the proletarian parties which had attacked his strong China policy. No doubt the left's substantial gains in the general election also influenced his decision. It is also likely that Tanaka, who had been plagued with serious political reverses, saw here an issue that might be exploited.[64]

The Tanaka Cabinet also struck at leftist extremists by urging the Fifty-fifth Diet to approve quickly a revisional peace law bill. This bill, whose provisions were much harsher than the 1925 law, was sent to a committee of the House of Peers. Article One specified from five years to death as a sentence for leaders and organizers of groups trying to change the *kokutai*. Anyone joining a subversive organization, knowing its goals, was subject to over two years' imprisonment. The sentence of two years for those who violated the private-property clause remained unchanged. However, the new version separated the ideas of repudiating private property and altering the *kokutai*. The most

61. Kita Kazuo, *Nihon Kyōsantō Shimatsuki*, 43–44. For details of Tanaka's strong anticommunist speech at the opening of the Fifty-Fifth Imperial Diet see Maezawa Hiroaki (ed)., *Nihon Kokkai Nanajūnenshi*, I, 763–764.

62. Itō Miyoji, 7.

63. Kita, 35–36. For the full text of Article Eight see Wagatsuma Sakae (ed.), *Kyū Hōreishū*, 60.

64. George O. Totten, *The Social Democratic Movement in Prewar Japan*, 255–256.

significant change was that nonmembers could be charged with "furthering the aims" of an illegal organization. Since with the 1925 law procurators could only indict suspects who were formal members of the communist party, they supported the suggested amendment. Such a significantly broadened law would, the authorities hoped, close loopholes discovered during the mass arrest.[65] However, Suzuki's revision was not acted upon, due to the Diet's dissolution.

Tanaka's Cabinet had been blocked by the Diet, but only temporarily. There was another route for revising the 1925 peace law, that is, by reproducing it as an emergency imperial ordinance. Article 8 of the constitution permitted the enactment of law via imperial ordinance, when the Diet was adjourned, in order to maintain the safety of the nation. Such an ordinance was law until the next session of the Diet, when it could be either ratified or rejected. There were ample precedents for employing an imperial ordinance, and Tanaka's group could be certain of strong support from the conservative Privy Council which had to ratify their decision, particularly since Hiranuma was vice-president of the Council. Moreover, Railway Minister Ogawa Heikichi, who felt strongly that the law should be quickly revised, was available to aid Justice Minister Hara Yoshimichi draw up the revised law draft, and to help get it through the Privy Council. It should also be noted that Maeda Yonezō, who had chaired the Diet committee that passed on the draft of the 1925 peace-law bill, was now head of the board of legislation, and he, too, went out of his way to help Tanaka's group draw up the revision; he also urged Privy Council members to support the ordinance. This was probably unnecessary, since Hiranuma and President of the Privy Council Kuratomi Yuzaburō had secretly pledged their support.[66]

Near the end of June, the Privy Council held special sessions, with the emperor and Cabinet in attendance. Hiranuma, as chairman of the committee that examined the bill, said that under current conditions it was extremely urgent to act quickly. It was, of course, too bad that the Diet had not acted, but under the Meiji Constitution an imperial

65. For a police view of the revision bill see Japan, Kōchi Ken Tokubetsu Kōtōka, *Tokubetsu Kōtō Keisatsu Kankei Hōki Kaigi Shūroku*, 3.
66. Ogawa, 621. Kawahara, "'Chian Ijihō' no Suishinshatachi," 5.

ordinance was legal. Justice Minister Hara Yoshimichi pointed out that quick action was needed to meet the threat of communist publications which were daily growing bolder in their antistate comments, and were aiming at corrupting farmers and soldiers.[67]

Although the government got its ordinance, five of the twenty-six privy councillors took strong stands against it. Egi Senshi, who had a long political career in the Home Ministry and House of Peers before entering the Privy Council in 1924, said that he had never before read such a peculiar report. Why did the government not extend the Diet, if the law was so urgent? And if it was such an urgent matter, why did the House of Representatives' shorthand record not even once mention that fact? What had occurred during the last several weeks to make the matter so urgent? Did the Cabinet feel that the *kokutai* was so weak that it could not withstand comments in leftist publications, at least until the Diet met again? Besides this, Egi felt that it was the duty of the Diet to pass the bill, and not the Privy Council. Then, there was the matter of the death penalty which he felt was unwarranted, especially on the eve of the enthronement ceremony.[68] Other opponents of the bill made similar comments. Privy Councillor Matsumuro Itaru said that while few people disagreed with the bill, he felt that a death penalty was too harsh, but he believed that in the end the bill would be passed by the Diet. Therefore, it was his duty to point out to the emperor that for the Privy Council to act in place of the Diet was a serious mistake.[69] Ishiguro Tadanori urged those present to think about what would happen if the Diet did not confirm the Council's actions. Then, all those given a death penalty—and the emperor's signature would be on the law —would be saved by the Diet. This would make good propaganda material for subversives.[70] Ogawa wrote in his diary that he could not understand why Egi and Matsumuro refused to support the bill, noting that he suspected the latter had become senile.[71]

67. Okudaira, GS, XLV, 115–116, 124–125.

68. *Ibid.*, 127–129. The increase in respect for the emperor, which the government constantly encouraged, was further strengthened by the elaborate enthronement ceremonies for Emperor Hirohito. Although he succeeded to the throne on December 25, 1926, the enthronement ceremonies did not take place in Kyoto until November 10, 1928.

69. *Ibid.*, 130–133.

70. *Ibid.*, 138.

71. Ogawa, 622.

The government issued an Emergency Imperial Ordinance (Number 129) with the Privy Council's blessings, and the law was put into practice on June 29, 1928. Although the Cabinet's actions drew strong criticism, the following January the House of Representatives voted 249 to 170 to accept the law, and on March 19, the House of Peers also passed it. [72]

At the time the revision was being debated, much attention focused on the death penalty which was, in fact, not the most important item. Even more significant was the matter of the prosecution of nonmembers who supported an organization, who were now to be treated like ordinary members. A few years later this "furthering the aims" clause, which was originally intended to aid in the prosecution of those promoting communist-front groups, was reinterpreted to include noncommunists even when they were not connected with an illegal organization. In 1928 few persons, including politicians, sensed the full significance of the revised law.

Authorities, shocked at the events of March 15, decided to tighten up things in the educational field. Students, they had discovered, were playing an important role in communist party activities. One newspaper headline read: "MAJORITY OF STUDENTS ARRESTED ARE IMPERIAL UNIVERSITY STUDENTS   AUTHORITIES ARE ASTONISHED STUDENT PARTICIPATION ON A NATIONAL SCALE." Such vivid proof that the nation's stability was threatened gave the government an excuse to suppress students' freedom of activity. [73]

After student participation in radical activity was revealed in the Kyoto Student Association case (during the winter of 1925–1926) the Education Ministry had become stricter, but officials were not yet seriously alarmed. Minister Okada Ryōhei had ordered selected associations which were considered dangerous to dissolve, and others were put under strict supervision. [74] Lists of proscribed books and

72. *Dai 50-Kai Oyobi Dai 56-Kai*, 27–28, 289, 481, 485–486.

73. Quoted in Smith, 200.

74. *Ibid.*, 194–195, and n. 17. The Okada directive, which was issued in May 1926, extended an earlier prohibition of group study of leftist literature to individual study. Student clubs were placed under stricter supervision and off-campus activities were tightly regulated. The form of Okada's order is unclear, but it probably was a *kunji* (oral explanation), given by Okada at an educators' conference.

magazines were circulated, the spy network was enlarged, and leftist suspects were blacklisted. Although there was some talk about discharging leftist professors, education officials were mostly content to let university authorities deal with the thought problem.[75] However, the response of education authorities in 1928 was quite different. Where the earlier directive had simply provided administrative guidelines for each school, the new instructions were specific and stressed complete control.[76]

In a Cabinet meeting on April 13, Education Minister Mizuno Rentarō placed the blame for student radicalism on leftist professors. Hereafter, it was decided, teachers, students, and social science research groups would be strictly regulated.[77] The new policy was explained in the Official Gazette: "Cultivation of the Idea of *Kokutai*." All imported ideas were to be thoroughly "Japanized," abnormal thought was to be purged, and educators must firmly support the *kokutai* and truly understand its meaning. Mizuno went on: "We must especially concentrate upon preventing youth from catching this disease. We must teach them about our nation's creation and explain in clear terms the real meaning of the *kokutai*." Finally, teachers were ordered to monitor student thinking to prevent disturbance by outside influences.[78]

Mizuno's statement was implemented in the following months. A Student Section was established in the Bureau of Special Education.[79] In addition to collecting material and evaluating student movements, this central organ did basic research and published information. Its publications were to carry articles on the background of the Kyoto Student Association case, on Fukumotoism, on leftist activities in high schools, and on social science study groups.[80] Within the Student

75. Kikukawa, 458–460; Matsuo, 72, 75; A. M. Young, *Japan in Recent Times*, 327–328; Harry E. Wildes, "Japan Returns to Feudalism," *The Nation*, CXXIII (October 27, 1926), 436–437.

76. Smith, 200.

77. Kita, 54.

78. *Ibid.*, 47–50.

79. Smith, 201. The Student Section was later expanded into a larger Division, and then into a Thought Bureau, and finally into an Education Bureau. See Appendix III. Also, Chapter 6, the section on "Thought Guidance."

80. Uyehara, 342–343.

Section was a committee to supervise student thought, using reports sent in by each school. Direct control was introduced into schools by appointing "student supervisors" whose double mission was to ferret out illegal organizations and to advise students. To show that it meant business, the Education Ministry dissolved social science associations and purged radical professors like Kawakami Hajime of Kyoto Imperial University.[81]

As for the Home Ministry, despite its long involvement in watching radicals, its officials were shocked by the large number of elite students apprehended; the fact that the poison had spread to Tokyo Imperial University, from which the next generation of leaders would emerge, spurred them to action. Consequently, the number of thought police in Tokyo was increased and thought police were assigned to all prefectures. Up to this time, there were Special Higher Police units in Tokyo, Osaka, Kyoto, Kanagawa, Aichi, Hyōgo, Fukui, Nagano, Yamaguchi, Fukuoka, Nagasaki, and Hokkaido. Agents were also stationed in Peking, Shanghai, and Harbin. In requesting a special budget to expand the coverage of the thought police, the Home Ministry pointed out that part of the funds would be used to install special telephone lines between Tokyo and other cities, and to send personnel to places like Berlin, London, New York, and Chicago, to keep watch on overseas Japanese and foreign radicals.[82] Behind the scene, the thought police issued a secret directive that broadened the scope of the Peace Preservation Law: Now, the administrative decision said, "anyone who appears as if they *might want* to change the absolutism of the emperor [italics mine]" was to be arrested. "We will define them as people who are going to change the *kokutai*."[83]

Significant changes took place in the Justice Ministry. The Supreme Court, seven appeals courts, and ten main district courts were assigned "thought procurators" (*shisō kenji*). They were ordered to prosecute

81. Smith, 201. Beckmann and Okubo, 157. Odanaka, "San'ichigo Yon'ichiroku Jiken," 136. Ōuchi Tsutomu, *Fashizumu e no Michi*, 86. Walker G. Metheson, "Japan Dams 'Dangerous Thoughts,'" *The Nation*, CXXVII (November 7, 1928), 504.

82. Sasaki Yoshizō, *Tokkō Zensho*, 4. Kobayashi Gorō, *Tokkō Keisatsu Hiroku*, 190–191. Kyoto Daigaku Bungakubu Kokushi Kenkyūshitsu (ed.), *Nihon Kindaishi Jiten*, 426. Suzuki Kisaburō Sensei Denki Hensankai, *Suzuki Kisaburō*, 274–275.

83. Japan, Kōchi Ken Tokubetsu Kōtōka, *Tokubetsu Kōtō Keisatsu Kankei Hōki Kaigi Shūroku*, 5.

"thought criminals" whose illegal actions were called "thought crimes" (*shisō hanzai*). Thought procurators' duties were outlined in May 1928 in an eight-point directive from the head of the Criminal Affairs Bureau. They were to handle crimes rising from the leftist thought movement, especially those which violated the Peace Preservation Law, the Public Peace Police Law (1900), and other statutes; certain crimes specified in the Criminal Code (for example, against the emperor); publication crimes (for example, those with alteration of thought as a motive); crimes based on reactionary movements (these might include crimes by rightists); crimes connected with labor, tenant, or Suihei movements; and the crime of sedition, if ideology was involved.[84] Thus, a thought crime was not limited only to violations of the peace law, but extended to any criminal action in which ideology played a role. The final decision was up to each procurator. Later, as the meaning of the term "thought crime" was stretched to cover the involvement of other than radical leftists, identification became largely an administrative matter, not a legal one in the strict sense; and the courts usually accepted the wider interpretation. Besides this, the Thought Section in the Criminal Affairs Bureau was expanded. Concurrently, the June 1928 issue (number seven) of its journal changed its name from *Shisō Chōsa* to *Shisō Kenkyū Shiryō* (Thought Research Materials). Courts were strengthened by adding new judges and secretaries.[85]

Despite the detailed directive outlining thought crimes, and the supposed concern only with overt actions which resulted from holding a particular ideology, the real meaning of a thought crime remained clouded. Procurator Sakamoto Hideo, whose detailed research on this subject was widely circulated within the Justice Ministry, wrote in late 1928 that "any action which infringes upon the present social order is a thought crime." Even though it was easy to spot ideology in the

84. Sakamoto Hideo, "Shisōteki Hanzai ni Taisuru Kenkyū," in SK, VIII (6), December, 1928, 6. Japan, Shihōshō, *Shihō Enkakushi*, 420. Table 3, Chapter 6, contains a list of the appeals courts and district courts. The Justice Ministry was given a supplementary budget for the establishment of a nationwide system of thought procurators. Okudaira, "Some Preparatory Notes", 64. Budget information is scarce. See comments in note to Appendix II, Chart 1.

85. Omori, 3. Japan, Shihōshō, *Shihō Enkakushi*, 420.

background of crimes, the concept of an ideological offense "is so abstract that you cannot help but feel that the outline is vague." Not even the Justice Ministry's May directive to thought procurators had cleared up this haziness. Many books and documents explained the contents of various kinds of social thought, "but I could not find anything that explained well the thought crime itself. . . . We cannot escape from this unclear idea about thought crimes."[86]

Nonetheless, the Supreme Court consistently rejected appeals by those convicted under the peace law. The first decision on *kokutai* and "changing the *kokutai*" came in May 1929, when the court rejected an appeal of defendants at the Sapporo Appeals Court. The *kokutai,* said the court, means "an unbroken line of emperors held the supreme power." *Kokutai* was a proper, exact legal term. As for the second item, attempting to establish a proletarian government was just the same as trying to destroy the *kokutai*.[87] Other appeals based on the meaning of the "denial of private property" (April 1929), the meaning of the term "organization" (April 1932), the meaning of "joining an organization" (June 1934), and the meaning of "activities for carrying out the purpose" (November 1930) were also rejected.[88]

Certain that Bolshevization was, as Maruyama Masao puts it, "a profound menace to Imperial Japan,"[89] the state reacted strongly to the events of March 15. The continuing arrests, which soon netted over two thousand people, convinced government leaders that the rot had spread into their stronghold as well. Even though one mass arrest after another crippled and then killed the communist party, the Japanese continued to be haunted by the specter of communism, and by the late 1930's the charge of being a "Red" had come to be a generic catchall used to attack any foe of those in power.

The Expanding Political Influence of Justice Officials

The enactment and application of the Peace Preservation Law enhanced the power and prestige of justice officials, sometimes at the expense of bureaucrats in the powerful Home Ministry. Among those

86. Sakamoto, in SK, 4–5, 7.
87. Okudaira, GS, XLV, 580.
88. *Ibid.,* 585–628.
89. Maruyama Masao, *Thought and Behaviour in Modern Japanese Politics,* 76, note.

who most conspicuously advanced were the procurators linked to Hiranuma and Suzuki. It was the Hiranuma faction that was most active in planning and drafting the peace-law bill, in seizing the initiative from the police in the Kyoto Student Association case, and in taking the leading role in the March 15 incident. Application of the new peace law certainly cast procurators and other justice officials in an important role, since they best understood the new legal terminology and most readily learned how to handle the new-type criminal. As a result, Justice Ministry bureaucrats saw the thought-war era as an opportunity for expansion of their power and prestige; the new breed of thought procurators expanded from their Tokyo base, and during the 1930's they became an important political force. As a consequence of the war against radical thought, the Peace Preservation Law system coalesced, with thought procurators at its center: their numbers grew, the peace law was strengthened, a supplementary budget was given the Justice Ministry, and a ''think tank'' was established in Tokyo to research ideological crimes and related subjects.[90]

90. Okudaira, ''Some Preparatory Notes,'' 64–65.

4 Handling Ideological Offenders

The Japanese government, while proud of its legal code and modern system of courts, was well aware that the mass arrests would attract foreign attention. A special effort was made, therefore, to conduct the arrests, trials, and other proceedings in a legal manner. During 1928 and 1929, this meant that for the most part those arrested were treated like ordinary defendants. However, as the number apprehended climbed into the thousands, hardpressed police and prison officials began to consider alternative methods. Old techniques were criticized not only because of the numbers involved, but also because the authorities discovered that they were dealing with a different type of radical. Indeed, many of the new breed were young people of promise from good families who came from the same elite imperial universities as did the authorities. They were in fact part of the establishment, and quite different from the old-style radicals of the Meiji period. Thus, in light of the "fundamental respectability" of the new radicals, the state was forced to reconsider its traditional criminal procedures. Old methods of strict surveillance and executions, as in the case of the high-treason incident when Kōtoku was hanged, were inadequate.[1]

1. Henry D. Smith, *Japan's First Student Radicals*, 266–268. According to Maruyama Masao, parents worried mainly about two things: that their children might become *moga* or *mobo*, or that they might be captured by dangerous thought. "The situation appears very similar to that of late Meiji when these two tendencies were lumped together as frivolous and subversive. This time, however, the extent of the infiltration of 'dangerous thought' into the intellectuals and students was far greater and what was more, those students who had been regarded as exemplary were found to be the transmitters of this dangerous thought." Maruyama Masao, "Patterns of Individuation and the Case of Japan," in Marius B. Jansen (ed.), *Changing Japanese Attitudes Toward Modernization*, 519.

There were also other forces at work promoting a special treatment for thought offenders. The concept of rehabilitation had a long tradition in Japanese society,[2] and penal system reforms reinforced this idea. Influenced by German and other foreign methods, modern Japanese penologists were engaged in constructing a "progressive stage treatment system" for ordinary prisoners. The efforts of Shiono Suehiko (he left the Tokyo District Court in September 1930), as the new Director of the Prison Bureau, and Masaki Akira, as a member of the Prison System Research Committee, were rewarded in July 1931 with the establishment of a more lenient parole system, and in January 1934 with the introduction of the progressive stage system. Their enlightened policies strengthened the argument of other officials who urged the creation of a special parole system to rehabilitate thought criminals.[3] Moreover, the concept of rehabilitation had deep roots within the procuratorial corps as well. This is illustrated not only by Shiono's attitude, but also by that of Sakamoto Hideo. Sakamoto spent a three-month period in Tokyo researching and discussing thought crimes, outlining his ideas in a voluminous report published late in 1928. Penal punishment and strict laws, he wrote, were by themselves inadequate; it was a mistake to depend only upon the overly harsh Peace Preservation Law, and, since wrong ideology could only be countered by correct ideology, the nation's strongest weapon in the thought war was "love." "We must make the proletarians love the country and the country must also love them."[4] Thus, the urge to reform instead of punish, to suspend sentence instead of imprison, was strongly felt in justice

2. Like the Chinese, the Japanese attached great importance to an admission of guilt and a promise to repent. Those who surrendered and confessed might even be exempt from punishment. For the Chinese background see W. Allyn Rickett, "Voluntary Surrender and Confession in Chinese Law," *The Journal of Asian Studies*, XXX, August, 1971, 797. This concept was preserved in the Meiji Criminal Code. Ishii Ryōsuke, *Japanese Legislation in the Meiji Era*, 344–345. The 1922 peace-law bill followed this tradition by offering a reduction in sentence or freedom to anyone who informed authorities. Amnesty or reduction of punishment was promised in the 1925 law also.

3. Masaki Akira, *Reminiscences of a Japanese Penologist*, 62–63, 69, 71, 131. Masaki felt that in order to be rehabilitated a prisoner required love and hope. There were four stages in the progressive system, and, as a prisoner was promoted, he enjoyed more privileges. *Ibid.*, 46, 71.

4. Sakamoto Hideo, "Shisōteki Hanzai ni Taisuru Kenkyū," in SK, VIII (6), December, 1928, 659–660.

circles; and from this basic feeling evolved a positive policy of parole and reintegration for the majority of thought offenders.

Procedures for Arrest, Preliminary Trial, and Trial

Since many of those taken in the mass roundups of March 1928 and in arrests continuing into 1929 were treated like regular defendants, let us briefly look at the route from arrest to trial. After preliminary interrogation of the suspect, police drafted two documents: a Written Report of a Criminal Investigation and a set of Police Notes. These were sent, with perhaps a confession, to the public procurator. He was required to drop charges or request, citing the laws involved, that a preliminary judge order the suspect's detention and interrogation. Next the procurator interrogated the suspect, with the objective of securing a confession. It was very important to obtain a confession, and if a suspect refused to cooperate the procurator might order further police interrogation. The procurator then compiled another Written Report of a Criminal Investigation which contained basic statements of fact, including a statement by the suspect. Next, after a formal indictment, a preliminary judge read the procurator's report and then questioned the suspect. The suspect might be questioned only once or many times—Nabeyama Sadachika's examination, for example, stretched out into forty-three sessions. Long periods of interrogation were not at all unusual in 1928 and 1929, because the judges were first learning about communism and the structure of the communist party. A judge could release a suspect, if he felt that the crime was not serious, or if he discovered extenuating circumstances, or if no crime had occurred. The Preliminary Examination Record, the only legal proof at the regular trial, was produced at this stage by the preliminary judge who also wrote a summary of this document containing the main facts of the case, the reason for the crime, and the laws violated. Next came the formal trial.

What follows will add substance to this brief outline. Not all of those apprehended during 1928 and 1929 were scooped up in mass arrests. Instead, many were captured one by one in police ambushes. Those caught in August 1929 are a graphic example of the falling-dominoes style of arrest.

This series of arrests began when two Osaka police inspectors got a tip that Kawai Etsuzō was hiding in Tokyo. Kawai, who was chief of the local communist committee in Niigata and Nagano prefectures, had been to the Soviet Union in 1927 and had participated in the party's central committee meetings. Helped by Tokyo police, the Osaka officers finally located Kawai's hideaway. Early on the morning of August 4, police rushed into the building, but Kawai, after first igniting party documents, attempted to flee over the rooftops. He was pursued and caught, and the fire was extinguished. Luckily for the authorities, not all of the documents had burned. Under interrogation Kawai claimed to be someone else, insisting that a mistake had been made. Meanwhile, a police detail had staked out Kawai's neighborhood, and the next evening they seized a young man. A search turned up an issue of *Red Flag* hidden in his collar and a message in his hat band. Under interrogation, the suspect gave his real name, told the police who had given him the note, and confessed that he had studied in Russia at the Eastern Workers Communist University. Moreover, he admitted to knowing four other graduates. Police arrested them the same evening. They also apprehended a young woman who carried an important message from the central committee ordering party members to suspend all meetings and correspondence and to hide or burn all documents, addresses, and maps. After the young woman confessed her party connection, and to cohabiting with a party member, police trapped her lover, and the common-law wife of another party member. Other arrests followed. Early August 14, police raided a house in Chiba (east of the metropolis), arresting two communists, seizing a mimeograph machine, printing supplies, and copies of *Red Flag*. Another police stakeout and another arrest implicated Professor Arima Tsuyoshi of Tokyo Imperial University. On August 16, thought police discovered Arima hidden in a teahouse in Tokyo. Visitors to his home were arrested. And so it went, with other names being added to the list day after day. Thus, the first confession touched dozens of party members and sympathizers, like ripples spreading across a quiet pond.[5]

After their arrest, suspects were interrogated by police before being

5. Japan, "Keishi Sōkan no Kenkyo ni Kansuru Tshūhō (August, 1928)," in Yamabe (ed.), GS, XVI, 65–70.

sent on to procurators. Many Japanese and foreign scholars have written about the brutality of the Japanese police during these interrogations. Yamabe Kentarō, for instance, says that torture was used not only by police to force confessions, but also by procurators, even though the procurators might not have been directly involved.[6] Certainly, all this smoke indicates some fire, but did this brutality reflect government policy, and is it not possible that tales of police brutality have been magnified? It appears that the answer is no to the first and yes to the second. Mistreatment of prisoners was usually carried out by lower-ranking personnel, a not unusual situation even in the United States today. Moreover, when compared with the club-swinging, head-cracking approach employed by German riot police in 1927 to subdue communists, or the techniques used by modernizing communist states, Japanese actions were mild. This is not meant to whitewash instances of police cruelty, but only to indicate the need for more serious analysis of this subject to replace sweeping statements about prewar police brutality.

In the final analysis, those who indict the police for brutality often point to Kobayashi Takiji's fate and his novel, *The Fifteenth of March, 1928*, which exposed police tactics in Otaru, Hokkaido. A more balanced view would also include a look at official policy statements. For instance, in 1927 Procurator-General Koyama Matsukichi spoke on this subject to procurators and to police. Koyama said that examples of beating and torture had come to his attention. It was the duty of procurators to teach low-ranking policemen the meaning of the Criminal Code and to correct this regretful behavior. Those who disobeyed must be strictly punished. Speaking to senior police officers in strong language, Koyama repeated his message, reminding them that the revised Criminal Code was based on "moral principles" and was designed to "protect human rights."[7] Koyama said nothing about legal ways to pressure suspects into confessing, but we can suspect that police used them. Furthermore, harsh living conditions in jail, plus

6. *Ibid.,* viii.
7. Japan, Shihōshō, Shihō Daijin Kanbō Hishoka, *Kunji Enjutsu Shū*, 266, 268. Articles 194–195 of the Criminal Code prohibited police, justice, and prison officials from cruelty or acts of violence against a suspect or criminal. William J. Sebald, *The Criminal Code of Japan*, 142.

anxiety over the indeterminate length of detention while awaiting trial, became a kind of "psychological torture" which was more effective in producing conversion than an occasional beating.[8] During this stressful time, cut off from friends and without the right to call an attorney, suspects were inclined to bend and confess.[9]

After their police interrogation, suspects were passed on to district court procurators. Many of the party's small fry reacted like Kaneko Kenta, a thirty-year old organizer. Kaneko gave a full confession to the Special Higher Police, telling of his contacts with Kanto area party members, of his orders to create a new cell organization, and other information. In his confession, Kaneko displayed remorse, appealed for mercy, and promised to cut all ties with the communist movement. Kaneko's interrogator at the Tokyo District Court, Procurator Okada Minoru, used this police document as a point of departure. Between April 28 and May 2, 1928, Kaneko was thoroughly interrogated four times. Okada probed deeply into his early life, work experience, union-movement activities, reasons for joining the communist party, and for details of party organization and contacts. At their final session, Kaneko told of party activities during the February election campaign, specifically in support of Naniwa Hideo for the Okayama Prefectural Assembly. From this information, Okada compiled a dossier fully illustrating Kaneko's complicity in party activities and his motivation.[10]

During the preliminary trial examination, Kaneko confessed to Judge Tsukada Shōzō the inner workings of the party, giving information as to exact roles of party leaders, dates of organizational changes, party tactics and plans, and his own activities. The judge took special pains to extract detailed information about contacts between party headquarters and each cell.[11] Kaneko's frank admissions were not unusual, since many party leaders also made lengthy statements. Indeed, what began

8. Life history statements written by thought suspects for the authorities indicate the psychological stress they were under. For instance see Akita Ujaku, *Gojūnen Seikatsu Nenpu*, 198–202.

9. Chalmers Johnson, *Conspiracy at Matsukawa*, where Chap. 4 has an interesting section on the role of confession in Japanese society.

10. "Shihō Keisatsukan Oyobi Kenji no Torishirabe Kiroku (1928)," in Yamabe (ed.), GS, XVI, 71–74, 82–94.

11. *Ibid.*, 75–80.

as scattered comments by a few became a torrent of words by many. Thus, by the time for trial, the prosecution had obtained more than sufficient evidence for convictions. There were several reasons for this urge to tell it all. Tokuda Kyūichi and others spoke during the preliminary examination in order to counter statements being made by those who wished to dissolve the party organization. Yamabe Kentarō thinks that Tokuda began talking in order to keep the record straight.[12] Tokuda said that he spoke because he expected execution and wanted to clarify the shape of the party. Moreover, Tokuda felt that he had to counter what was being said by two other defendants, Sano Manabu and Nabeyama Sadachika. Later Tokuda regretted his actions, since the police used his statements to persuade others to confess.[13] Besides a strong desire to keep the record straight, personal differences and tensions stimulated tongues to wag. Sano felt that Tokuda's Ryukyuan background caused him to dislike mainland Japanese.[14] Additional friction was generated by the rivalry between those arrested in 1928 and those caught a year later. Nabeyama, who was caught last, accused Tokuda and Shiga Yoshio of failing to organize jailed party members. Nabeyama felt that Tokuda and Shiga did not properly struggle and instead "talked excitedly with government officials."[15]

Justice was swift for many of the communist suspects. While authorities in Tokyo were engaged in lengthy investigations, local trials were carried out with dispatch. The first trial began in Okayama District Court on October 31, 1928. Because of their youth or slight involvement in the party, the defendants got only one to two years in prison.[16] At the Osaka District Court, ninety-seven prisoners were sentenced on February 1. Kasuga Shōjirō, the area's chief organizer, received the heaviest penalty of eight years. Most of the defendants were sentenced to under three years.[17]

A few party leaders defected. Even before he was bailed out of an

12. Yamabe (ed.), GS, XVI, xi, and XIX, vii.

13. Tokuda Kyūichi and Shiga Yoshio, *Gokuchū Jūhachinen*, 58–59. Beckmann and Okubo, 215–216. Travers E. Durkee, "The Communist International and Japan" (unpublished doctoral dissertation), 167–168.

14. Nabeyama Sadachika and Sano Manabu, *Tenkō Jūgonen*, 101.

15. Yamabe (ed.), GS, XX, xvii. Nabeyama and Sano, 55–56.

16. Kita Kazuo, *Nihon Kyōsantō Shimatsuki*, 67–69.

17. *Ibid.*, 121–148.

Osaka jail, Kawai Etsuzō had second thoughts on the party's demand for destruction of the imperial system. He suggested that this be eliminated and that instead the party call for the removal of corrupt men around the throne, and a process of systematic reform. As he thought about this, he concluded that there was no need for a communist party or for contact with the Comintern. Kawai's arguments persuaded others, who took a similar position at the Osaka Court of Appeals in June 1929.[18] At that time, however, authorities did little to exploit this crack in communist solidarity, since Kawai and the others were not high-ranking figures, and the time was not yet ripe. An open trial in Tokyo and an upsurge of nationalism, triggered by fighting in Manchuria, changed the mood of communists who began to apostatize in large numbers.

The Public Trial in Tokyo

At the urging of Procurator Shiono Suehiko, following the mass arrest in March 1928, the government decided to hold a special open trial of communists at the Tokyo District Court.[19] The purpose of the carefully staged trial was to re-educate those who had slipped into the heresy of communism, and to publicly blacken the image of the Japanese Communist Party. It was hoped that a public trial would dispel the aura of mystery surrounding the party and shake the faith of communists. Moreover, an ideological victory would be scored if party leaders would publicly recant. There were other compelling reasons: Tokyo's courts would have choked on individual trials for nearly three hundred suspects, and a unified trial of party leaders would help the government understand the party and its tactics. The defendants cooperated in the open trial, because they wanted to use the courtroom as a propaganda platform.

For such an important event, the government carefully picked an all-star cast: Chief Justice Miyagi Minoru of the Tokyo Appeals Court and Thought Procurators Hirata Susumu and Tozawa Shigeo. The defendants were respresented by skillful lawyers such as Fuse Tatsuji. The communist leaders on trial were party kingpins: Sano Manabu,

18. Beckmann and Okubo, 184.
19. Yamabe (ed.), GS, XVI, xvi.

chairman of the party central committee; Nabeyama Sadachika, central committee member; Tokuda Kyūichi, central committee member until 1927; Shiga Yoshio, chief editor of *Marxism*; Takahashi Sadaki, a leader in the Communist Youth League; Kokuryō Goichirō, central committee member and member of the labor union department; and Ichikawa Shōichi, who headed the party in 1927 while other leaders were in Moscow.

Judge Miyagi, who was forty-four years old in 1931, first put on judicial robes in 1913. In 1927, after a research trip to Europe and the United States, he was promoted to Chief Justice of the Tokyo Appeals Court. It is unclear why the government chose Miyagi, but his experience as a senior judge in the capital area must have been a compelling reason. At any rate, his appointment to the Tokyo District Court for the duration of the trial proved a good choice—from the government's viewpoint. The trial, from Miyagi's, point of view, presented a challenge. It was an opportunity, he felt, to display the importance of the judicial branch at a time when the military and police had become very strong.[20] Moreover, Miyagi fully understood the trial's importance and the need to "clear up what the communist party really was."[21] Furthermore, Miyagi's personal ambition should also be considered; a successful completion of this difficult trial would ensure him of an honored place in the history of Japanese justice.

Miyagi prepared for this trial like a general prepares for a decisive battle. Every aspect of the procedure was discussed in detail. As part of his painstaking preparation, Miyagi made a thorough study of communism, reviewed techniques used in political trials, read books in German on tactics employed by German communists, and closely analyzed transcripts of the trial of communists in Osaka.[22] Miyagi was concerned with every detail of the coming trial, even the order in which the defendants were to enter and depart from the courtroom. He decided to reverse the usual order and have court officials enter the courtroom

20. Miyagi Minoru, "Watakushi no Keiken Yori Mitaru Kyōsantō Jiken no Shinri ni Tsuite," in Yamabe (ed.), GS, XVI, 603–604. SKST, LVII, February, 1939, 69. Nabeyama suspected that the government was holding an open trial "in order to give this system a testing," Nabeyama Sadachika, *Watakushi wa Kyōsantō o Suteta*, 138.

21. Miyagi, 604.

22. SKST, LVII, 51–53.

first, and after each session the defendants would leave first. This would serve as a restraining influence. The handling of spectators, the control of improper speech, the scope of newspaper coverage, and the punishment for infractions of rules were also decided.[23] Such careful preparation helped Miyagi anticipate the actions of defendants and maintain the dignity of his court.[24]

Since Miyagi's chief concern was to conduct the trial quickly and smoothly, he reached a compromise with the defendants. As long as they policed their own ranks and prevented disruptions which had marred earlier trials of communists, the open trial would be allowed to continue. Miyagi, Hirata, and other justice officials met in a series of bargaining sessions with selected party leaders (Sano, Tokuda, Shiga, Nabeyama, and others), in order to reach agreement on rules for the trial. Based on these discussions, Sano prepared a nine-point list of demands which were submitted to Miyagi: (1) that the defendants arrested at different periods be given a single unified trial; (2) that the trial be held soon; (3) that it be open; (4) that the preliminary examinations be concluded with dispatch; (5) that the defendants' representatives be permitted to speak about specified subjects; (6) that the representatives be allowed to form a trial committee which would negotiate with the court and be responsible for the actions of defendants; (7) that those in prison be released on bail; (8) that prison committee members be allowed to attend trials in other districts to act as witnesses; and (9) that they be permitted to carry reference materials and notes into the courtroom. Miyagi agreed to all but number seven.[25]

The carrot and stick strategy employed by Miyagi was effective, since the defendants badly wanted the court's "gift" of an open trial. Whenever the defendants departed from Miyagi's ground rules he could, and he did, close the trial to the public. Furthermore, the court kept a tight rein on the defendants by trying them in three groups, with top leaders included in each group. Of course, there was a practical

23. *Ibid.*, 52, 54, 58. Miyagi, 603. Yamabe (ed.), GS, XVI, xxx. "Kōhan Hōdō ni Kansuru Shimbun Taisaku (1931)," in Yamabe (ed.), GS, XVI, 583.

24. SKST, LVII, 49, 52–53.

25. Odanaka Toshiki, "San'ichigo Yon'ichiroku Jiken," in Wagatsuma Sakae (ed.), *Nihon Seiji Saiban Shiroku, Showazen*, 203–204. Beckmann and Okubo, 216–217.

reason for this as well: no courtroom was large enough to contain all of them.[26]

The trial began on June 25, 1931, and lasted until July 2, 1932 (108 sessions), with sentencing on October 29. The defendants were charged with violating either the 1925 Peace Preservation Law or the 1928 revision. Trial of the first group was completed on September 29, the second during November, and the third by July 2.

Some Home Ministry officials, including members of the Tokyo Metropolitan Police Board, were uneasy over Miyagi's "soft" treatment of the communist defendants, and his permission to let them speak out to the public. Their dissatisfaction was leaked to the *Tokyo Nichi Nichi Shimbun* which printed it on July 4, 1931. The Home Ministry, said that the article, was concerned over the way the trial was being conducted and over the bad influence it might have on the public. Miyagi also heard via the official grapevine that the Home Ministry was considering legal steps against him. Miyagi felt the hot breath of a few justice officials who thought he was being too easy on the defendants. His critics, in both ministries, were especially angered by the agreement he had made with party leaders which had set the ground rules for the trial. Threatening letters from fanatics of the left and right added to this pressure. Efforts to change his method of handling the trial were resisted by Miyagi, however, who was simultaneously receiving words of strong encouragement from other important judges. Finally, Miyagi had a face-to-face meeting with Home Ministry officials; he agreed to stop the trial or eject spectators, if the defendants acted improperly. Official objections to his methods ceased, and the Tokyo District Court Procurator Bureau gave a sigh of relief. As for Miyagi, he was pleased at the outcome; now the government side could present a unified front to the public.[27]

During the trial, the communists did not allow internal bickering to interfere with their main purpose of propagandizing. They insisted that they were political prisoners, and that their testimony would provide the public with a true picture of the party.[28] Despite minor problems, the

26. Odanaka, 204–205. Miyagi, 603.
27. SKST, LVII, 65–66.
28. Odanaka, 192–199. Beckmann and Okubo, 218–219.

trial went along smoothly. Miyagi followed his prearranged plan of constantly reminding the defendants that he had the power to hold the trial in camera. This fear, Miyagi felt, did much to restrain the defendants.[29] Communists and their supporters outside the courtroom carried out demonstrations and published details in the leftist press about prison conditions and the brutality of guards. However, the outbreak of fighting in Manchuria, in September 1931, quickly overshadowed the courtroom drama. Those on trial denounced the ''imperialistic'' war and preached against sending troops, but they misunderstood the public mood, and their antiarmy campaign backfired.[30]

Procurator Hirata wanted the defendants strictly punished since their crime of fomenting rebellion was so serious. The prosecution, therefore, devised a punishment scale for consideration by the court. Imprisonment for five years was asked for party members, and additional time for those who engaged in party activities or who ''carried out the goals'' of the party. Especially heavy penalties should be given to those who refused to express remorse.[31] The defense team denied charges that their clients attacked the *kokutai* and private property; they condemned the ''terrorism'' directed at the defendants, and pointed out that the court behaved improperly when it closed the trial to the public or ordered the defendants to leave the courtroom. The procurators were charged with playing politics, the provisions of the Peace Preservation Law were judged faulty, and the sentences requested were called excessive.[32]

Near the end of the affair, demonstrations and plots to rescue the defendants jangled the nerves of authorities to the point that the court was surrounded by hundreds of policemen, and the road from prison was lined with others. Sentence was passed on 181 defendants (the

29. Miyagi, 603. Miyagi sought to maintain court discipline by closing the trial either two or three times. On July 11, 1931, Sano was ordered to stop talking about the proletarian dictatorship, and since he refused to continue under this restriction, the court adjourned. On April 19, 1932, as Sano spoke on violent revolution and destroying the emperor system, spectators were cleared from the courtroom until he finished. For the most part, spectators were quiet, but several times people were asked to leave for applauding defendants' statements. Odanaka, 211.

30. Beckmann and Okubo, 219.

31. Odanaka, 211–212, 215–216.

32. *Ibid.*, 216–217.

balance had been removed for various reasons): Nabeyama Sadachika, Mitamura Shirō, Sano Manabu, and Ichikawa Shōichi, life confinement; fifteen years for Takahashi Sadaki and Kokuryō Goichirō; ten years for Shiga, Tokuda, and ten others; and so on.[33]

The final act of the drama was played at the Tokyo Court of Appeals. It was made clear to the defendants that they would be given a reduced sentence if they renounced the party. And for those who cooperated, the prosecution kept its bargain: Sano's and Nabeyama's terms were reduced from life to fifteen years, Takahashi's from fifteen to twelve, and so on. The sentences of die-hards like Shiga, Tokuda, Kokuryō, and Ichikawa were confirmed, and they were refused a review by the Supreme Court.[34]

The state declared in this sensational trial that those who trespassed the Peace Preservation Law would be dealt with severely. The decision to give stiff penalties to party leaders, but to execute no one, was shrewd. Without executions there could be no martyrs. Once established, this policy was never changed.

Judge Miyagi was awarded a silver medal and an appointment to the Supreme Court. If this political trial posed a personal dilemma for Miyagi, he kept silent. Some years later he observed that "the trial was not only a judicial problem, but also a national problem." Thus, for Miyagi there was no conflict between the state's needs and judicial independence; the former clearly superseded the latter, and communism's threat overshadowed the issue of executive interference in the trial process. However, Miyagi did insist upon authority to run the proceedings in the courtroom, including his requirement of full legal rights for defendants.[35]

Tenkō

One startling result of the trial was the sensational "conversion" (*tenkō*) by Sano and Nabeyama. Because of their prestige, the party received a mortal wound at their conversion, and hundreds of other imprisoned communists followed their lead. The term *tenkō* began to

33. *Ibid.*, 218–219.
34. *Ibid.*, 221–222, 225–227.
35. SKST, LVII, 54–55, 58.

have a special ideological meaning in the late Taisho period, when the proletarian parties were debating a change in direction. As used here, however, it described a change in ideological position on the part of former antigovernment radicals who had undergone self-criticism and who had returned to the ideological position supported by the state.[36]

Sano and Nabeyama did not quickly adopt such a drastic course. Indeed, Sano had begun to question the subservient relationship between the party and the Comintern in 1929, when he began to suspect that high ideals might not be a replacement for nationalism. Earlier doubts were reawakened by the fighting in Manchuria, the wave of patriotism sweeping the nation, and his own feelings of depression which resulted from the intense effort expended at the Tokyo District Court. It appears that the assassination of Prime Minister Inukai Tsuyoshi by rightists (May 15, 1932) and terror tactics used by communists also distressed Sano.[37] Central to their conversion, however, was their sharp sense of defeat. They hoped to make a fresh start, the first step of which was a scathing criticism of the party for its ineffectiveness and alienation from the people. Their aroused nationalism sticks out all too clearly. Nabeyama wrote: "If we had stuck to our party line, we would have been advocating the defeat of our own country. . . . After the war started, I could not possible say that my country should be defeated. . . . I could not even think such a thing."[38] One scholar thinks that their experience is best described as ideological *re*conversion. In order to make up for the failure of the party, the disillusioned communists decided to make a fresh start "by trying to

36. Fujita Shōzō, "Showa Hachinen o Chūshin to suru Tenkō no Jōkyō," in Shisō no Kagaku Kenkyūkai (ed.), *Tenkō*, I, 33–34. Tsurumi Shunsuke defined *tenkō* "as the change of one's thought under the coercion of power." By this he meant the application of state power. "The means of coercion include both direct and indirect violence. Arrest by police, torture, court trial, imprisonment, and death belong to the former; job discrimination, praise or denunciation through mass communication media, and social pressure of various kinds belong to the latter." Quoted in Tsurumi Kazuko, *Social Change and the Individual*, 37.

37. Durkee, 168–169. Nabeyama and Sano, 86–87. Beckmann and Okubo, 245. After 1931, some civilian and military rightists sought to forcefully overthrow the government. The approximately twenty military men and twenty civilians involved in the unsuccessful coup of May 15, 1932, planned to kill the prime minister, party leaders, and to topple other parts of the conservative establishment. They succeeded only in killing Inukai.

38. Quoted in Tsurumi Kazuko, 50.

identify themselves with the majority of the people. . . . The majority of the people, they observed, adhered to Emperor worship and supported Japan's war aims. Therefore, they could switch from advocacy of the abolition of the Emperor system to support of it, from an antiwar stance to the endorsement of Japan's war aims, and at the same time still maintain their original position—'sincerity' and service to the masses of the people.''[39]

Near the end of May 1933, Sano and Nabeyama informed authorities of their conversion in a long memorandum. On June 10, 1933, newspapers broke the story, which came as a total surprise to party members. Their May memorandum repudiated the party's antiemperor stance. The Comintern, they wrote, did not comprehend the emperor's pivotal position for the Japanese. Each country must carry out its revolution based upon national characteristics and historical conditions, and in Japan's case this meant leadership by the emperor. Moreover, Japan, as one of the superior nations, had a duty to annex weaker neighbors. Hence, they fully supported Japan's actions in Manchuria. Furthermore, they criticized the Japanese Communist Party's kowtowing to the Comintern. A new communist party operating under imperial guidance should be substituted.[40]

Delighted justice officials circulated their statement to other prisoners. At first communists were stunned by this defection, but soon others followed their example. By the end of July, a trickle of recantations had swollen to a river, with thirty percent of the nonconvicted and thirty-six percent of the convicted communists following Sano and Nabeyama's example.[41] Many justice officials had hoped for this, since one of the purposes of the open trial was to create just such a situation. However, it is interesting that the strongest push for more emphasis upon recantation and less upon standard punishment came primarily from procurators.

39. *Ibid.*, 52.
40. Ibid., 47–48. Aoki Sadao, *Tokkō Kyōtei*, 166–182. Beckmann and Okubo, 246–249. Besides allowing Sano and Nabeyama freedom to work together on their joint statement, authorities released it to the press and published it in an official journal. Copies were distributed to communist prisoners, and Sano and Nabeyama were encouraged to meet with other party members. Tsurumi Kazuko, 47.
41. Tsurumi Kazuko, 47. Odanaka, 220–221.

In April 1928, justice officials meeting in Okayama debated the problem of handling thought criminals, and again in Sapporo in June. After that it was discussed at nearly every meeting. Procurator Shiono Suehiko, who promoted the open trial, also pushed for a "recantation" policy. It is logical that new concepts for handling thought offenders germinated in the procuratorial corps and not at the Tokyo headquarters, since it was the procurators who had somehow to process great numbers of suspects. The defection of Kawai Etsuzō and his followers, in the spring of 1929, encouraged thought procurators to more fully develop the idea of recantation and reintegration. Certain that the negative approach of arrest and punishment was insufficient, procurators sought to weld the positive aspects of conversion to traditional procedures. Finally, the topic was discussed at a Conference of Administrators in Tokyo, and on March 27, 1931, in Instruction Number 270, conversion was approved for the handling of cases violating the Peace Preservation Law. Then procurators were empowered to withhold prosecution, depending upon the defendant's attitude.[42]

A majority of procurators and judges attending a Conference of Administrators held early in November expressed support for conversion and probationary techniques. Procurator Inoue Nagamasa (Urawa District Court) reminded everyone that the report issued after the third meeting (May 1927) had allowed that if thought offenders showed "repentance" (*kaishun*) they should be put on some kind of probation. Officials were urged to give offenders proper reading material, place them under the guidance of good people, grant paroles to those who had reformed, and locate employment for them. Unrepentant persons should be dealt with severely.[43]

Statistical evidence presented at the November conference reinforced the opinion of those who advocated a liberal policy. Procurator Miyazato Tomehachi from Hiroshima referred to his bureau's experience. Among the 111 people given some kind of probation or parole about sixty percent appeared to reform. Of the three who had served a full sentence, however, none had reformed.[44] These figures

42. Shiono Suehiko Kaikoroku Kankōkai, *Shiono Suehiko Kaikoroku*, 592. Hasebe Kingo, Shisōhan no Hogo ni Tsuite, in SK, XXI (10), March, 1937, 53–56.
43. Japan, Shihōshō, Chōsaka in SK, XVI, August, 1932, 113–114, 116, 121.
44. *Ibid.*, 118–119.

illustrate that Miyazato's bureau was less interested in gaining court convictions and stiff prison sentences and more in converting thought offenders; and his statistics suggest that a positive parole policy was succeeding. Thus, we see an early example of an administrative solution to the problem rather than a strictly judicial one (that is, by trial and punishment).

The Tokyo open trial was a resounding success; it was smoothly completed, mass conversion was induced, and the communists were humbled. However, the trial produced new problems for justice officials. What, for instance, was to be done with thought offenders who recanted? Although the need for a quick decision was obvious, a well-considered reintegration plan could not be created overnight. Even more immediate was the discovery that ultranationalists took a dim view of recantation and reintegration. Charges of "soft on communism" filled the air. The sensational revelation that some officials had communist leanings and were under investigation brought forth rightist demands for a thorough housecleaning of the Justice Ministry.[45] Rightist pressure was exerted in several ways: personal visits to officials, rallies, demands for impeachment of officials, and even demands that Justice Minister Koyama commit suicide.[46] Some rightists viewed justice policies as utter foolishness. Sano and others, one wrote, had not truly had a change of heart; they were merely playacting to escape punishment.[47]

New Techniques

Procurators led the way in devising new methods for handling thought criminals, with the Tokyo District Court bureau in the vanguard. Despite a manpower shortage, the Tokyo bureau created a reasonably efficient system to investigate, interrogate, and prosecute large numbers of suspects. They displayed ingenuity, flexibility, and an ability to experiment with new methods. Work was delegated to Justice Police,[48] and procurators even exploited thought suspects whose

45. Japan, Kōan Chōsachō (ed.), *Senzen ni Okeru Uyoku Dantai no Jōkyō*, I, 585.
46. *Ibid.*, 25, 48–50, 582, 585–586.
47. Ayakawa Takeji, *Fuon Shisō no Shinsō to sono Taisaku*, 155–156.
48. Justice Police investigated crimes and obtained evidence. Legally, they were completely subordinate to procurators during the course of criminal investigation, and

autobiographical notes served as an unintentional contribution to the study of how to handle thought criminals. By September 1932, special techniques not only kept suspects within close reach, but also kept them out of jail, thus easing the strain on prison facilities. Moreover, procurators were investigating the underlying psychological reasons for thought crimes.

Tokyo District Court procurators became too busy for close investigations. However, this problem was partially solved by transferring more of the investigative work to Justice Police.[49]

A difficult problem was deciding which suspects to prosecute and which to release or parole. Sometimes those released again joined the communist party or in some other manner committed a thought offense. Such mistakes prompted procurators to experiment with new methods of control. Until the fall of 1932, three documents were used as guidelines: the Criminal Procedure Code, the Public Procurator-General's Instructions, and Official Note, Number 270, March 27, 1931 ("Handling of Incidents in Connection with the Japanese Communist Party's Violations of the Peace Preservation Law"). According to these regulations, procurators were to investigate each suspect's attitude toward destruction of private property, his willingness to engage in violent revolution, the seriousness of his crime, and his chances for reform. Difficulty in keeping track of those released, suspicion that they had not fully renounced communism, and the arrest of repeaters indicated that these regulations needed modification. Tokyo procurators, therefore, developed a new system of delayed procedure which was outlined in Secret Order, Number 2006, September 22, 1932 ("Official Regulations for the Procedure of Charges Withheld for Thought Offenders").[50]

The new technique of "charges withheld" (*ryūho shobun*) gave procurators wide powers, allowing them to hold suspects in a suspended state directly under their thumb. This system was a middle-of-the-road

they often acted as office help for procurators in both regular and thought cases. Nonetheless, they did belong to the Home Ministry, an arrangement which sometimes led to split allegiances. Takai Kenzō, *Shihō Keisatsu Ron*, 14–15, 18, 80–81.

49. Tozawa Shigeo, "Shisō Hanzai no Kensatsu Jitsumu ni Tsuite," in Yamabe (ed.), GS, XVI, 19–20, 22.

50. *Ibid.*, 26–27.

method which fell between the extremes of release and prosecution, and is a prime example of short-circuiting criminal law procedures by replacing laws with administrative techniques. While the legal proceedings were suspended, procurators and others pressured suspects to renounce their dangerous ideas, a process analogous to the group think induced by brainwashing. A suspect was put in the custody of a proper guarantor—this could be a responsible person or institution, even his family. The suspect returned to his occupation, but during a probationary period of six months or longer the guarantor submitted monthly reports to the procurator describing the suspect's thought, friends, correspondence, living conditions, health, feelings of guilt and remorse, and other items. Simultaneously, police were ordered to maintain a discreet watch. They were cautioned not to take any action which might cost the suspect his job, since that would be counterproductive.[51]

Tokyo strongly urged other bureaus to adopt this procedure. The new technique was an improvement over the old system under which suspects sometimes felt that they were forgiven and that their crime was acceptable: "It was as if the authorities had given their stamp of approval." But under the new scheme the suspect clearly understood that he was neither released nor forgiven until he had proven himself worthy. Tokyo procurators cited another compelling reason for favoring the new arrangement: it reserved limited prison facilities for more serious cases, keeping thousands of borderline cases out of jail but under supervision. Between January and the fall of 1933, the Tokyo District Court bureau handled more than 1,100 cases in violation of the peace law, with most processed as "charges withheld" (fewer than 400 were prosecuted).[52]

Methods of interrogation were perfected in Tokyo as well. Proper techniques, they discovered, could convert even extremely recalcitrant persons into cooperative partners. To create a favorable impression and open a path between potential partners, procurators were instructed never to laugh or ridicule suspects, to use a direct and friendly approach, never to employ threats or lies, to be kind, to be a good

51. *Ibid.*, 27.
52. *Ibid.*

listener, and to be persistent. This approach would inspire trust, and a suspect would then naturally turn to his interrogator for consolation, expressing his feelings, discontent, and hopes. Although this method was time consuming, haste could ruin cases before they reached the preliminary court.[53]

Procurators were dependent upon police and keenly aware of the need for cooperation. In order to provide increased efficiency, the Tokyo District Court bureau closely supervised the work of police; regular conferences were held with Special Higher Police from each of the city's eighty police stations. Detailed instructions were given about preparing depositions and notes, and special pains were taken to make these instructions easily comprehensible. These procedures spread nationwide.[54]

A properly done deposition included information about the suspect's family and employment, influential books read by the suspect, his involvement in social protest movements, and changes in his ideological position. One section of the new deposition ("Knowledge about the Japanese Communist Party") was designed to aid police who had no firsthand knowledge of the 1928–1929 arrests. Suspects were quizzed on where they had learned about the party and why they had joined. This section was to draw out what each person knew about party organization, activities, objectives, and theory. Was the suspect a party member? An admission was the beginning of a confession, a crucial item in the procurator's case. Questions were asked about procedures for joining, official positions held, and payment of dues. This last point was important, since paying dues was considered as "unshakeable evidence." In addition, the suspect was to tell how he felt about being arrested.[55]

Writing autobiographical statements also began in Tokyo. This technique was not unheard of, but it was more fully exploited after March 15, 1928. It began by accident, when a suspect complained about the way in which a procurator was writing his deposition, especially the terms employed to describe party development. The alert procurator

53. *Ibid.*, 21–22.

54. The Justice Ministry urged all thought procurators to maintain close contact not only with thought police but also with a wide range of other officials and civilians.

55. Tozawa, 23–24.

responded by allowing the suspect to write out a statement, and then used the suspect's brief memoir as a guide. This method not only saved time, but also, as a statement in the suspect's own handwriting, it was solid evidence. Quickly, this method spread to other bureaus, with the police adopting it as well. The Tokyo bureau discovered other advantages to this system. Many troublesome suspects "softened" when allowed to write and sometimes even took pride in doing a skillful job. Moreover, by "allowing them to write about it in their own words, their actual feelings came oozing out."[56] It was only a short step from an autobiographical statement to writing a confession. Both justice officials and prisoners were familiar with the concept of a public apology in the form of a written confession—an old tradition in Japanese law.[57] The technique of having suspects take brush or pen in hand, therefore, worked in naturally with the increasing emphasis upon *tenkō*, and was in fact a preliminary step in that process.

Procurators used police labor to collect statistics. For instance, police were encouraged to fill out "personal affairs" forms, even though they duplicated deposition information. These forms were used by procurators to trace changes in a suspect's ideological position. Questions were raised about dialectical materialism, international communism, violent revolution, *kokutai*, the family system, and the state political structure. Why had the suspects adopted radical views? Or why had they renounced communism? Such information was useful in determining if a suspect was truly repentant and fully renouncing radicalism.[58]

In October 1933, Tokyo District Court Procurator Tozawa Shigeo addressed a Conference of Thought Administrators.[59] A procurator's duty, he said, did not end with interrogation, but extended to overseeing the court to prevent it from straying away from the main point. A successful trial resulted from close cooperation between procurators,

56. *Ibid.*, 24–25. As an example, see Akita Ujaku, 204.

57. A deposition was not lawful evidence unless a suspect signed it and applied his stamp, and even then he could repudiate it in court. Therefore, a brief autobiographical note in the suspect's own hand, properly signed and stamped, was added insurance that the suspect would not deny the deposition. Tozawa, 25.

58. *Ibid.*, 25–26.

59. This was the first meeting using the new title: "Shisō Jitsumuka Kaidō." Japan, Shihōshō, *Shihō Enkakushi*, 468.

judges, police, and prison personnel. Judges were in a position to strike a heavy blow against uncaptured communists. Party leaders who had converted should be tried first, since this stimulated surrender by others. "If you judges who are present today will lead suspects properly during the trial, it can be proven that they carried out the objectives of the Japanese Communist Party." Even nonmembers and fellow travelers who had only a "thin" knowledge about party activities could then be successfully prosecuted. Unrepentant communists, he said, like dangerous germs, must be removed from healthy society.[60] If they all pulled together, it would be easy to slip a legal noose around the neck of the communist party and strangle it. Indeed, one of the Peace Preservation Law's "charms," said Tozawa, was that "it could be interpreted so many different ways." They should "interpret the law for their own convenience."[61]

Meanwhile, the Thought Bureau's think tank was busy, analyzing the causes for deterioration of thought, explaining techniques used in detecting and punishing offenders, and reviewing applicable laws. In connection with *tenkō*, researchers systematically investigated the psychology involved in accepting alien ideology and rejecting it. *Shisō Geppō* (Monthly Report on Thought) appeared in July 1934. Mainly these reports were in four sections: research, reference materials, statistics, and miscellany. Studies of the communist, nationalist, proletarian, and other movements were in the first section. The second explained peace-law-related court decisions. Statistics on indictments and convictions were in the third.[62] Despite such efforts, justice bureaucrats remained dependent upon the thought police for much of their raw data.

Thought Police

The Peace Preservation Law was used more as a threat (of surveillance, arrest, temporary imprisonment, and pressure to convert) to hang over the heads of radicals than as a regular law in which punishment was given after a trial. The state was inclined to employ an

60. Tozawa, 28–30.
61. *Ibid.*, 30.
62. Cecil H. Uyehara, *Leftwing Social Movements in Japan*, 33–34.

administrative solution rather than a strictly judicial one. Hence, since its effectiveness rested on administrative restrictions which could not be enforced by justice officials alone, the thought police played an important role. This is illustrated by the disposition of Peace Preservation Law cases from 1928 to 1941. Out of 62,000 suspected communists fewer than 5,000 were prosecuted. Under 9,000 got some form of probation.[63] A huge majority, therefore, were neither formally charged nor put on trial. Both justice and police officials used the law in an administrative manner, as a threat to pressure people into conversion and to suppress those who might upset the social order.

The role of the thought police was to discover and suppress anyone who violated, or might violate, the peace law or who might in any way upset the social order. These questions, then, should be asked: What was the mission of the thought police? How did they define thought crimes? What were their main duties? How did they carry them out? What was their attitude toward justice officials?

The primary mission of the thought police was the investigation and control of social movements. Thus, they required an understanding of the origins and ideology behind each protest movement, of each group's propagandizing methods, and of their public impact. To accomplish this difficult task, each officer had to be alert for dangerous ideas. Spies and regular police units aided the thought police in carrying out a continual canvass of society.[64] After 1932, the Special Higher Police was enlarged and given the status of a full department, with six sections. Thought police were by then in each prefecture. In 1928, there had been only seventy thought police in the Toyko headquarters, but just four years later there were three hundred and eighty. The expansion in Osaka was similar. The thought police were the nation's most important intelligence-gathering organization.[65]

63. Higuchi Masaru, "Sayoku Zenrekisha no Tenkō Mondai ni Tsuite," in SKST, XCV, August, 1943, 5–6. The figure for arrests under the Peace Preservation Law (Table 1, chap. 5) is several thousand higher, because noncommunist leftists are included.

64. Sone Chūichi, *Tokkō Keisatsu to Shakai Undō no Gaisetsu*, 7–8. Sasaki Yoshizō, *Tokkō Zensho*, 3–6, 168, 248, 254. Japan, Keisatsu Kenkyūkai, *Shakai Undō ni Chokumenshite*, 77–78.

65. Sasaki, 4–5. Kobayashi Gorō, *Tokkō Keisatsu Hiroku*, 190. Suzuki Kisaburō Sensei Denki Hensankai, *Suzuki Kisaburō*, 274–275. For the growth of the Thought

Enforcing laws was perplexing, and was made more difficult by the vague terminology of the peace law, the unclear nature of a thought crime, and the general trend toward more laws. Police were caught in a dilemma. The holding of an ideological position, if it was not acted upon, was not illegal. Yet the authorities continually urged prevention of thought offenses. As a result, police erred on the side of too much control rather than too little. Police pressure was amply justified by the system.

Since prerequisite for thought control was an understanding of forbidden ideologies, police attended lectures, read books, and learned during their daily work.[66] As one textbook put it: "You must know Marxist theory well enough to understand which part acts as a magnet for students. Also, you must be well versed in the theory against it."[67] Police publications were no more successful than Justice Ministry pronouncements in dispelling the vagueness clinging to "dangerous thought." Nevertheless, all publications stressed prevention.[68] One manual, published in 1930, did differentiate between "thought" and "action," and forbade interference with thought itself. The duty of the police was to "control actions based on thought, when these actions disturb public peace."[69] A 1932 publication by the Police Research Institute viewed dangerous ideas as those held by communists and anarchists, and anyone else who attacked the *kokutai*.[70]

Thought police could investigate anyone and anything. They watched people on surveillance lists, unions, political parties, and ideological groups. Printed matter came under their scrutiny. Rumors and reports by spies were checked. Educational organizations, as well, were put under surveillance.[71] Meetings and demonstrations got special attention. Before each meeting, they looked at items for discussion, posters

---

Police see Appendix I, Charts 1–4. Information gotten from Ōkasumikai, *Naimushōshi*, IV, 734.

66. Japan, Keisatsu Kenkyūkai, 84–87, 90.

67. Quoted in *ibid.*, 84–85.

68. Sasaki, 247. Sone, 6. Japan, Keisatsu Kenkyūkai, 78. Ishihara Masajirō, *Shisō Keisatsu Gairon*, 43–44.

69. Sone, 7.

70. Japan, Keisatsu Kenkyūkai, 77–78, 83.

71. *Ibid.*, 111–117. Sasaki, 3–4. Japan Naimushō, Keihokyoku, *Tokkō Keisatsu Reikishū* (Part III), 4–5.

and handbills, and at the people involved. Officers listened to speeches and took notes. Even nonpolitical gatherings did not escape their notice. Demonstrations were tightly regulated, with the size, route, order of march, and written slogans prescribed.[72]

The police favored indirect and secret methods of investigation: "To discover the truth about a person you need not ask him. You can instead ask his family, relatives, friends, neighbors, and others. . . . From such people, you can discover the suspect's thought tendencies." A common method was the house-to-house canvass. If, while drinking a cup of tea and chatting with the occupants, the officer saw or heard anything unusual, a secret watch was established. Many times this resulted in an arrest.[73]

In 1932, the Police Research Institute advised officers to cooperate with justice authorities, and to discuss with them methods for conducting arrests. Moreover, the Home Ministry issued directives in 1932 and 1934 ordering close cooperation with procurators.[74]

A Bill to Revise the Peace Law

By 1934, techniques for dealing with thought offenders were streamlined, and a conversion and rehabilitation system was put into operation. Nonetheless, the new system was not striding along on two strong legs but rather had the gait of a peglegged sailor. Investigation, interrogation, and prosecution—the strong leg—were going well; but the other leg—conversion and rehabilitation—was weak. Most justice officials saw that more precise standards were required for conversion; better coordination between bureaus was needed, and more money was necessary, and these things could best be secured by passing a new law which would centralize the loose system of local option and would also provide adequate funds.

Pressure for a more rational system came both from Tokyo and from other areas. Ikeda Katsu, a Thought Section official, pointed out that between 1928 and 1933 "suspension of indictment" (*kiso yūyo*) was used 3,288 times, and a "stay of execution" (*shiko yūyo*) in 607 cases. Supposedly, most of these people had renounced communism. Sase

72. Japan, Keisatsu Kenkyūkai, 155–173.
73. *Ibid.*, 188–191. Sasaki, 255–256.
74. Japan, Keisatsu Kenkyūkai, 82. Japan, *Tokkō Keisatsu Reikishū* (Part III), 4–5.

Shōzō, who researched at the ministry in 1934, was alarmed over such large numbers of suspects being released without proper supervision. Although he felt acceptance of sincere repentance and rehabilitation was a good idea, it made him "shiver to think that society has no defense against those who have recanted and left prison." If thought criminals were "cured" without "de-escalating their . . . dangerousness," they remained a danger to society.[75] Procurator Moriyama Takeichirō, a specialist on this problem, was also worried. To show the need for greater supervision, he pointed to an industrial area near Tokyo which was a gathering place for released, supposedly converted, offenders. Might not these unsupervised people slip into their old ways? A procurator from the Nagano area pinpointed another problem: the need to locate jobs for released criminals. In this manner, pressure grew to enact legislation that would create a nationwide system supported by relevant agencies. Thought procurators saw themselves as the linchpin of the new structures.[76]

On February 1, 1934, a bill to revise the Peace Preservation Law was introduced into the House of Representatives. The bill provided for protection and supervision (*hogo kansatsu*) and for preventive detention (*yobō kōkin*). The former was designed to keep track of thought criminals released for one reason or another, and the latter was designed to provide for the incarceration of incorrigible prisoners for longer periods than required by their court-imposed sentences. The system for keeping track of thought criminals was in fact already in use, but the new law was intended to standardize techniques and provide funds.[77]

Justice officials were quizzed by legislators about the yardstick used in determining successful conversion. Would it be correct, asked one representative, to say that *tenkō* was synonymous with *kaishun* (repentance)? Justice Minister Koyama agreed. Representative Hirajima Toshio expressed strong doubt about the sincerity of Sano and Nabeyama, since even though they said they accepted the *kokutai* they did not recognize private property. Were they, therefore, still criminals, even though their crime was a "lighter one"? Perhaps they had

75. Sase Shōzō, *Seiji Hanzairon*, iii, 177, 201–202.

76. SKST, XVI, October, 1934, 135.

77. Naimushō, Keihokyoku, *Dai 65-kai Teikoku Gikai Chian Ijihō Kaisei Hōritsuan*, 146–147.

converted only because it was politically expedient. Then Hirajima asked about the criterion for accepting a conversion. Koyama admitted that there was room for doubt about the fullness of Sano's and Nabeyama's conversion, but insisted that their thinking had radically changed. Therefore, they had undergone conversion, even though not a full one. The Justice Ministry saw a complete change of heart as a total renunciation of all illegal thought.[78] Representative Tachikawa Taira felt that most of the so-called converts had adopted temporary camouflage to escape punishment. Some justice officials shared this pessimism. Chief of the Criminal Affairs Bureau Kimura Naotatsu, for example, was worried over Sano's and Nabeyama's plan to create a new communist party under the imperial system. Were they perhaps scheming to subvert the state in this circuitous manner?[79]

Koyama defended the bill, by pointing out that it merely formalized a system which had been used since 1932. As for the new preventive detention part, it would be used only to extend prison sentences of hard-core communists who would not reform. This approach would not only protect society, but would also be good for incorrigibles; prison officials would make a special effort to convert them.[80]

Interpellation of Koyama revealed that the bill strengthened the position of the procurators. Besides their pivotal role in the protection and supervision system, they would be given new powers to move cases from one court to another and to issue arrest warrants (under the old law only judges could do this). In addition theirs would be a decisive voice in the preventive detention system.[81]

The policies of the Saitō Makoto Cabinet (May 1932–June 1934) came under fire during the debate. Saitō's national cabinet was charged with failure to control the spread of communism and to properly educate the people. We need, said one legislator, a Spiritual Cultural Research Center to examine the theory of *kokutai* and explain it. Moreover, research and action for correcting dangerous thought was too scattered, with each ministry going its own way. A new Social Ministry should be created to coordinate government actions. This was unnecessary,

78. *Ibid.*, 1–3.
79. *Ibid.*, 4–5.
80. *Ibid.*, 107–112.
81. *Ibid.*, 147, 172.

replied Koyama. Indeed, Home, Justice, and Education Ministry officials were meeting to discuss thought problems and were working in concert. The movement toward interministerial coordination had culminated in 1933 with the Deliberative Committee on Thought Control.[82]

Another legislator saw little that was new in the bill except the idea of preventive detention. Actually, it was common practice for police to seize suspects without warrants and in other ways to infringe upon civil rights; the government, therefore, was attempting to legalize what was being done. Moreover, why was the government not more interested in controlling the outrageous actions of rightists?[83] Such a question was natural in light of the Blood Pledge Corps incidents (Ketsumeidan Jiken) in 1932 (the assassins of Dan Takuma and Inoue Junnosuke had gone on trial on June 28, 1933).[84] Others also pressed the government for a clarification of the rightist issue. One pointed out that justice officials had not said a word on this subject. Yet, hiding behind patriotism and the *kokutai*, ultranationalists were attempting to destroy Japan's economic and political system. Were their actions really so different from those of the communists? Koyama insisted that the government was concerned about rightists, and was using the Criminal Code to control them. Justice officials preparing the bill had been instructed to add a clause covering rightists, but, after deep thought, they were unable to reach agreement, and the idea was dropped.[85] Another revealing statement came from Matsumoto Manabu, Chief of the Police Bureau, Home Ministry. Rightists were dangerous, he said, and they were being investigated and sometimes arrested, but they were far less dangerous than leftists, because they did support the *kokutai*.

82. *Ibid.*, 147–150.

83. *Ibid.*, 151.

84. The Blood Pledge Corps incidents were two in a series of rightists-inspired violent events in 1932 that shocked politicians and the public and that marked the decline of parliamentary dominance. The incidents of February 9 (former Finance Minister Inoue was shot) and March 5 (Dan, the director general of the Mitsui company, was killed) were staged by radical young military officers and rural terrorists in an effort to solve the economic, political, and social crises brought on by the strains of rapid modernization and the depression. Inoue and Dan were two of twenty prospective victims whom these fanatics considered responsible for national weakness and rural suffering. Police intervention ended the murder series after Dan's death.

85. Japan, Naimushō, Keihokyoku, *Dai 65-kai,* 26, 28, 157, 159.

Moreover, terror tactics employed by them were but a temporary phenomenon.[86]

An amended bill was passed by the House of Representatives on March 16, 1934, and was sent on to the House of Peers the same day. After making some modifications, the upper house returned the bill to the lower. Then, at the request of the lower house, a joint session was held. However, by the time a compromise was reached the Diet adjourned.[87]

Two months later, thought procurators met for a three-day conference. Yazu Keiji (Fukuoka) mourned the bill's failure and urged the Justice Ministry to "create something no matter what we call it." Could it not be done by an imperial ordinance, he asked? The head of the Criminal Affairs Bureau replied that although he, too, was pained by the bill's failure, an imperial ordinance was impossible. Thought procurators must continue to get along as best they could.[88]

Conclusion

By 1934, the Peace Preservation Law system was coalescing. Stimulated by the war on domestic communists and other subversives and by events in Manchuria and China, justice officials devised new methods for handling ideological offenders and also set the stage for a system of mass thought control which would soon become so pervasive as to touch everyone's lives. The bleak wintertime era for free thought and expression, however, had not yet arrived in 1934; a chill was in the air, but the intellectual world went about its business not realizing how soon a thought-killing frost would strike.

From the government's viewpoint, efforts to perfect the mechanism for thought control were meeting success: the Japanese Communist Party was nearly destroyed; the Tokyo trial was a triumph, and had been followed by a flood of conversions; procurators had created a positive policy of parole and reintegration; and interministerial cooperation was formalized in 1933. At first glance, a reasonably unified and efficient thought-control apparatus appeared to be in operation; a closer look,

86. *Ibid.*, 18–22, 29–31.
87. Shakai Bunkohen, *Showaki Kanken Shisō Chōsa Hōkoku*, 29.
88. SKST, XVI, 137–138.

though, revealed the imperfections. Shortages of funds and personnel plagued justice officials; disputes arose over the way in which thought criminals should be treated—police were sometimes too harsh, and justice and education officials were sometimes too soft; procurators in remote bureaus felt neglected and complained that information sometimes failed to reach them; and secret publications were not always willingly shared by the Home Ministry. The Home Ministry, for example, despite repeated official requests by the Justice Ministry, refused to share copies of *Tokkō Geppō* (Monthly Special Higher Police Report) and other publications.[89] While this problem was partially solved by individual procurators who exchanged publications, including the *Tokkō Geppō,* with nearby thought-police units, it was a knotty one which was never fully solved by central bureaucrats. In short, the longstanding rivalry between justice and police officials refused to die, even in the face of the thought problem.

89. SKST, LXIV, September, 1939, 266.

CHAPTER 5 Administration of *Tenkō* (Conversion)

The idea of confession and rehabilitation had deep social roots, and this approach to the thought problem had been incorporated into the 1925 peace law (by promising amnesty or reduction of punishment for those who turned themselves in). In March 1931, conversion was officially approved as a method for handling cases, and rules were devised to enable police and procurators to weigh each suspect's degree of repentance. Thus, officials developed a *tenkō* policy, rather than a harsher one of mass jailings, executions, or exile. The most important reason for adopting this approach was the official feeling that, after all, the suspects too were Japanese. The common origins of both offenders and officials "provided the hope—even the expectation—of rehabilitation." Procurator Hirata Susumu summed up this view: No "thought criminal was hopeless. . . . Since they were all Japanese, sooner or later they would all come around to realizing that their ideas were wrong."[1] Hirata was simply expressing a fact about Japanese society which many scholars have noted: that a feeling of familylike intimacy has long pervaded the nation.[2]

1. Quoted in Patricia G. Steinhoff, "Tenkō: Ideology and Social Integration in Prewar Japan" (unpublished doctoral dissertation), 70.
2. Nakamura Hajime, "Basic Features of the Legal, Political, and Economic Thought of Japan," in Charles A. Moore (ed.), *The Japanese Mind*, 157. Other evidence suggests that this was a common attitude. During the Privy Council debate on revising the Peace Preservation Law (June 27, 1928), Justice Minister Hara Yoshimichi remarked that the leader of the Social Democratic Party had cried while reading a poem by the Meiji emperor. This, said Hara, made me think that after all, they are Japanese, too. Okudaira, GS, XLV, 126. Also see Higuchi Masaru, "Sayoku Zenrekisha no Tenkō Mondai ni Tsuite," in SKST, XCV, August, 1943, 51.

By 1931, the state's policy toward communists was aimed at conversion. Justice Ministry Instruction Number 270 (March 27) approved this method for thought cases.[3] Therefore, when Sano's and Nabeyama's conversion statement broke the dam, and hundreds of other communists followed their example, justice authorities were prepared. Prison authorities responded by establishing a five-step scale of "repentance," with the term "converted" applying to the top three levels and "semiconverted" to the bottom two: (1) the person renounces revolutionary thought and pledges to give up all social movements; (2) the person renounces revolutionary thought and in the future plans to work in legal social movements; (3) the person has renounced revolutionary thought but is undecided about his position regarding legal social movements; (4) the person's revolutionary thought has been shaken and it is anticipated that he will renounce it in the future; and (5) the person does not renounce revolutionary thought, but he has pledged to give up all social movements in the future.[4]

Thus, it is clear that while the 1925 peace law was aimed at illegal actions by groups and individuals, by the early 1930's justice officials were no longer satisfied with confessions and prison sentences, or confessions and promises of reform by released offenders. Instead, they aimed at pressuring offenders into a full purge of their radical thoughts. Actually, a policy aiming at the total renunciation of all illegal ideological belief was surfacing several years prior to the publication of the prison authorities' scale. One research report, on people who repeatedly violated the peace law, stated that in 1931 authorities realized the necessity not only to make converts take an oral pledge, but to put the concepts of the *tenkō* idea into daily practice and fully reform themselves.[5] Judge Miyagi's decision to execute no one blended in smoothly with the growing inclination to solve the problem by effecting a change in the thinking of thought offenders. Therefore, by 1932 the graft of *tenkō* onto the body of the 1925 peace law had taken hold, resulting in a unique solution to the thought problem. The nation's

3. Tozawa Shigeo, "Shisō Hanzai no Kensatsu Jitsumu ni Tsuite," in Yamabe (ed.), GS, XVI, 26.

4. There was, of course, a final category for stubborn persons who refused to make any attempt to convert. SKST, XXI, May, 1935, 178–179.

5. Higuchi, 8.

social and legal traditions reinforced this approach. However, since it was a new procedure, it required specific administrative and legal action.

Reforming Thought Offenders Prior to 1936

Prior to 1936 the organization created to reform thought criminals was surprisingly weak, limited in personnel, funds, and facilities, and greatly dependent upon a generous public. Besides these faults, it suffered because it was a system of local option, with inadequate control from the top. Moreover, there were only three or four protection groups especially designed for ideological offenders, and only a few others involved in rehabilitating former convicts.[6]

Not unexpectedly Tokyo's roughly two-dozen rehabilitation groups were the largest and best supported. Through the Thought Protection Enterprise Research Association (whose president was the chief procurator of the Tokyo Appeals Court), justice officials were able to exert some control over the rehabilitation groups. Besides receiving semiofficial direction from justice officials, rehabilitation groups were in close contact with the National Spirit and Culture Research Institute (Kokumin Seishin Bunka Kenkyūjo) sponsored by the Education Ministry. In June 1933, these private groups held their first conference to discuss thought criminals with about fifty scholars, representatives from protection groups, and National Spirit and Culture Research students attending.[7] Despite such activities, government funds for rehabilitation were scarce, and the rehabilitation groups functioned chiefly because of the good will of volunteer workers and the benevolence of philanthropists.[8]

Best known among the protection groups in Tokyo was a branch of the Teikoku Kōshin Kai (Imperial Rehabilitation Club). This relief agency for former convicts was financed by the emperor and the business world, with Judge Miyagi Chōgorō as president. At first the club accepted only thought offenders who had completed their prison terms, but later it expanded its operations to include those who were not

6. SKST, LVII, February, 1939, 34.

7. Suzuki Kisaburō Sensei Denki Hensankai, *Suzuki Kisaburō*, 154.

8. SKST, XXII, September, 1935, 50–52, 59, 60. Special Higher Police units also gave some aid. Japan, Naimushō, Keihokyoku, *Tokkō Geppō*, March, 1936, 5–9.

jailed. A former communist, Kobayashi Tojin (he had converted for religious reasons), headed the special section for thought offenders. Kobayashi was a main reason for the club's success. Since he was a former communist, and interviewed all candidates for membership, he was able to pick those who were sincerely interested in making a new life. Great stress was placed on finding proper employment. Some became small businessmen, like noodle peddlers or dealers in children's toys; others worked on a club farm in Ibaragi Prefecture. This hand-picked group of about 100 members was very successful; up to May 1934 none of its converts had dropped out.[9]

Osaka had protection organizations, but they absorbed few of those who needed jobs or ideological guidance, since that city lacked a coordinating body and funds.[10] In Nagoya, sponsored by the court of appeals, a society entitled the Meitoku Kai (Illustrious Virtue Association) was struggling to extend its influence. In Hiroshima, where there was no protection association, procurators at the district court had begun to sponsor round-table conferences with former thought criminals.[11] Shizuoka, and many other areas, had no guidance organizations, and procurators had to accept help from thought offenders' relatives and others who generally had little understanding of the problem.[12] Although the situation was little better in Fukuoka, procurators had established a protection center staffed with civilian volunteers. There, thought offenders met in round-table conferences with procurators and police to discuss problems, and, in addition, money was available to finance loans to members.[13] Nationally, however, the reintegration program faced several substantial obstacles: a shortage of funds, personnel, and jobs.[14]

Even within the prison system, because of poor planning and shortages of qualified personnel and equipment, the conversion effort had floundered. In spite of a system for classifying the degree of conversion, those who had not renounced communism were treated

9. SKST, XVI, October, 1934, 136–137. Shiota Shōbee, "Kazoku Kokka no Omomi," *Asahi Jānaru*, VII, June 20, 1965, 74–75.

10. SKST, XXII, 82–83, 86.

11. *Ibid.*, 72.

12. *Ibid.*, 64, 66–67.

13. *Ibid.*, 66.

14. *Ibid.*

exactly the same as those who had. For example, thought criminals served their sentences in regular prisons side by side with conventional felons; thought prisoners seldom had contact with the prison chaplain who was one of the key figures in the government's plan for converting recalcitrant ideologists—before an offender's sentence was decided he was visited only once per year, and after the sentence was given, even though visits were scheduled once every three months, they did not occur unless the prisoner made a written request. An Osaka procurator viewed the situation as just short of hopeless: "Anyhow, today's prison chaplain has so many other things to do I suspect that he cannot do much proselytizing among the prisoners on an individual basis."[15]

Outside of the ideological adjustment faced by all, finding a job was the most serious problem. The public and employers shunned them. Procurator Hanawa Nagaharu (Shizuoka District Court) saw the irony in this situation. In the past the government propaganda machine indoctrinated the people with a great fear of communism. Unfortunately, "that propaganda worked too well among the citizens. Once you say someone is a red, and only because of that word, a skilled working man faces the disaster of losing his job."[16] A procurator from Hiroshima felt that the program could not function properly in the midst of a hostile public. Consequently, the first task was to begin a national campaign through the various news media to make people understand the need to aid thought criminals.[17]

Among other problems was that of thought policemen who failed to adjust their techniques, and who continued to operate in a manner more appropriate to an earlier period when incidents of unnecessary repression had occurred. Released people were sometimes visited at work, and when their employers learned that they were "Reds," they were often discharged; some lost one position after another.[18]

15. *Ibid.*, 71, 83.
16. *Ibid.*, 69.
17. *Ibid.*, 61–62.
18. *Ibid.*, 37, 58, 60, 70. The Home Ministry did publish directives ordering police to "avoid causing the suspect to be discharged from his position." Furthermore, police were told not to mistreat suspects during questioning. Japan, Naimushō, Keihokyoku, "Kyōsanshugisha no Tenkō Hōsaku-Miteikō" (typewritten about 1935), 5, 12. By 1937, Moriyama Takeichirō felt that police treatment had improved. Moriyama, *Shisōhan Hogo Kansatsuhō Kaisetsu,* 175.

A story told by procurator Sakurai of Hiroshima is illustrative of the social problem involved. One day a lawyer came to visit Sakurai, explaining that his young nephew had been arrested. Sakurai recalled that the student had renounced his radical ideas, had been released on bail, and had joined the local branch of the National Spirit and Culture Research Institute. Sakurai felt that he had completely reformed. However, the uncle had not come to discuss him, but the case of his elder brother. Soon after the arrest, the elder brother was discharged by a large firm. The uncle was certain that it was a case of guilt by association. Even though Sakurai tended to doubt the story, his investigation confirmed it. "Therefore, if the older brother is receiving this much persecution, you can imagine how much is being given to former thought criminals. In other words, society has no understanding at all about what kind of people converted thought criminals are."[19]

School authorities were sometimes as narrow-minded as businessmen. Judge Ishii Kanzō (Kobe District Court) reported that few schools wanted former thought criminals,[20] and comment like his was not uncommon at meetings of justice officials prior to 1937.

In order to determine the rehabilitation system's effectiveness, the Justice Ministry compiled statistics on repeaters (those who claimed to renounce communism but who actually rejoined the movement or supported its goals). Based on analysis of the years 1928 to 1934, the figure was a modest three percent, with the percentage remaining constant for each category investigated (charges withheld, suspension of indictment, stay of execution, and those who served their sentences).[21] When compared with the average for repetition among common criminals (e.g., robbers and other kinds of thieves), which was about sixty percent,[22] the ratio for thought offenders seems amazingly low. Nevertheless, thought officials viewed the three percent figure as a "very serious problem," and suggested ways to lower it: better indoctrination while in prison, fuller cooperation from the Special Higher Police, improved liaison between the penal administration and

19. SKST, XXII, 60–61.
20. *Ibid.*, 80.
21. *Ibid.*, 48.
22. SKST, LVII, 42.

the procurator bureaus, deeper investigation of each case before requesting the penalty, better organization of the network of protection associations, and fuller, more frequent publications by the Justice Ministry.[23]

Tozawa Shigeo, Yoshimura Takeo, and others emphasized that although the Diet had not yet created a government system, it was important not to wait, but to skillfully utilize private associations. In spite of financial handicaps, and the fact that most procurators were already overworked, they were, as Tozawa and Yoshimura pointed out, in a key position to encourage the growth of the guidance system. Not only was it necessary to increase the number of protection centers, but communications had to be established between each center and government organs engaged in similar work. Prison officials, police, education officials, procurators, and judges must all support this effort. However, only civilian volunteers who understood the problems of ideological offenders should be picked, and financial contributions should be investigated before acceptance.[24]

One procurator suggested the establishment of committees to help find employment. Members might be a procurator, a prison official, the head of a local employment agency, and an influential layman, each of whom would cooperate with the local protection society. Police, Shinto priests, Buddhist priests, social workers, and others might also help by reviewing the released person's thought tendencies. They would report to the head of the protection association who would in turn inform the local procurator. The procurator's duty would be to give advice, provide books on proper conversion methods, and interview offenders. Since "the family and love of home is the most important item," in the decision to discard radical ideology, it was important for the director of a protection association to open a dialogue with relatives. Judge Ishii from Kobe agreed, adding that it was crucial "to destroy the way of thinking that says that the protection association is somebody else's business and has nothing to do with us. Instead, make them [each Japanese] fully understand that as an influential member of society they have a responsibility for such an enterprise." The best way to

23. SKST XXII, 48.
24. *Ibid.*, 49–51, 59.

accomplish this, he said, was to bring many useful local people into the system.[25]

Tozawa was concerned over the quality of guidance. He advocated more extensive use of the "charges withheld" category because of the "psychological impact upon the suspect." Like a stay of execution, the use of charges withheld gave the criminal hope, as well as considerable motivation to reform in order to avoid punishment. However, it would work properly, he felt, only if a thought criminal received proper guidance. Protection associations could play an important role in giving such guidance, by encouraging offenders to read good books and listen to good lectures, and by helping reformed offenders keep their jobs.[26]

In 1935, Justice Minister Ohara Naoshi felt that the organization and real effectiveness of the Japanese Communist Party was destroyed, but successful suppression of the party had produced another serious problem: the reintegration of ideological criminals.[27] From 1928 until the end of 1935, over 58,000 communists and their supporters were arrested. Of this group, some of those who had renounced communism were backsliding and others were unable to find employment; they were, in short, becoming a serious social problem. Since justice officials were anxious to prevent thought crimes, they were forced to become deeply involved in the offenders' personal lives, responsible for ideological guidance, job placement, and livelihood aid. Moreover, since thought crimes could not be handled in the manner of regular crimes, procurators spent a good deal of time reflecting upon the standards for *tenkō*.[28]

The Thought Criminals' Protection and Supervision Law

Justice officials were eager to institutionalize the technique of conversion and rehabilitation, but legislation was required in order to formalize their new system. Such legislation failed to win Diet approval in 1934 and 1935 because of its connection with a bill for revising the Peace Preservation Law and the debate centering on Professor Minobe

25. *Ibid.*, 69–70, 79.

26. *Ibid.*, 53–54. The "charges withheld" category was dropped in late 1936, after the enactment of the protection and supervision law.

27. SKST, XXII, 34–36.

28. *Ibid.*, 52, 88–89, 92.

Tatsukichi's "organ theory."[29] Then the Justice Ministry, in 1936, presented the Sixty-Ninth Imperial Diet a separate bill dealing only with *tenkō*.[30] Justice Minister Hayashi Raisaburō explained the Thought Criminals' Protection and Supervision Law (Shisōhan Hogo Kansatsuhō) bill to the House of Representatives (May 16) and the House of Peers (May 22). The state's control over the numerous thought offenders who had been either released without prosecution or paroled from prison was too lax, Hayashi said. The new law would prevent unreformed offenders from repeating their crimes, would isolate them from others, and would aid all offenders in their mental and economic struggles.[31]

After enactment of this crucial legislation, Protection Division Chief Moriyama Takeichirō announced that the "father-and-mother-type policy to control thought crimes has been established."[32] The proportion of strictness and tenderness depended upon the nature of each crime and the attitude of each offender. Passage of this bill was a logical result of the public policy defined by the Justice Ministry. It was obvious that standard criminal procedures would not necessarily remove the ideology behind thought crimes. Hence, it was imperative not only to destroy subversive organizations, but also to create a method of formally reintegrating those individuals who had legally been cast out of society. The 1936 law filled this need; the category of "thought criminal" was solidly established in the legal system.

The new law (passed on May 29) did not go into effect until the issuance of Imperial Ordinance Number 403 (November 13, 1936); issuance of administrative orders which outlined the composition and duties of Protection and Supervision Centers, and other administrative details, were completed (on November 20). Twenty-two Centers were created throughout the nation. Attached to each district court was a Protection and Supervision Examination Commission, with a staff of procurators, judges, police, and prison officials.[33] They were to review

29. Moriyama, 19–20.
30. SKST, XXII, 62.
31. Okudaira, GS, XLV, 273.
32. Moriyama, 20–21.
33. For a definitive study of the law's background and contents see Hasebe Kingo, *Shisōhan no Hogo ni Tsuite*, SK, XXI (10), March, 1937.

cases of a suspension of indictment, a stay of execution, a release on
parole, or completion of sentence.[34] When a person needed further
economic or spiritual aid, the Commissions referred him to one of the
Centers. The Center then decided how to deal with the case.[35]

Moriyama, who had helped draft the new law, explained at a justice
conference in November, that it was designed to keep thought criminals
under indirect surveillance, to guide them positively in reforming their
thinking, and to help them find employment; it was also intended
to keep them from backsliding into another thought crime.[36] A
Nagoya-based procurator felt that each offender should do more than
what was minimally required: "Progressing further, as in the spirit of
our protection law, we must endeavor to resurrect them from the
left-wing to be Japanese, and those who are in unresurrected uncertainty
must be completely resurrected."[37]

Moriyama also explained the "standard" to be used by Protection
and Supervision Examination Commissions. At that time *tenkō* was
divided roughly into three categories: perfect (a person who had
renounced all revolutionary ideology); semi- (a person hanging in the
balance); and unchanged (a person who had not expelled revolutionary thought). These broad categories could, of course, be further
subdivided. However, using only the broad categories, it was clear that
those within the second and third groups needed guidance, as well as
some in the first, since even if their thoughts were pure they might need
help finding jobs. Moriyama also pointed out that the Commissions had
to set a time limit for protection and supervision; a standard time was
two years, but each Commission could adjust this.[38]

Working closely with the twenty-two Centers, Commissions placed
each person in the hands of either a probation officer, a private

34. Among the roughly 60,000 people arrested for violating provisions of the Peace
Preservation Law by 1936, over 10,000 were covered by one of these categories, SKST,
XXXIV, December, 1936, 43.

35. Hasebe, in SK, 77–78. SKST, XXXIV, 31–32. Hirata Susumu was the Tokyo
Center's first director. See Appendix II, Chart 2 for the distribution of the centers and
their position within the administrative structure of the Justice Ministry.

36. SKST, XXXIV, 32, 37.

37. *Ibid.*

38. *Ibid.*, 32–33.

guardian, or an institution such as a temple, shrine, church, hospital, or business. Many thought offenders had several legal guardians: perhaps a relative, the firm for which he worked, and the Center. Periodical reports were required on his activities and ideological development. Authorities were empowered to place restrictions on residence, social intercourse, correspondence, and reading material. Financial assistance was given to those unable to work because of illness or for whom suitable employment could not be secured.[39]

After centralizing the system and institutionalizing it, the Justice Ministry lost no time in raising the criterion for full ideological conversion—a perfect conversion would be different than in the past. No one would be certified fully converted until he fully changed his mental attitudes; in a perfect conversion, a person would discard not only his revolutionary ideology, but would also recognize the awakening of his feelings of nationalism.[40] War with China in July 1937 caused the government to increase pressure in order to force conformity. The offender, by the new standards, was expected to give a positive demonstration of his total acceptance of the Japanese spirit and of his patriotism. In 1940, Judge Ishii Kiyoshi (Takamatsu District Court) said that one good standard for *tenkō* would be whether or not the subject "worshipped the emperor as a personal god."[41]

Protracted warfare in China and the diplomatic crisis with the United States during 1941 ushered in new standards for conversion. It was held that the thought offender must awaken to the fact of being Japanese, put his Japanese ideas into daily practice, fully accept and understand the concept of *kokutai,* and discard the unassimilable portions of Western culture (e.g., individualism, liberalism, Marxism, and other "inferior" ideas). Furthermore, he must be ready to help other Japanese liberate the entire world from Marxism.[42] Justice officials remained confident that the few die-hards who had not yet come around would in time convert. Eventually, they would find their way out of the swamp of "modern individualism and materialism" which had prevented them

39. Moriyama, 70–76, 154–158. Hasebe, in SK, 74. SKST, XXXIV, 38. The Foreign Affairs Association of Japan (ed.), *The Japan Year Book, 1940–1941*, 625–627.
40. SKST, XXXIV, 34–36.
41. SKST, LXXXVI, May, 1941, 151.
42. Higuchi, 40–42.

from realizing their true Japaneseness. "Since they are Japanese, we feel that some day they will awaken to this fact."[43]

For Judge Higuchi Masaru, the author of an important document on converting leftists, the crucial point to investigate was the offender's attitude about loyalty and filial piety. Higuchi illustrated this by using a story circulating at that time. An army officer asked his men why they were loyal to their emperor. One replied because the ruling line went back to the beginnings of the nation; another said because the Japanese *kokutai* was incomparable; and the third answered that the emperor was benevolent to the people. They were all wrong replied the officer in an angry tone. Their loyalty had a reason; it was a conditional loyalty. True loyalty, he said, has no conditions and no reason, "It is pure loyalty to the emperor."[44]

This story, which exalts loyalty over all other requirements for a complete conversion, is a graphic example of officialdom turning its back on the rational legal system so painstakingly constructed after 1868. By making this the chief yardstick not only for a true conversion, but the most important virtue for all citizens, Judge Higuchi was stating that the imperial will coincided with ethical axiom. Indeed, the identification of the emperor with standards for moral value had deep roots in Japanese tradition. Uesugi Shinkichi, Hozumi Yatsuka's leading disciple, carried this argument to its logical extreme in a 1913 article which is recognizable as quite similar to Higuchi's story about the officer speaking to his men. Uesugi was discussing commentaries on the Imperial Rescript on Education:[45]

None of those commentaries . . . answers correctly the basic question: Why should the Japanese people obey the rescript? They offer the following explanations: that the rescript embodies human morality; or that it expresses Japanese morality; or that it is based on the teachings of Confucius and Mencius, the doctrines of Buddha and Jesus, and the customs of Japan. In short, they argue from its content. Such discussions of content are useful in praising the rescript, but they do not explain why the Japanese people must obey. The answer . . . is simple: because it is the word of the emperor. . . . "The will of

43. *Ibid.*, 51.
44. *Ibid.*, 230, 237.
45. Richard H. Minear, *Japanese Tradition and Western Law*, 182.

the emperor is absolute, and the standards of conduct of Japanese subjects depend solely on his will. . . . It transcends relative merits; it transcends right and wrong; it is the commandment which all people must respect absolutely.''

While conversion began as a ''personal emotional commitment'' it eventually became ''a social form which could be utilized by individuals and groups alike to express symbolically their integration into Japanese society.'' The public pledge of support for the government, and the repudiation of the popular front policy by the Social Masses' Party, is one example of an organization using conversion as a means of ''symbolically'' reaffirming its integration.[46] Businesses, as well, announced their conversion, in order to escape public criticism of past policies and to identify more fully with the nation's mood. A year after the assassination of Baron Dan Takuma, the managing director of Mitsui Gōmei (Holding Company) began a public-relations campaign to improve its image, a campaign which was soon referred to as the *zaibatsu no tenkō* (*zaibatsu* conversion).[47]

By 1938, Protection and Supervision Centers had handled about 13,000 people. Protection Division Chief Moriyama felt that the new system was working moderately well, in spite of shortages of funds and personnel: the number of repeaters was a low one percent;[48] the total of privately supported protection groups had shot up to about 130; public distrust had declined, with some businessmen making special efforts to hire offenders; the Education Ministry was permitting students and teachers involved in thought cases to return to schools; and over two hundred offenders had journeyed to North and Central China to visit

46. Steinhoff, 253–255. The Social Masses' Party (Shakai Taishūtō), formed in 1932, was anticommunist, antifascist, and anticapitalist. Representing leftist moderates, and profiting from some antimilitarist feeling, this party polled half a million votes in 1936 and won eighteen House of Representatives seats.

47. Arthur E. Tiedemann, ''Big Business and Politics in Prewar Japan,'' in James W. Morley (ed.), *Dilemmas of Growth in Prewar Japan*, 291.

48. This one percent covers thought offenders in protection groups. SKST, LVII, 43. If others are included, the percentage in 1933 was about six, and by 1937 it had jumped to twenty-nine. But this bald figure is deceptive, since the number of people involved dropped sharply during the same period, from 3,775 to 779. Thus, although the percentage increased, the number of repeaters remained about the same (just over 200 in 1933 and 1937). These were the hard-core incorrigibles. For a chart on repeaters see SKST, LXXIX, August, 1940, 542.

Japanese troops, and upon their return had made a good impression by giving patriotic lectures.[49]

Lack of funds and personnel were neatly circumvented by Moriyama and his assistants. The budget allowed the employment of only fifty junior probation officers for the twenty-two centers, but the Justice Ministry solved this problem by enlisting almost 1,000 part-time volunteers. Administrators from the central and provincial bureaucracy were asked to serve, as were people from the fields of business, religion, labor, and medicine. Extra funds were acquired by appealing for aid to private protection groups. Thus, the protection and supervision enterprise owed much of its success to public support. Moriyama was distressed by the lack of government funds but understood that the money was needed for the war effort. "Therefore, we must allow the protection groups to spend money and help us carry out the . . . probation work smoothly."[50]

An Administrative Solution

Undoubtedly, the Peace Preservation Law system was extremely effective: the communist movement was crushed; Western ideology in general lost favor among intellectuals; and, between 1928 and 1940, the recidivism rate was a low eight percent. These repeaters represented 1,036 people who had either served time in prison or been given one of the special dispositions (i.e., stay of execution, suspension of indictment).[51] Why was the peace law so effective? Part of the answer, of course, lies in the nature of Japanese society and the strict application of the law, but an important element was the special disposition system created by thought procurators. Over the years, the solution of the thought problem involved more instances of handling cases by administrative disposition than of treatment by applying punishment after a trial. Indeed, the majority of offenders were never indicted, and the success of the system was based upon these administrative dispositions.

49. SKST, LVII, 19, 24, 34, 39, 43. In May, 1938, the Justice Ministry began to publish Shisō Hogo Geppō (Thought Protection Monthly).
50. SKST, LVII, 32, 35.
51. Higuchi, 13.

A look at records on enforcement of the law shows that although conviction rates were very high, the ratio of indictments to arrests was extremely low. Out of nearly 66,000 persons arrested (1928–1941) only about 5,500, or approximately eight percent, were prosecuted; about 6,200 received a suspension of indictment; and charges withheld was applied to about 2,700; a total of under 12,000. (See Table 1.) It should be recalled that there was one execution of a Japanese under the provisions of this law. Hence, we must conclude that strict enforcement alone does not explain the law's success. The employment of the *tenkō* system, which accounted for the high rate of suspended sentences and the extremely high rate of people released, was the reason for the law's success.

The creation of the conversion system and the use of special dispositions brought the enforcement of the law into the sphere of administrative discretion. Thought procurators could, then, direct prosecution only against hard-core communists and could use suspension of indictment or charges withheld for less serious cases. And the majority of those arrested were, from the viewpoint of authorities, only lightly tainted red; they converted easily and totally cut themselves off from the antistate movement.[52] By using these dispositions, authorities readily convinced those who were released that Big Brother was keeping an eye on them. Authorities were especially eager to rescue students who knew Marxist theory but who had little actual experience in the movement.[53] Students who repented and wrote a conversion statement were given a suspension of indictment. (See Table 1.) While technically their cases were still pending, usually the procurator considered them closed, but the students were not informed, and they went back to school suspecting that they were still under close watch. Students for whom charges were withheld were similarly treated, but release was given even before the preliminary steps toward indictment had been taken. (See Table 1.) Justice officials considered this disposition to be a great success.[54] After Sano's and Nabeyama's conversion, convicts as well as suspects were included in the expanding

52. *Ibid.*, 7.
53. *Ibid.*
54. *Ibid.*, 7–8.

Table 1. Disposition of leftist-related violations of the Peace Preservation Law
(January 1928–October 1941)*

Year	Arrests	Indictments	Suspension of indictment	Charges withheld†	Total
1928	3,426	525	16		541
1929	4,942	339	27		366
1930	6,124	461	292		753
1931	10,422	307	454	67	828
1932	13,938	646	774	717	2,137
1933	14,622	1,285	1,474	1,016	3,775
1934	3,994	496	831	626	1,953
1935	1,785	113	269	186	568
1936	2,067	158	328	56	542
1937	1,312	210	302		512
1938	937	240	382		622
1939	723	388	440		828
1940	817	229	315		544
1941	823	162	295		457
Total	65,921	5,559	6,199	2,668	14,426

*Source: Higuchi Masaru, "Sayoku Zenrekisha no Tenkō Mondai ni Tsuite," 3–5.
†Dropped after the passage of the Thought Criminals' Protection and Supervision Law.

tenkō system, with court and prison officials becoming involved in its
administration. The 1936 protection and surveillance law centralized
the *tenkō* system, and the category of thought criminal was written into
the legal code for the first time. This law clearly spelled out a policy
already in operation: reconverting ideological heretics and reintegrating
them. Once authorities were convinced that the thought criminals fully
repudiated leftist radicalism, they were fully forgiven.

The Phenomenon of Tenkō

Thousands of thought criminals underwent ideological conversion.
While some element of government, public, or family pressure was
usually behind each conversion case, one scholar suggests that there
was a strong faddish element involved. Young people, who were caught
up in the communist current because it was new and exciting, gave it up
with few qualms when pressure was applied. Only a very few were

really dedicated Marxists ready to die for the cause. Around 1927–1928 many bourgeois writers suddenly switched to the proletarian camp; Takami Jun, Takeda Rintarō, and Kataoka Teppei are but a few of the more famous converts. Then, almost as suddenly, proletarian writers fled the revolutionary literature movement in a panic as increased police pressure and an upsurge of nationalistic sentiment swept the country.[55]

Some conversions began because of difficult conditions in jails and prisons, during a time when an offender's physical and mental defenses were lowered. Signs of an illness such as tuberculosis, in which long confinement probably meant death, coupled with real or imagined physical torture were enough to break the resistence of many. The author Murayama Tomoyoshi's conversion novel, *The White Night*, well illustrates this fear: "Sitting in the dark corner of his prison cell, visualizing the scene of torture by the police, he tried to torment his own body, and he ended up with the full recognition that he could not stand up to such conditions."[56]

An equally important reason for conversion was psychological. Anxiety was heightened by the indeterminate length of detention between the time of arrest and final sentencing. An isolated life in jail, a far cry from the intense activity prior to arrest, forced each prisoner to rethink his position and consider death. Prisoners in this state were extremely susceptible to pressure from their families and close friends. Family relationships, which had been neglected during the offenders' active period as a party member, suddenly came back to life during his isolation. Guilt over past neglect further disturbed prisoners who might then relieve this unpleasant feeling by converting.

Recapture by familism was, undoubtedly, as many justice officials said, a cardinal reason for conversion. In *The White Night*, Murayama writes a vivid scene of what happened to a person after two years in prison, a scene in which he describes the change from a rational person holding universalistic ideas to an irrational one accepting particularistic notions, and dependent upon his family: "After his second summer there, absolutely shut away from fresh air, his mind was eroded by

55. Iwamoto Yoshio, "Aspects of the Proletarian Literary Movement in Japan," in Bernard S. Silberman and H. D. Harootunian (eds.), *Japan in Crisis*, 168, 180.

56. Quoted in Tsurumi Kazuko, *Social Change and the Individual*, 58–59.

something undefined and invincible. He felt as though . . . something mysteriously a part of his own father and mother, and of their forebears from time immemorial. . . was eating away his existence, which was after all an infinitesimally small particle of their posterity. However hard he tried to cry out at them, to push them aside, and to drive them out, it was of no avail.''[57] This confrontation with his spiritual core, which was brought on by police pressure and jail, led Murayama to abandon communism.

Many Japanese communists must have shared Sano's and Nabeyama's reservations about communism, and as members of the party's leadership their conversion alone was enough to influence many others. While there is no need to repeat the reasons Sano and Nabeyama listed in their statement of conversion (see Chap. 4), the major one was the emperor system. To destroy the emperor system, which was one of the party's main goals, would be to deny the deep attachment and respect felt by the people, according to Sano and Nabeyama.

A complete conversion required three mental steps, which need not come in any particular order. The first step might involve doubts over party policies (the emperor was a sore point), contradictions within the party (theory and practice, for example), and disillusionment (a natural feeling after arrest). As the second mental step, an excuse for conversion might be supplied by the example of party leaders defecting, or by a decision that one's family was more important. Perhaps the most difficult part came next: accepting conversion. In many cases, this required finding a new ideology to replace what had been lost. Nabeyama claimed that after his public conversion it took him seven more years to fully stamp out doubts over his action.[58] A common way to fill the emotional void after rejecting communism was to heartily embrace ultranationalism. One of those best known for taking this path was the writer Hayashi Fusao who was first arrested while a student at Tokyo Imperial University during the Gakuren affair (1926). After his reconversion, he became ''a champion of right-wing emotional populism whose hero he found in the antiestablishment rebel and

57. Quoted in *Ibid.*, 59.
58. Steinhoff, 151, 153.

expansionist of the Meiji period, Saigō Takamori."[59] Hayashi's book, *Tenkō ni Tsuite* (Concerning *Tenkō*), which was published in 1941 with Justice Ministry cooperation, is one of the better known of the conversion statements and autobiographies done by converts.[60]

There were three basic types of conversion: political, common-man, and spiritual. Sano and Nabeyama were the prototype for the first, the next centered on a need to return to a normal life; and in the last communist ideology was exchanged for something else. These categories can be roughly equated to psychological, educational, and social-class differences. Less educated laborers tended toward the common-man type; intellectuals toward the spiritual; and the political path was followed by a mixed group.[61]

The few communists who managed to withstand pressures to convert were less susceptible to police, family, patriotic, and cultural pressures. For example, Tokuda Kyūichi's natural immunity resulted from his Okinawan birth and the fact that his mother was a second-generation prostitute. Rejected by mainland Japanese, and free of the usual family pressures, he sought his identification with the communist party. Shiga Yoshio escaped the net by establishing close emotional ties with the Soviet Union which he managed to keep as a long-term idealized image.[62]

A discussion of *tenkō* is not complete without a few words on *gisō tenkō* (false conversion), since some thought offenders undoubtedly fell into this category. That this problem was recognized by officials who formulated guidelines for the rehabilitation program is clear. False converts, however, were not a serious threat to the rehabilitation program, as long as they supported government policies and did not express their doubts publicly.

Conclusion

Behind the Justice Ministry's extraordinarily successful *tenkō* policy

59. James W. Morley, "Introduction: Choice and Consequence," in Morley, *Dilemmas of Growth in Prewar Japan*, 15.
60. SKST, LXXXVIII, October, 1941, 160–161.
61. Steinhoff, 159–161.
62. *Ibid.*, 219–221.

lay the basic nature of Japanese society; it was an unusually homogeneous one, in which individualism and universalistic concepts
were subordinated to group solidarity and particularistic views.
Certainly, the conversion program in great measure owed its success to
the nation's tightly structured family system, with the pull of the family
being a decisive reason for an about-face. The majority of Japanese
associated with the communist movement were highly vulnerable to the
official and social pressures waiting for them after 1928. Moreover,
since many never fully escaped their heritage, they were never fully
integrated in the communist movement. Thus, it was natural for them to
buckle under pressure, and to choose the path leading back to their
families and emperor. Furthermore, serious organizational flaws in the
party, like the demand by the Comintern for total subservience, helped
drive them away. While this was tolerated in earlier years, it was always
a sore point. Then, as Sano and Nabeyama pointed out, the nationalistic
upsurge together with the rapid change in world affairs made it
intolerable to continue under Russian leadership.

Nevertheless, those who converted were responding to more than
their cultural heritage, to more than the family system and the upsurge
of nationalism after 1931. In fact, arrest, torture (or fear of it),
interrogation, trial, imprisonment, and fear of death certainly played as
important a role as traditional sociocultural factors. As Tsurumi
Shunsuke points out, "duress was the major factor involved in the
process of ideological transformation. . . . Ideological transformation is
the best term available because it implies both external duress and
personal spontaneity."[63] The majority of leftists converted, then, for
mixed reasons, but state power was fully as important as any other. The
situation was unique in that justice officials deliberately promoted it as a
new solution. Without official direction and encouragement, and
without the shock of arrest and prison, the campaign to convert thought
offenders would not have been so effective.

The thought-control apparatus produced exceptional results, with
the nation entering the Pacific War highly integrated and loyal. An
overwhelming majority of those prosecuted had accepted conversion.

63. Tsurumi Shunsuke, "Cooperative Research on Ideological Transformation,"
Journal of Social and Political Ideas in Japan, II (April, 1964), 54.

For instance, from among 500 authors who had been members of leftist literary groups, more than ninety-five percent converted.[64] Statistics published by the Justice Ministry in March 1943 were equally dramatic. Out of a total of 2,440 communists prosecuted, 1,246 were classified as converted; 1,157 were semiconverts; and only thirty-seven were unreformed.[65] The rate of success appears to have been equally high among those who were arrested but not prosecuted.

64. Tsurumi Kazuko, 42.
65. *Ibid.*

**6 Toward Total
Integration
of the Nation**

Japan faced an unprecedented series of crises after 1931: the Manchurian problem, the collapse of a liberal interpretation of the Meiji Constitution, an attempted army coup d'etat in Tokyo (1936), protracted war with China, and a continuing "Red" scare. While the leadership did not agree upon the causes and solutions for these crises, they did agree upon the urgent need to promote harmony and unity. Therefore, as the nation slipped into a state of semiwar, toleration of dissent decreased. Communists and antiwar protestors were early targets, with socialists, liberals, Christians, and even some Shintoists and Buddhists coming next. A rising current of anti-Westernism led to the condemnation of individualism and other corrupting importations. Some think that the foreign-policy crisis may have become exaggerated in the minds of Japanese leaders,[1] and perhaps domestic problems were blown out of proportion as well. However, these crises seemed shockingly real at that time.

Under such pressure, the Japanese tended to reject Western ideas and solutions and to turn instead to the emperor cult. The modern state had always "relied more heavily on an emotional approach which, in appealing to the national consciousness, dramatized the unique character of the nation and the racial homogeneity of the people to effect a national unity."[2] Such attitudes were easily aroused during the 1930's

1. Edwin O. Reischauer, "What Went Wrong?," in James W. Morley (ed.), *Dilemmas of Growth in Prewar Japan*, 503.
2. Matsumoto Sannosuke, "The Significance of Nationalism in Modern Japanese Thought," *The Journal of Asian Studies*, XXXI (November, 1971), 52.

because a majority of the population had been heavily indoctrinated with concepts of loyalty in the primary schools. Even though Minobe Tatsukichi's theory that the emperor was an organ of the state had for decades commanded respect in university circles, Hozumi Yatsuka's view that "the emperor is the state" had maintained a tight grip on the lower rungs of the educational ladder. Among the university-educated elite, trained in rational-scientific concepts, were many who were emotionally susceptible to government propaganda. No doubt Maruyama Masao is right: most intellectuals did feel that "fascism was stupid" and "were certainly not positive advocates of the driving force of the fascist movement."[3] Nonetheless, it is clear that important intellectuals did support state policies.[4] Most thinkers, it seems, possessed a hard core of indoctrination which instinctively drew them toward the emotional slogans tied to the emperor system.

Thought Guidance

Shocked by the number of students arrested as communists, the Education Ministry created a special organization for guiding student thought. The discovery that teachers, too, were involved, plus an upsurge in student arrests, let to the expansion of the former Student Section first into a larger Division and then into a Thought Bureau (June 6, 1934). This Section (Division) produced a stream of research materials on student politics, life, and thought. In addition to *Thought Investigation Materials* (Shisō Chōsa Shiryō), a periodical which appeared several times yearly, a wide range of reports analyzed the student movement.[5]

To undercut economic causes for radicalism, student welfare facilities were created: an employment service, scholarships, reduced tuition, discounts on supplies, loans, and new dormitories. Besides this "soft" approach, radicals were closely watched and pressured into recantation. A special on-campus police force dealt with difficult cases.[6] Left-wing activity of any sort was strictly limited at all universities. Campus

3. Maruyama Masao, *Thought and Behaviour in Modern Japanese Politics*, 58, 63.
4. James B. Crowley, "Intellectuals as Visionaries of the New Asian Order," in James W. Morley (ed.), *Dilemmas of Growth in Prewar Japan*, 319, 373.
5. Henry D. Smith, *Japan's First Student Radicals*, 203.
6. *Ibid.*, 201–205, 223–224.

control was so tightened by 1933 that any student who persisted in agitation could be sure of eventual arrest and punishment.[7]

"Thought guidance" was construed to mean a dual approach to the problem: that of clarifying the meaning of *kokutai* and that of attacking Marxism and other hostile ideologies. Well-known political figures and scholars were mobilized to lecture and write in support of government policy. One pamphlet, published in late 1929, contained articles by Hiranuma Kiichirō and Professor Nitobe Inazō. Pointing to a poem by the Meiji emperor, which glorified brotherhood and cooperation, Hiranuma urged that its example be followed. Nitobe said that it was necessary to unify national thought. Individualism and freedom of thought should be permitted, but antistate thought had to be punished.[8]

Beginning in 1930 anti-Marxist scholars lectured in higher schools, while a government-sponsored project translated Western anti-Marxist material. New courses were introduced on the history, ethics, religion, and culture of Japan, and new editions were published of classical Japanese literature.[9]

Thought guidance was reinforced through newspapers and magazines. Semiofficial publications like *Shisō Tōsei* (Thought Control), first issued on December 1, 1931, carried articles on various aspects of the thought problem. Most of the writers contributing to this issue felt that dangerous ideology could be wiped out in the school system by putting more emphasis on moral education and less on alien ideas and techniques. The Education Ministry also published guides to good books.[10]

Education officials created the National Spirit and Culture Research Institute (1932) to review the impact of alien ideas upon the nation and to make the *kokutai* more readily understandable. The Institute re-educated teachers in traditional ideas and promoted Japanese studies. Among its many other projects, it researched the personality and motivation of leftist students.[11] Moreover, the Institute also provided

    7. *Ibid.*, 205.
    8. Hiranuma Kiichirō, "Showa Ishin," in *Kyōka no Shiryō*, 8–13. Nitobe Inazō, "Kokui wa Uchi yori Soto e," in *ibid.*, 36–37.
    9. Smith, 203.
    10. *Shisō Tōsei*, December, 1931, Preface, 113–117, 143. Japan, Monbushō Gakuseibu, *Shisō Mondai ni Kansuru Ryōsho Senshō*, March, 1933.
    11. Smith, 204.

guidance and spiritual nourishment for former leftists who had converted.[12] In 1941, the government stepped up its program for the re-education of educators, with the construction of a People's Training School. Up to that time the efforts of the National Spirit and Culture Research Institute had been limited to training teachers during summer and other vacations, but the new organizations' program was more ambitious.[13]

For the most part thought guidance was successful. At the imperial universities a few secret Marxist study groups survived until 1941, but the leftist movement was dead. Government policies "had a tremendous psychological impact on graduates and students of colleges and universities. Fear of prosecution was so great that it established in the students a sharp sense of the limits beyond which they must not think rationally."[14] Thus, while there was a lingering undercurrent of revolt on campuses, it was muted because of either fear or indifference. Commenting on the attitude of his fellow students, one third-year Tokyo Imperial University student wrote in his diary for October 1938: "There is something really despicable and hateful about indifference and callousness of Imperial University students. They are no more than a flock of thorough-going opportunists. Eager pawns of the capitalists, whose dictates they meekly obey, they are self-protecting to the end."[15]

The Assault on the Organ Theory

Minobe Tatsukichi's constitutional theories were regularly attacked by supporters of the emperor cult who could tolerate neither his concept of emperor as an organ of the state nor his spirited defense of parliamentary democracy. Articles denouncing his views began to appear as early as 1912,[16] and Hiranuma lectured justice officials on the

12. Okudaira, GS, XLV, xxvii. In 1933, the government created a committee to develop a comprehensive plan for promoting good thought. The major political parties reacted by jumping on the bandwagon and issuing their own plans for promoting proper thought. Okudaira Yasuhiro notes that it quickly turned into a thought counterplan "boom." *Ibid.*

13. *Ibid.*, 301.

14. Tsurumi Kazuko, *Social Change and the Individual*, 112.

15. Smith, 230.

16. The Imperial Military Reserve Association's publication attacked him in 1912. Richard J. Smethurst, "The Military Reserve Association and the Minobe Crisis of 1935," in George M. Wilson (ed.), *Crisis Politics in Prewar Japan*, 9, n. 33.

evils of Minobe's ideas: "Those who say the Emperor is an organ of the state are treasonous. The Emperor is the essence of our government. To say that he is but an organ of the state is to say that he is not the essence."[17] Nevertheless, Minobe's views were widely accepted by scholars and officials until 1935, when he was heavily criticized. The attack upon Professor Minobe's constitutional theory was significant because he was the outstanding symbol of constitutional liberalism—his defeat and humiliation paved the way for the rise of intensely nationalistic and authoritarian groups.

What caused Minobe's fall from grace and why did the attack come in 1934–1935? Modernization was really responsible; the elite of society had been comfortable with Minobe's ideas, but when his ideas penetrated into the mass culture they called forth vehement rebuttals.[18] In addition there were at least two other reasons why Minobe became a target. Minobe, with his usual frankness, had announced with respect to the controversy over the London Naval Disarmament Treaty (1930) that Prime Minister Hamaguchi Osachi was correct and that the navy general staff had no right to interfere in the disarmament issue. Minobe's strong support of the constitutional right of the civilian prime minister to reach a decision on national defense contrary to that of the navy staff and of the supreme war council brought the professor into a direct confrontation with the military. In addition, the elder statesmen Saionji Kimmochi suspected that behind the attack upon Minobe lay the machinations of Hiranuma who was really after Ichiki Kitokurō, the head of the Privy Council, who was identified with Minobe's theories.[19]

Shortly after his retirement from Tokyo Imperial University and after his appointment to the House of Peers, Minobe was heavily criticized. The opening shots were fired in February 1934 by retired Major General Kikuchi Takeo, a member of the House of Peers and the Kokuhonsha (Hiranuma was president of this organization). Kikuchi was angry not only about Minobe's use of the word "organ" (kikan), which was used to denote subordinate parts of organizations and machinery, but also because his theory placed the military in a subordinate position.[20] The

17. Richard Yasko, "Hiranuma Kiichirō and Conservative Politics in Pre-war Japan" (unpublished doctoral dissertation), 110.
18. George M. Wilson, Radical Nationalist in Japan, 121.
19. Yasko, 111. Frank O. Miller, Minobe Tatsukichi, 208–209.
20. Smethurst, 4.

attack was resumed with vigor early in 1935, when Kikuchi denounced Minobe in the House of Peers. Minobe's enemies also brought a suit in Tokyo District Court, charging the professor with writing statements disrespectful to the emperor. Meanwhile, others joined in the attack: opportunists in the Seiyūkai party who were out to break the Okada Keisuke Cabinet (1934–1936); rightist agitators such as Minoda Muneki, who had long been eager to bring down Minobe; and members of the Imperial Military Reserve Association, who had opposed Minobe's denigration of the emperor, by calling him a mere "organ."[21] Once the uproar over the organ theory began, Hiranuma immediately supported the clarification movement.[22]

Reservists flooded Tokyo with telegrams and resolutions, demanding that the government silence Minobe and clarify the *kokutai*. A delegation from Nagano burned his books in front of Tokyo's Meiji Shrine, and denounced his "non-Japanese, blasphemous, Europe-worshipping ideology which ignores our . . . tradition."[23] On March 26, the House of Representatives condemned the organ theory, and a few days later the government banned the sale of three of Minobe's books.[24]

As the political typhoon developed, the Okada Cabinet, which at first had tried to ignore the issue, was forced to press an investigation against Minobe; he was interrogated three times by justice officials. The legal case against Minobe was closed, however, after he made a written admission of error and resigned from the House of Peers.[25] Pressured by the service ministries, the Cabinet promulgated a declaration clarifying

21. *Ibid.* Maruyama, *Thought and Behaviour in Modern Japanese Politics*, 62. Miller, 208–209.

22. *Ibid.*

23. Quoted in Smethurst, 9.

24. *Ibid.*, 10.

25. Maruyama *Thought and Behaviour in Modern Japanese Politics*, 61–62. Miller, 243–244. Yasko, 111. Tokyo District Court thought procurators investigating Minobe were caught in an embarassing situation, since many of them had been his students. Tozawa Shigeo, who was in charge of the case, was concerned over what to call Minobe when he faced him during interrogations. Should it be *sensei* (teacher) or *anata* (you)? Finally, he decided on *hakase* (doctor) which met with everyone's approval, including Minobe. The mood among the eleven thought procurators at the Tokyo District Court was, at first, that Minobe was not in violation of either the publications or lese-majesty laws. However, in order to clarify the case, they divided into two groups, with half defending Minobe and half attacking him. These discussions sometimes developed into hotly argued debates. At last a consensus emerged; the organ theory was bad, but Minobe had never had any intention to commit lese majesty, so that charge should be dropped. Then, chief

the *kokutai*, explaining that the emperor was sovereign and that any foreign theory which held differently would be suppressed.[26] Besides labeling Minobe's views as un-Japanese, the government stepped up pressure on all liberal and progressive forces.[27]

One interested observer of the Minobe affair was Professor Kawakami Hajime who was serving a five-year term in Kosuge Prison. The fifty-six year old Kawakami was arrested in August 1932, interrogated, and pressured to sign a statement of ideological conversion. He refused to renounce Marxism, but he did promise to retire from political activity. Since his reply was unsatisfactory, he was jailed. His prison diary for September 18, 1935, notes that Minobe "had changed his way of thinking." In other words, Minobe had undergone *tenkō* to save himself, his family, and his friends. "I thought that he had decided on jail," wrote Kawakami, "but it seems that nobody likes to go to jail. It is, I think, natural."[28]

The "clarification" campaign caught the imagination of all social classes and spread like wildfire, not fading away with Minobe's political death. The Okada Cabinet created a Council for the Renovation of Thought in November 1935, which was charged with promoting the *kokutai* and recommending methods to keep out dangerous ideas.[29] Military and civil bureaucrats joined forces to crusade against venomous ideas from the West.[30] Education Minister Hirao Hachi-

---

procurators from the seven appeals courts met to discuss the case with Tozawa. They also were divided, with Miyagi Chōgorō and Shiono Suehiko against the organ theory. Tozawa claims that at no time did he ask the Justice Ministry for its opinion, nor did they ever express one. Miyazawa Toshiyoshi, *Tennō Kikansetsu Jiken*, I, 241, 245; II, 650, 653–654.

26. Miller, 243–244.

27. *Ibid.*, 245, 344. Dorothy Borg and Shumpei Okamoto, *Pearl Harbor as History*, 501.

28. Kawakami Hajime, *Gokuchū Nikki*, 52.

29. Guenther Stein, "Through the Eyes of a Japanese Newspaper Reader," *Pacific Affairs*, IX (June, 1936), 180. Charles N. Spinks, "Indoctrination and Re-education of Japan's Youth," *Ibid.*, XVII (March, 1944), 63–64.

30. Galen M. Fisher, "Revisiting Japan," *Amerasia*, I (July, 1937), 220. They felt an obligation to free China of dangerous thought as well, and often justified expansion there on the grounds that it was an extension of their domestic anticommunist crusade. Association for the Study of International Socialistic Ideas and Movements (ed.), *Japan's Conflict with the Evil of Bolshevism in the Far East*, 24, 62, 77, 90–92.

saburō said: "We have imported too many Western ideas. . . . What we have to do now is to turn to our traditional culture which kept us an ideologically homogeneous nation in the past and can make us such again."[31] Early in 1937, *Kokutai no Hongi* (Fundamentals of Our *Kokutai*) was issued by the Education Ministry.[32] This important book sought to still the confusion in the thought world and to clarify the *kokutai*. As the backbone for the revised ethics course, it was at the center of an intensive propaganda effort directed at school children and teachers. It glorified service to the state and strongly opposed liberalism and individualism. Ideological and social problems were blamed on the failure to digest imported alien ideas, and a new synthesis of Eastern and Western thought, firmly grounded upon the indigenous tradition, was promoted.

Narrowing the Range of Legal Dissent

The Justice Ministry responded to the demands for harmony and unity by narrowing the range of legal dissent. At first their new interpretation of the peace law appeared to affect only communists, but it had future implications for socialists, liberals, and Christians, and for adherents of "radical" indigenous religions, and for rightists as well.

Spurred by the Comintern's popular front policy of 1935, Japanese communists infiltrated legal labor unions, legal political parties, and other legal organizations. In order to escape police detection, the party

31. Quoted in A. F. Thomas, "Japan's National Education," *Transactions and Proceedings of the Japan Society London*, XXXVI (1938–1939), 50. The state promoted Buddhism as part of its antiradical crusade. However, the idea of using Buddhism to foster nationalism was not new. In 1926, Tokyo area businessmen employed Buddhist priests to correct dangerous ideas among their workers. Hosono Nagamori, *Shisō Akka no Moto*, 163–164. For an interesting article on the Buddhist-Shinto synthesis which regarded Japan's *kokutai* as much dependent upon Buddhism as upon Shinto, see Edwin B. Lee, "Nichiren and Nationalism," *Monumenta Nipponica*, XXX (Spring, 1975). For an overview of the state's manipulation of religion see A. M. Young, "Religious Revival in Japan, How it Serves the Purposes of Nationalism," *Asia*, XXXV (September, 1935), 542.

32. Robert K. Hall (ed.), *Kokutai no Hongi*, 52, 175–183. "This handbook echoes many if not all of Hozumi's themes: reverence for the emperor, absolute loyalty, the amalgamation of the individual into the national group, the origins and dangers of individualism, and so on." Richard H. Minear, *Japanese Tradition and Western Law*, 185.

had decentralized and combined illegal and legal activities.[33] It was easy for justice officials, who had for years been worried over the activities of closet communists, to convince themselves now that communists were somehow in the background of all political and economic disputes. Once this premise was accepted, the distinction between communists and ideological Marxists collapsed, with a crackdown on those who had previously enjoyed borderline legal status. The scope of Article One of the peace law was extended, in an administrative fashion, to insure successful prosecution of these formerly legal people and groups.

Communists in the Social Masses' Party and the labor movement had discarded old slogans and used new legal ones such as "lower taxes," "establish a labor union law," and "revise the law for retirement payments." Communists infiltrated rightist organizations and even protection groups caring for reformed thought criminals. Their propaganda was subtly spread in legal publications.[34] The most important two were *Rōdō Zasshi* (Labor Magazine) and *Taishū no Seiji Keizai* (Popular Political Economy), with the former aimed at the general laborers and the latter at the leaders.[35]

A police raid on the academic and literary world in July 1936 and again in December was the government response. By the following June, about 200 people who had previously enjoyed borderline legal status had been arrested.[36] That month justice officials met to discuss the proper manner in which to handle these people, and from the conference emerged a "new counterplan."[37]

Procurator Kuriya Shirō (Tokyo District Court) summarized the new situation. Communists were trying to absorb the people legally, he said. Few of those arrested in his area could be prosecuted using the Peace Preservation Law, since, unlike earlier incidents, their violations were difficult to spot. Communist publications, for instance, no longer carried explosive antigovernment material, but, instead, contained legal

33. George M. Beckmann and Okubo Genji, *The Japanese Communist Party*, 254–255, 360–361.
34. Quoted in SKST, XXXVII, July, 1937, 34–37, 54–55, 119.
35. *Ibid.*, 31–32. Beckmann and Okubo, 260.
36. Beckmann and Okubo, 263. SKST, XXXVII, 30, 61.
37. SKST, XXXVII, 1.

terms. Also, the old patterns of secret organizations and clandestine meetings were gone. Thus, secret illegal activities which were formerly punished easily did not exist. Moreover, suspects were usually connected with legal organizations and did not appear to have the direct purpose of rebuilding the Japanese Communist Party or the illegal Nihon Rōdō Kumiai Zenkoku Kyōgikai (National Conference of Japanese Trade Unions), or Zenkyō. In spite of these obstacles to indictment and conviction, Kuriya urged the suppression of this "frightening thing," which was "directly absorbing the people."[38] A spokesman for the Osaka District Court confirmed Kuriya's opinion.[39]

Kuriya suggested that the Justice Ministry follow the Comintern lead and modify its policies. Common sense tells us, he said, that we must discard our old notions about a communist organization. While not many of those arrested were guilty of advocating a change in the *kokutai* or in the ownership of private property, they had supported the Comintern's popular front. The Comintern still recognized a Japanese branch and had urged that legal actions be used to establish an illegal party. Therefore, even legal activities, if they made the party stronger, should be considered illegal. People engaged in such "legal" activities should be prosecuted for "furthering the aims" of the communist party. He concluded that the Justice Ministry should suspect "that communists are involved in the background of any dispute."[40] A judge from Kobe told of guidelines set for prosecuting difficult cases in which the suspect's communist connections were vague. Prosecution might take place based on furthering the aims of the party if: (1) the suspect knew about decisions of the Seventh Congress of the Comintern, (2) the suspect had received *Red Flag* from an illegal organization, (3) the suspect knew of the existence of the Japanese Communist Party, and (4) the suspect sympathized with communist ideology.[41]

Others suggested that the peace law be strengthened in order to narrow the bounds of legal activities and to aid in the prosecution of people in the twilight zone. With former leftists moving into the

38. *Ibid.*, 36–38.
39. *Ibid.*, 67–68.
40. *Ibid.*, 39–41, 44.
41. *Ibid.*, 167.

rightist camp, radicals of both camps into the religious field, and some rightists intimidating and brutalizing society by assassinations and antigovernment plots, the law needed adjustment to fit the times.[42] This was not, of course, the first time officials had called for an expanded peace law. For instance, Sase Shōzō, a researcher in the Justice Ministry, wrote in March 1936 that one comprehensive law to cover all extremists should be enacted.[43]

After war began in North China, authorities tightened the vise on the previously legal Rōnōha (labor-farmer faction) and other theoretical Marxists. This group of Marxist intellectuals, centered on the former communist Yamakawa Hitoshi, had for years expressed its views openly in *Labor-Farmer*. The legal case against the labor-farmer faction, therefore, was prepared with painstaking care. The prosecution recognized the group as an ''organization,'' as specified in Article One of the peace law, which advocated the destruction of the *kokutai* and the system of private property. Their group held monthly meetings, had formal membership provisions, assigned members to different tasks (e.g., magazine, political party, labor union, and farmers' union sections), and put policy decisions into practice. Their goals were outlined in *Labor-Farmer* and in a document entitled *Our Position*. The organization had passed a resolution in 1933 supporting the latter's contents, and an article in *Labor-Farmer* amplified it. Confessions supported captured documents. Tokyo District Court procurators decided that the group's ultimate goal was communism in Japan.[44]

Change in interpretation of the peace law is well illustrated by the arrest and trial of the liberal-socialist Kawai Eijirō. Until 1938 he had been considered by many to be a progovernment scholar, and justice officials saw nothing dangerous in what he said or wrote. He was, indeed, one of their star attractions in the student thought-guidance program. However, as the idea that ''liberalism is the seedbed of communism'' took hold, the state placed restrictions on liberal scholars and thinkers, and Kawai was made an example of in order to silence others. He lost his position at Tokyo Imperial University, then his

42. *Ibid.*, 69, 72.
43. Sase Shōzō, *Seiji Hanzairon*, 321.
44. SKST, XLV, August, 1938, 49.

publications were prohibited, and next he was charged with a peace-law violation. Although he was found not guilty in the first trial, he was later punished for writing an antistate article and was forbidden to publish.[45]

Although some scholars and thinkers continued to show great courage after 1937, most bent under government pressure, with few putting up any real resistance. Some retreated into introspection and noninvolvement while others became active promoters of government policies. Except for a few "heretics," says Maruyama Masao, all Japanese moved along with the current of the times.[46]

Spreading the Police Net

During the 1930's, Japan moved gradually from a state of semiwar into a protracted war on the Asian mainland. The Special Higher Police, as one of the main agencies for dealing with the public, naturally became more deeply involved in the daily life of each citizen. To enforce greater social conformity, the Home Ministry developed stronger institutional controls for its thought police: new regulations and fuller, more detailed reporting on all aspects of national life. Moreover, rightist plots and assassinations prompted thought police to refocus their investigations. Prior to 1932 police publications said little about the so-called patriotic groups, but from February onward each monthly issue carried detailed accounts.[47] Furthermore, after mid-decade, religious groups got more attention: Christians because of their clear foreign connections, and Shintoists because they might be a front for revolutionary rightists. Following the 1936 army revolt in Tokyo, the government served notice of its intention to deal more harshly with subversive activities of military and civilian rightists.

Violence and threats by rightists must have cost police and justice officials some sleepless nights, but the right was seldom viewed as dangerous as the left (after all the right did support the *kokutai*). Also, it was difficult to prosecute rightists under the existing peace law, so they

45. Zadankai, 569, 574–575. Wm. T. deBary (ed.), *Sources of Japanese Tradition*, II, 325.

46. Ivan J. Morris, *Nationalism and the Right Wing in Japan*, xviii. Resistance by some of these "heretics" is the subject of Dōshisha Daigaku Jinbun Kagaku Kenkyūjo, *Senjika Teikō Kenkyū.*

47. Omori Megumu (ed.), *Tokkō Geppō: Sō Mokujishū.*

Table 2. Number of rightists arrested and prosecuted from 1935 to April 1943

	Arrested	Prosecuted
1935	147	132
1936	37	22
1937	49	8
1938	115	12
1939	61	39
1940	61	40
1941	53	31
1942	39	21
1943	7	7
Total	569	312

were apprehended under the provisions of the Criminal Code and other laws. As a result, only 569 rightists were arrested and only 312 were prosecuted from 1935 to 1943 using the Peace Preservation Law. (See Table 2.)[48] Most ultranationalists were viewed by officials more as a nuisance than as a serious threat. There were, of course, exceptions, and authorities certainly took seriously the sensational assassinations and attempted coups of the 1930's. On balance, though, "Reds" continued to be the primary concern.

According to Home Ministry Order No. 569 (May 1935), people were placed under special surveillance for connection with a thought crime or subversive activity. Those on the list were classified as either extremely dangerous or less dangerous, with subdivisions for communists, socialists, anarchists, Koreans, Taiwanese, and others. Their correspondence, meetings, travel, and other activities were closely watched.[49] Investigation of such people, coupled with other Home Ministry activities, required a huge amount of paperwork: reports on specific incidents, fourteen monthly reports, twenty-five semiannual reports, and twenty-four annual reports.[50]

The Home Ministry and other authorities such as the army and navy further expanded restriction of the press and other important media. The Army Ministry acted immediately after fighting broke out in

48. Okudaira, GS, XLV, 651.

49. Nihon Kindai Shiryō Kenkyūkai (ed.), *Taisho Kōki Keihokyoku Kankō Shakai Undō Shiryō*, 5.

50. Japan, Naimushō, Keihokyoku, *Tokkō Keisatsu Reikishū*, 1939, Section I, 24–34, and Japan Hyōgo Ken Tokkōka, *Tokkō Keisatsu Reikishū*, 1935, Table of Contents.

Manchuria, by issuing an order warning newspapers and periodicals against publication of military news prior to obtaining official approval.[51] Every aspect of life was colored by the emergency and the semiwar conditions existing after 1931. And antiwar expression in the press, magazines, broadcasting, movies, plays, and records was suppressed by the Home Ministry. Mass media was manipulated by the government to release the "real facts" (the official view), and, for the most part, the government's viewpoint was accepted, with conflicting information dismissed as untrue. "Thus, rather than attempting to influence the actions of the government, the Japanese mass media merely rationalized each change in the political situation as it occurred."[52] Indicative of the press response to increased government pressure is the fact that no major paper protested the treatment of Professor Minobe during the "organ theory" affair. As one Japanese scholar neatly put it: "Instead of struggling for freedom, they dug their own graves."[53] Expansion of the Sino-Japanese conflict after July 1937 triggered increased government control of the press. The Home Ministry issued regulations to smother antiwar or pessimistic expression. Inadmissible subjects were: any antimilitary or antiwar arguments, or any report which might weaken public support of the military; any report which suggested that Japan was warlike; or any account which confused the public and disturbed public peace.[54] To centralize and tighten its censorship agencies, the government created the Cabinet Information Division (Naikaku Jōhōbu) in September 1937 and then expanded it into the Cabinet Information Bureau late in 1940. Since the goal of this new agency was to guide the thoughts of newspapermen into the proper channels, it provided them with "correct data." Among other things, newspapers were "to inspire an enduring, untiring spirit into the mind of the people."[55] Not only newspapers but all other aspects of mass media came under the scrutiny of the Cabinet Information Division and Bureau which imposed an enormous variety

51. Okudaira Yasuhiro, *Political Censorship in Japan from 1931 to 1945*, 13.
52. Kakegawa Tomiko, "The Press and Public Opinion in Japan, 1931–1941," in Dorothy Borg and Shumpei Okamoto (eds.), *Pearl Harbor as History*, 539–540.
53. Okudaira, *Political Censorship in Japan from 1931 to 1945*, 14.
54. *Ibid.*, 21.
55. *Ibid.*, 24–25.

of restraints. Finally, the harsh National Defense Security Law of March 1941 silenced most critics: anyone convicted of intentionally revealing to foreign powers secret information on diplomacy, finance, industry, and other important national affairs could be executed; life confinement could be the punishment for publishing such information.[56]

By the end of 1940, the Cabinet Information Bureau employed 600 people sent by the Army, Navy, Foreign, and Home Ministries, with the most important positions reserved for the military. Details of the power struggle between Home Ministry officials and the military are unclear, but the outcome is not; the Home Ministry lost its near-monopoly over censorship which was absorbed by the new Bureau.[57]

Spiritual Mobilization

Soon after war began in North China in 1937, the government set out to foster sentiment supporting its actions. Near the end of August the Konoe Fumimarō Cabinet (1937–1939) announced plans to promote a spiritual mobilization movement. Various civilian groups joined this bureaucratic effort to whip up mass support for the war. During its first six months, the movement's leadership sponsored rallies, lectures, radio programs, films, and publications. Special weeks were set aside in 1937 and 1938 to honor the people's spiritual awakening and the founding of the nation. Ceremonies for war dead, worship at shrines, and helping servicemen were other activities. The Home Ministry supported this movement, by ordering municipal officials to create town and village associations. However, since the town and village groups turned out to be too large, many were subdivided into "neighborhood associations" (tonarigumi), consisting of ten to twenty families. Caught up in a protracted and widening war with China, the government, in 1938, tried to strengthen the program for spiritual mobilization. Prime Minister

56. Kakegawa, 548. Thomas R. H. Havens, "Frontiers of Japanese Social History during World War II," *Shakai Kagaku Tōkyū*, XVIII (March, 1973), 13. On March 31, 1941, the Cabinet Information Bureau ordered all important publishers to furnish lists of subscribers, which lists were then passed on to the police. Nihon Jānarisuto Remmei, *Genron Dan'atsu Shi*, 102. For the law see Domei Tsushin Sha, *Wartime Legislation in Japan*, 1–28.

57. Okudaira, *Political Censorship in Japan from 1931–1945*, 27. Some information on sectionalism, and the Home Ministry's fight to preserve its powers are in Uchikawa Yoshimi (ed.), *Gendaishi Shiryō*, XL, xix, xxv.

Konoe saw the movement as a way to psychologically prepare the people for the personal deprivations of a long war. The movement, therefore, was given funds, and two vice-ministers were placed on its board of directors.[58]

When Hiranuma took the premiership in January 1939, the spiritual mobilization campaign was reorganized to prepare the nation for constructing a new order in East Asia. Faced by what it viewed as a hostile international environment, the Hiranuma Cabinet redoubled efforts to instill self-confidence in the people. Mainly, the government relied upon moral exhortations for support of the war effort. For instance, Hiranuma addressed a Tokyo rally on April 12, 1939, and spoke of the need for moral rectitude and cooperation: "The most important factor in a long-term war of endurance is the intensification and sustenance of national moral force. . . . The virtues of simplicity, soundness, strength, stamina, positivism and enterprise must be encouraged." He concluded with: "Let your hearts be as one, do your best in your respective jobs, earnestly strive in public service and seek to repay the Imperial benevolence."[59]

While it may be true that the spiritual mobilization campaign was a failure, as stated by the *Asahi Shimbun* in April 1939,[60] the reactivation of neighborhood associations was significant. They, and the larger units of which they were a part, not only planned the people's moral training, but they also took over many of the services of local government: they collected taxes, kept order, helped the aged, promoted public works, provided liaison with police and fire officials, and assisted with sanitation and public health. Moreover, they were involved in savings and bond subscription campaigns and in arranging for shrine pilgrimages and Shinto ceremonies. Finally, in September 1940, the Home Ministry formally established town and village associations "as the basic organizations for planning for . . . spiritual unity, . . . enforcing the regulated economy as the local control unit in people's economic lives, and stabilizing people's livelihoods."[61] These de facto agencies of local rule (there were 210,000 town and village associations

58. Havens, 9–10, 18. Yasko, 131.
59. Quoted in Yasko, 133–134.
60. *Ibid.*, 134.
61. Quoted in Havens, 19.

and about 1,200,000 neighborhood associations) functioned reasonably well during the war years, but exactly why they worked is debatable. Perhaps their success was due as much "from the long-standing equipoise of Japanese society . . . as from the wisdom or effectiveness of the state's policies for social mobilization."[62] Thus, this offshoot of the spiritual mobilization campaign had more impact than Hiranuma's moralizing.

The Role of the Justice Ministry

Justice officials took Konoe's and Hiranuma's exhortations seriously. After years of fighting a "thought war" against radicals, it was easy for them to think in terms of regulating the thought tendencies of everyone. Hiranuma's follower Shiono Suehiko, by this time minister of justice (under three Cabinets between 1937 and 1939), saw the Justice Ministry's task as the "cultivation of healthy national thought."[63] Matsuzaka Hiromasa, head of the Criminal Affairs Bureau, felt that in order to win their "holy war" the Justice Ministry must strictly control any disturbance and maintain public peace.[64] Protection Division Chief Moriyama Takeichirō equated the Justice Ministry's role with that of the troops fighting in China. As guardians of the home front, it was the Ministry's duty to win the ideological battle. With reference to the way in which the Germans had lost that battle in World War I, it was said that "one of the main causes of their defeat was a crack which appeared in the solidarity of thought within the German nation."[65] Other officials agreed.[66] "Modern War is not just a war of military force or economics, but it is at the same time a war of ideology. In order to carry on, we must raise our national spirit, and under this spirit the people must be unified," said a procurator from Hiroshima.[67] In reality, said another procurator, the only difference between military and justice officials was the saber hanging at the side of the former.[68]

Officials were reminded of the importance of protecting military

62. *Ibid.*, 21.
63. SKST, XLV, 19.
64. SKST, LVII, February, 1939, 15.
65. SKST, LVII, 44–45.
66. SKST, LXXXVI, May, 1941, 74–75. SKST, XLVIII, January, 1939, 255–256.
67. SKST, XLVII, January, 1939, 17.
68. Aoki Eigorō, *Saibankan no Sensō Sekinin*, 56.

secrets, controlling rumors, capturing spies, supervising publications, and suppressing radicals of any kind. In order to mobilize the people behind the war effort, and secure the home front, procurators were encouraged to prosecute thought offenders vigorously, with one eye on the public's reaction. Moreover, they were urged to report more frequently, since the ministry was eager to take the national pulse.[69]

Under wartime conditions, the ministry expanded its role by obtaining additional funds, reorganizing the Criminal Affairs Bureau, and issuing new publications. The Thought Section within the Criminal Affairs Bureau was enlarged by dividing the Fifth Section (Thought Section) into two parts. The new part, called the Sixth Section, was to concentrate on rightists.[70] In addition, a new series of local conferences (Special Bloc Thought Research Conferences) were planned for each appeals court. Their purpose was to encourage the kind of frank discussions that were difficult at large national meetings. Bloc meetings were held at Hiroshima (July, 1938), Sendai (July), and Osaka (August).[71] Then, in October a special six-day conference was used to indoctrinate new thought officials, with about fifty judges and fifty procurators attending. Leading authorities gave lectures on the supervision and protection system, the famous open trial of communists, the rising rightists, the 1936 army rebellion, and the history of communism in Japan.[72]

The Tokyo headquarters decided to exploit its collection of documents more fully by creating a new system of Special Researchers on Thought (Shisō Tokubetsu Kenkyūin). Starting in June 1938, procurators and judges came to Tokyo for long periods to research and discuss cases they had handled. From their activities, the ministry hoped to formulate new methods to deal with thought problems.[73] New publications were issued as well: *Thought Materials Pamphlet* (Shisō Shiryō Pamfuretto) and *Thought Materials Pamphlet, Special Number* (Shisō Shiryō Pamfuretto Tokushū).[74]

69. SKST, XXXIX, October, 1937, 7, 10, 14–16, 217.
70. For information on this Division see Appendix II, Chart 3.
71. SKST, XLV, 25. SKST, XLVII, 11, 26, 88, 155, 164–165, 273.
72. SKST, LVII, February, 1939.
73. SKST, XLV, 25. SKST XLVII, 26, 165.
74. SKST, XLV, 25. SKST, XLVII, 26, 164–165. Cecil H. Uyehara, *Leftwing Social Movements in Japan*, 43.

Justice officials too began to modify substantially their thinking on ideological control. The stringencies of a wartime economy, with shortages of consumer goods and mounting inflation, pushed procurators into the field of economic control. In June 1939, the head of the Criminal Affairs Bureau announced that thought and economic crimes were so close that they could not really be separated.[75] In short, by an administrative decision, a criminal action in the economic sphere became a semithought crime, if not a full offense.

A Capstone for the Peace Preservation Law System

The never-ending conflict with the Chinese, coupled with the undeniable drift toward war in the Pacific, was the crisis background against which the Peace Preservation Law underwent its third revision. Justice officials had keenly felt the inadequacies of the peace law for some time, but it was not until a protracted war exerted pressure that the Diet became receptive to extensive alterations.

Early in February 1941, justice officials introduced a sixty-five-article peace law to a committee of the House of Representatives. This law bill, while it was a direct descendant of the 1925 and 1928 peace laws, was such a thoroughgoing alteration that the term revision seems an understatement; if the 1925 law was the seed, then the 1941 law was a huge tree casting its shade over the entire nation. The purpose of Part One was to dry up support for the communist party within legal organizations, by enlarging the definition of illegal activities. Furthermore, it was aimed at religious bodies which ventured into politics (See Appendix IV, for Articles 1–6, 9–16). Part Two invested thought procurators with broader powers than usual in arresting, examining, and detaining suspects. No more than two defense lawyers were specified, to be chosen from a pool designated by the justice minister; and the usual route for appeals was shortened, with the appeals court omitted (the Supreme Court remained). Thus, civil liberties were sacrificed in the name of efficiency; thought procurators could under this law move rapidly during the examination and speed up the trial and appeal process. Part Three was the result of numerous justice conferences in which the proper treatment of hardened thought

75. SKST, LXIV, September, 1939, 298–299.

criminals was discussed: they were to be kept in custody until reformed.
On February 12, Vice-Minister of Justice Miyake Shōtarō explained
the need for the proposed law and outlined its scope to a House
committee. He took special care to justify Articles 7 and 8 which were,
among other things, aimed at regulating semireligious organizations
such as Ōmotokyō (The Great Source Religion).[76] The leaders of this
organization disturbed the sacredness of shrines and the imperial house
and spread confusion about the true meaning of the *kokutai*. Regular
religious groups concentrated on individual salvation, he noted, but
these semireligious ones emphasized things like reforming society and
the *kokutai*, activities which naturally got them deeply involved in
illegal political activities. Yet, because of their religious camouflage,
the 1928 peace law was an awkward tool to use against these groups,
creating many frustrations for authorities in their attempt to crush the
organization rather than individuals.[77] Articles 7 and 8 were directed at
individuals and groups within the semireligious category,[78] and read as
follows:

Art. 7 A person who has organized an association with the object of
circulating matters disavowing the national polity or impairing the sanctity and
dignity of the shrines and Imperial Household or a person who has performed
the work of an officer or other leaders of such as association shall be punished
with penal servitude for a limited period not less than four years, and a person
who knowingly has joined such an association or a person who has committed
an act contributing to the accomplishment of its object shall be punished with
penal servitude for a limited period of not less than one year.

76. A thought-police report on Ōmotokyō is in Japan, Naimushō, Keihokyoku, *Tokkō
Geppō*, March, 1936, 77–93. The sect's leader Deguchi Wanisaburō was said to be
aiming at becoming Japan's ruler (under the emperor), and was charged with peace-law
and lese-majesty violations. The membership of Ōmotokyō was estimated at 50,000
to 60,000. *Ibid.*, 81, 85–86, 89. For additional information see Carmen Blacker,
"Millenarian Aspects of the New Religions in Japan," in Donald H. Shively (ed.),
Tradition and Modernization in Japanese Culture, 567, 570, 577, 579, 585, 588, 596.
One scholar views suppression of Ōmotokyō as a result of Deguchi's association with
army extremists and not primarily because Ōmotokyō's doctrines were in conflict with the
emperor system. Thomas P. Nadolski, "The 1921 and 1935 Suppressions of the Ōmoto
Religious Movement," *Abstracts of the Papers to be Read at 19th International
Conference of Orientalists in Japan* (May 24, 1974), 11.
    77. Okudaira, GS, XLV, 286–287.
    78. Domei Tsushin Sha, *Wartime Legislation in Japan*, 73–74.

Art. 8 A person who has organized a group with the object stipulated in the foregoing Article or a person who has directed such a group shall be punished with penal servitude for life or not less than three years, and a person who, with the object stipulated in the foregoing Article, has joined said group, or a person who has committed an act contributing to the accomplishment of the object stipulated in the foregoing Article in relation to said group, shall be punished with penal servitude for a limited period not less than one year.

Miyake next explained that Part Two of the proposed law was designed to bring the thought-control apparatus squarely under the control of procurators, by expanding their powers and streamlining the judicial process. Procurators would have full jurisdiction over the Thought Police. The technique of Preventive Detention (Yobō Kōkin) would be applied to die-hards who refused to convert, and who could not be handled by the protection and supervision system (Part Three of the draft law).[79]

Justice Secretary Ōta Taizō traced the development of the Peace Preservation Law for the committee. In the early years it was employed mainly against communists and anarchists, but occasionally it was used for nonleftist groups (e. g., semireligious groups, beginning in 1935), if they planned to change the *kokutai*. The revised peace law would be directed at anyone or any group, regardless of their political coloration, involved in a movement to change the *kokutai* or commit lese majesty.[80] Ōta's interpretation of the proposed peace law, together with the already greatly stretched 1928 version (under which a crime in the economic sphere could become a semithought crime), left few acts outside the scope of the law. Even a drunk who relieved himself in a dark corner of a neighborhood shrine might be charged with a violation.

The problem of leftists who refused to convert was of more than passing interest to officials in 1941, since many of the communist big shots captured in 1928 and 1929 were due to be released that year.[81] Prisoners, under the proposed law, who refused to convert could be detained for life. The preventive detention and the protection and supervision systems were meant to support one another. During his

79. Okudaira, GS, XLV, 287, 289. Domei Tsushin Sha, *Wartime Legislation in Japan*, 70.
80. Okudaira, GS, XLV, 294.
81. SKST, LXXXVIII, October, 1941, 73.

journey toward total reformation, a thought offender might be placed under both systems. A person discharged from prison would graduate to a protection and supervision center. After he fully reformed, he would be released from all forms of control. However, if at any time he became an apostate, he would be demoted to the level of preventive detention. Obstinate prisoners who refused to begin the process of conversion while in jail would, upon termination of their prison sentences, be sent to a preventive detention center. Then, if they were at least partially reformed, they might gain semifreedom under a protection and supervision center. An individual could, thus, spend an entire lifetime under the control of these two organizations.[82]

Broadening the law's scope and adding more rigid penalties were also part of the government's effort to tighten up the home front. Increasingly, procurators were occupied by crimes like hoarding and rumors, offenses that sapped the national will to fight. "Symptoms are appearing among the people that illustrate an early phase of fear. One such symptom is the appearance of rumors," said Tozawa Shigeo.[83]

Not all House committee members were satisfied with government efforts to suppress leftist radicals, even though an extremely broad and harsh piece of legislation was before them. Representative Inoge Toshisaka (Fukui Prefecture) fired a broadside at the Education Ministry for its supposed lack of supervision, and for its failure to dig out the roots of leftist radicalism which he said were deeply embedded in the university system. The thought problem, Inoge felt, stemmed from one source: communist infiltration of the educational field. How could the government hope to solve this problem by passing new laws, if subversive books continued to be published? It was ridiculous to make tough laws on the one hand, while on the other professors gave subversive lectures and published dangerous ideas. According to Inoge, it was the education minister's duty to tighten control over professors, especially those at Tokyo Imperial University who were the worst offenders. A solution would be to investigate the character of each professor, closely supervise lectures, and re-examine books. Inoge then pointed an accusing finger at several professors, and while he used no

82. SKST, XC, January, 1942, 169–170. SKST, XCI, June, 1942, 25.
83. SKST, LXXXVI, 67, 187–193.

names it was obvious whom he had in mind. From Inoge's viewpoint, to be prosecuted for a thought crime was the same as being convicted. There is a professor, he said, who was arrested, tried, and found innocent in a thought case; afterwards he was awarded the title professor emeritus by the Education Ministry and his university (Kawai Eijirō?). This man is today still publishing his bad ideas, concluded Inoge. Education Minister Hashida Kunihiko (second Konoe Cabinet [1940–1941]) replied that subversives were not tolerated in the university system, and that the government would prosecute any professor who gave improper lectures or who published improper books. Japanese education at all levels was based on the principles of *kokutai*.[84]

The new Peace Preservation Law was enacted by the Diet in February, promulgated on March 8, and put in force May 15, 1941. Procurators had their powers vastly expanded not only by this law but also by the new National Defense Security Law of 1941 which was intended to protect the nation from spies, subversive plots, and malicious propaganda.[85]

Soon after passage of the revised peace law, the Penal Administration Bureau began renovating a building at Toyotama Prison in Tokyo to use as the first preventive detention center. Space was planned for two hundred inmates.[86] Before launching their preventive detention system, the Japanese had closely analyzed Great Britain's. Like their model they decided to employ a separate facility, but, in an effort to improve upon it they decided upon a Spartan regime of plain food and intensive education. They were certain that daily indoctrination would reform even hardened thought criminals whose Japaneseness was bound to surface sooner or later. And since each was to be detained until he was fully cured, officials would have lots of time.[87]

Thought Procurators

Thought procurators played a key role in creating the Peace Preservation Law program and in the state's push to rally total support.

84. Okudaira, GS, XLV, 297–301.
85. SKST, LXXXVI, 1.
86. SKST, XC, 166–167.
87. SKST, LXXIX, 163–171. See Appendix II, Chart 4 (Justice Administration in 1941).

Yet, even though they held exceptional powers, very little has been written about them. What is available is usually critical; their program has been stigmatized with terms like *kensatsu fassho* (fascism of the procuracy), for going along with governmental policies. One American scholar says that use of the term *kensatsu fassho* indicates that "Continental procedures, Japanese personal values, the Imperial ideology, bureaucratization of the judiciary, and the capture of the government by the militarists all came together just before the war." The extension of the procurator's role produced a situation whose "worse manifestation was the procurator's framing a defendant (for political or personal reasons) by forcibly extracting a confession from him, and the court's acquiescence and even connivance with the procurator in doing this."[88] The postwar Justice Ministry regards *kensatsu fassho* as the exemplification of "the monoply of the power to prosecute held by the procurators which made it possible for them to exercise this power for political purposes."[89] Such explanations really tell us little about them. Also, in view of nearly everyone else's positive support of state policies, it seems strange to single out procurators as particularly "evil."

We have already analyzed the central role of thought procurators, unveiled their techniques, and mentioned the names of many. Justice Ministry documents can also supply information on their strength and location.

Prior to the passage of the Peace Preservation Law there were perhaps two thought procurators at the Tokyo District Court, but they were not in a special section. Three procurators stationed in Tokyo (Ikeda Katsu, Hirata Susumu, and Kurokawa Wataru) were the first to handle a thought case after 1925; they were dispatched to work on the Kyoto Student Association case (Hirata had not been involved in the arrest of communists in 1923; the other two may have been). Passage of the 1925 peace law, the mass arrests of 1928 and 1929, and other incidents resulted in the appointment of thought procurators throughout the nation. The Supreme Court, the seven appeals courts (Tokyo, Osaka,

88. Chalmers Johnson, *Conspiracy at Matsukawa*, 161.
89. Quoted in Hattori Takaaki, "The Legal Profession in Japan," in Arthur T. von Mehren (ed.), *Law in Japan*, 125, n. 50.

Sapporo, Sendai, Hiroshima, Nagasaki, and Nagoya), and the ten main district courts (the seven appeal areas plus Urawa, Kobe, and Yokohama) were staffed by July 1928.[90] However, the number of thought procurators remained small when compared with the hundreds of thought police, and the Justice Ministry was slow to place them at all courts. In September 1938, there were only nineteen thought bureaus.[91] Moreover, some remote country spots did not have thought procurators as late as November 1941.[92] This uneven distribution pattern, however, is deceptive, since most thought criminals and thought crimes were concentrated in the big cities, areas that were covered soon after the passage of the law.

It is difficult to know the exact number of genuine thought procurators for any year between 1925 and 1941, because the Justice Ministry, in order to cover an area, sometimes simply appointed a local procurator as the man in charge of thought, even though he was untrained. Also, some of those identified as thought procurators were primarily administrators. Table 3 estimates that there were seventy thought procurators in 1941 at all courts. There were fifty-two district courts, but thirty-two of them did not have a thought procurator.[93] Many thought procurators are identified in this book: Tozawa Shigeo (Tokyo District Court), Yoshimura Takeo (Osaka District Court), Ikeda Katsu (Supreme Court), Hirata Susumu (Tokyo District Court), Kurokawa Wataru (Tokyo District Court), Miyazato Tomehachi (Hiroshima District Court), Hanawa Nagaharu (Shizuoka District Court), Kuriya Shirō (Tokyo District Court), Ōta Taizō and Sano Shigeki (both of whom specialized on rightists), Katsuyama Takumi (Osaka Appeals Court), Imoto Taikichi (Tokyo District Court), Nakamura Toneo (Tokyo District Court), Mochizuki Takeo (Sapporo Appeals Court), and others. Justice officials like Shiono Suehiko, Matsuzaka Hiromasa, and Ohara Naoshi, while they did function for a time as thought procurators, are best remembered as administrators who directed others in the establishment of the thought-control system.

90. Japan Shihōshō, *Shihō Enkakushi*, 420.
91. SKST, LVII, 15.
92. SKST, XC, 215.
93. *Ibid.* This source claims that twenty-nine district courts did not have thought procutators. See Table 3 for an estimate of the number of thought procurators in 1941 at all courts.

Thought procurators in the ten principal district courts handled most thought offenders. (See Table 3.) This was natural, since communist intellectuals and workers were concentrated in these areas. Therefore, remote bureaus in nonstrategic spots were neglected in order to concentrate funds and trained personnel in the ideological hot spots. Here not only were funds and personnel more plentiful, but also research materials were available as well. Furthermore, police and judges in the big cities tended to be better trained in thought control.

The second-class status of bureaus far from Tokyo sometimes caused embarrassing situations. A procurator from Fukuoka complained at a

Table 3. Estimate of the number of thought procurators in 1941 at the Supreme Court, seven Appeals Courts, and District Courts

	Supreme Court	Appeals Court	District Court
Tokyo[ab]*	2	2	20 (including ward courts)
Yokohama[b]			2
Osaka[ab]		1	15 (including ward courts)
Sapporo[ab]		1	2
Sendai[ab]		1	2
Hiroshima[ab]		1	1
Kobe[b]			2
Nagasaki [ab]		1	1
Urawa[b]			1
Nagoya[ab]		1	2
Shizuoka			1
Nagano			1
Niigata			1
Kyoto			2
Wakayama			1
Yamaguchi			1
Okayama			1
Fukuoka			2
Kumamoto			1
Akita			1
Total for all categories:			70

*Superscript *a* indicates the appeals courts and superscript *b* the ten main district courts. This estimate is based on *Shisō Geppō*, XXIII, May, 1936, 529–532, and *Shihō Enkakushi*, 536.

conference in June 1938 that in a recent nationwide arrest his bureau was unaware that the target for arrest (Japanese Proletarian Party) was in violation of the Peace Preservation Law. They had not been instructed by the prefectural Special Higher Police. Afterwards the procurator requested that the Justice Ministry supply his bureau with advance information, in order to prevent such an incident from happening again. Chief of the Criminal Affairs Bureau Matsuzaka Hiromasa replied that he would do his best to keep them informed, adding that it was natural for them to feel as they did in "such a distant place."[94]

Preserving the Traditional Political Structure

The Peace Preservation Law was created by Hiranuma Kiichirō and other conservative members of the political elite in order to suppress those who sought to change the political, economic, and social order. Over the years the basic law, reinforced by revisions, administrative decisions, and supplementary legislation, developed into the "Peace Preservation Law System." This system, its supporters among the prewar conservative forces, and Hiranuma himself are often stigmatized as "fascist." Fortunately, recent books have retreated from the tactics of moralization and condemnation employed during the trial of Japanese "war criminals" by the victorious allied powers (1946–1948), and the anger voiced by Marxist scholars. Presently, scholars are spending less time excoriating Japan's "evil" leaders and are placing more emphasis upon investigating what really did happen.[95]

A good place to begin is with Hiranuma and his followers. Certainly, they were partially responsible for frustrating the expansion of parliamentary politics, and they did contribute, as did most others in Japanese society, to the expansion of military power during the 1930's. However, the Hiranuma clique also led the way in defending the Meiji constitutional structure against "new bureaucrats,"[96] service per-

94. Okudaira, GS, XLV, 86–90.

95. For an excellent review of historical interpretations of the interwar period see James W. Morley, "Introduction: Choice and Consequence," in Morley, *Dilemmas of Growth in Prewar Japan*. Also see Havens, 1–2, 40.

96. The primary characteristic of "new bureaucrats," or "revisionist bureaucrats," the generic name suggested by Robert M. Spaulding, was "their determination to change

sonnel, and others who attempted to overthrow the traditional system. Conservatives like Hiranuma, then, acted as a bulwark against a much more repressive system promoted by civilian and military radicals.

Together with other bureaucratic conservatives, Hiranuma fought to preserve inherited social and political values, and opposed foreign-oriented political ideologies, whether anarchist, socialist, communist, democratic, fascist, or totalitarian. During the late Taisho and early Showa periods he cooperated with rightists, but subsequently, as the radical rightists moved away from his position, he became an enemy of those who clamored for national reorganization; the Showa Restoration demanded by the radicals was the antithesis of the restoration Hiranuma had called for earlier. Thus, bureaucratic conservatives like Hiranuma acted in self-interest, and also to protect "their" state, when they broke with the radical right and attacked rightist plans to reorganize the political system. This was because the system the radicals envisioned undermined the position of the imperial bureaucracy and usurped its power. Hiranuma and his clique, who felt that imperial rule should be administered by a bureaucracy that combined moral rectitude and legal expertise, strongly resisted. That civilian and government-connected rightist extremists never managed to create a fascist movement in Japan was due not only to the nature of society but also to the hostility of conservatives toward the radical right.[97]

By the 1930's, the Hiranuma faction had become an important political force. Hiranuma, by the time he resigned as justice minister in 1923, had come to dominate the entire ministry, and continued to do

---

the status quo—in one or more of several ways, some contradictory." In general, revisionists were more willing than other bureaucrats to ignore traditional ministry boundaries and to seek cooperation with a wide range of civil and military officials. "All revisionists felt a general commitment to change the existing order—political, social, economic, or all three—for the purpose of increasing the nation's spiritual and military strength. They advocated either ideological purification, state control of the economy, or both." Spaulding, "The Bureaucracy as a Political Force, 1920–1945," in James W. Morley (ed.), *Dilemmas of Growth in Prewar Japan*, 61–62.

97. Yasko, 4–5. James Crowley suggests that the conservative Privy Council may have been a primary check "against a pure form of facism emerging in Japan." Quoted in George Akita, "The Other Itō: A Political Failure," in Albert M. Craig and Donald H. Shively (eds.), *Personality in Japanese History*, 337.

so through his personal following built up during his years as procurator-general. One by one his followers moved into the top administrative positions. After 1931, most Cabinets had his followers as justice ministers, including even the war-period governments of Tōjō (Iwamura Michio, 1941–1944), Koiso (Matsuzaka Hiromasa, 1944–1945), and Suzuki (Matsuzaka, 1945). Besides a dominant position in the Justice Ministry, Hiranuma extended his power into the Privy Council which acted as the emperor's highest advisory body. This gave him close contact with top leaders in all fields, including the Imperial Palace. After 1926, when he became vice-president of the Council, Hiranuma took over the day-to-day management of that body while the seventy-four-year-old president (Kuratomi Yūzaburō) handled the ceremonial functions. Prior to Hiranuma's appointment, the Council had been inactive, but after 1926 it reasserted itself, and Hiranuma had a good deal to do with its expanded influence.[98] Between 1936 and 1939 he was president of the Council. Besides his close relationship with the Seiyūkai party, Hiranuma had a strong support group in the 80,000-member Kokuhonsha until it disbanded in 1936. Guided by Hiranuma and his justice clique, this group pulled together a broad cross section of civil and military bureaucrats. Hiranuma strove to achieve political power in a multicentered institutional system. Therefore, he built power bases within different parts of that system and created a factional alliance. In 1939 his faction best represented the national consensus, as determined by imperial advisors, and he became prime minister.

Like other political hopefuls, Hiranuma was forced by the nature of the multicentered political system to engage in political intrigue, with the purpose of toppling the Cabinet. Therefore, it is not unexpected that his faction played an active role in the political battle over the ratification of the London Naval Disarmament Treaty (1930).[99] Prime Minister Hamaguchi got his treaty, but the sharp debate over it led ''to a

98. Yasko, 60, 62, 69.

99. Itō Takashi, "Conflicts and Coalitions in Japan, 1930: Political Groups The London Naval Disarmament Conference," in Sven Groennings et al. (eds.), The Study of Coalition Behavior. Itō Takashi, "The Role of Right-wing Organizations in Japan," in Dorothy Borg and Shumpei Okamoto (eds.), Pearl Harbor As History, 492–493, 495, 497.

general shift in the delicate balance among the plurality of contending political groups. The nationalist propaganda disseminated by Hiranuma and other antitreaty forces helped to crystalize the fluid ideas of the activist right wing. Elements of these romantic revolutionaries would soon directly eliminate many of the more moderate actors . . . from the political stage."[100] Itō Takashi concludes that after the treaty struggle "radicals" and "conservatives" in Hiranuma's faction "found themselves more and more in basic agreement," and that "large parts" of this union supported and encouraged the assassinations and terror of later years.[101]

It seems that this episode did much to brand Hiranuma as a "fascist" and a radical rightist, which he was not. Although Hiranuma used political turmoil to further his political ambitions, he repudiated assassinations and any kind of terror tactics, and soon after the London Naval Disarmament Treaty fight he began to disassociate himself from the radical extremists. Writing in 1934 in the monthly *Kokuhon Magazine*, he warned those who were using violence to impose a military regime on the country that they were violating the *kokutai* and exceeding their roles of assisting the emperor.[102] This was not the thinking of a fascist or a totalitarian, both of whom rely upon and actively promote terror and violence to achieve political objectives.[103] The February 26, 1936, army revolt in Tokyo, with its demands for social revolution, shocked Hiranuma. This incident, and the connection of Kokuhonsha radicals with it, promoted the notion that the Kokuhonsha was a "fascist" group. Hiranuma reacted by quietly departing from the organization, and a few months later it disbanded.[104] Thus, by the mid-thirties Hiranuma had made his position clear.

By the time Hiranuma formed his Cabinet in 1939, political liberals and other antimilitary groups had been severely weakened by intense pressure from the extremist right. To gain control of the state, the radical right had first of all to neutralize the strong bureaucracy. Under

100. Yasko, 88–89.
101. Itō, "Conflicts and Coalitions in Japan: 1930," 174.
102. Yasko, 114.
103. Carl J. Friedrich and Zbigniew K. Brzezinski, *Totalitarian Dictatorship And Autocracy*, 9–10, 107, 131, 135, 137, 141, 299.
104. Yasko, 118.

the guise of war mobilization, the radical right sought to reorganize the multicentered institutional system by various political and economic reforms, including the elimination of the traditional party system which was to be replaced by one national party. Hiranuma viewed their actions as no less a threat than those of his leftist foes. Any change which would realign existing political forces was distrusted by Hiranuma who was concerned about preserving the political influence of conservative bureaucrats. Hence, he viewed plans for political realignment as poor imitations of foreign totalitarian systems.[105] Although Hiranuma's coalition government broke apart after the shocking news of the German-Russian Nonaggression Pact of August 1939 reached Tokyo (Japan and Germany were negotiating a military alliance; hence, the resignation of Hiranuma who felt betrayed), he repulsed efforts by reformers to change the constitutional balance of power.

The political-action programs of the radical left and radical right had by this time become so similar that it was "possible for members of some left-wing groups to join right-wing groups without changing their positions."[106] Officials in Hiranuma's home base, the Justice Ministry, were concerned about this phenomenon and frequently commented on it.[107] Tozawa Shigeo felt, in June 1938, that the leftists and rightists has become so alike in their organization and tactics that it was difficult to separate them.[108] Sano Shigeki, a specialist on rightists, said in October that the difference between the left and right was "only the thickness of a piece of paper." For example, he noted that some rightists regarded Kita Ikki's book on the national reconstruction of Japan as full of communist ideas while others called it "their holy Bible."[109] In April 1941, a procurator at the Tokyo District Court announced at a justice conference that many former leftists were entering rightist groups like the Taisei Yokusan Kai (Imperial Rule Assistance Association).[110] If

105. *Ibid.*, 120, 126–129.
106. Itō, "Conflicts and Coalitions in Japan, 1930," 174.
107. SKST, XXXVII, July, 1937, 72.
108. SKST, XLV, August, 1938, 40.
109. SKST, LVII, February, 1939, 98.
110. The Imperial Rule Assistance Association was created in October 1940, under the Second Konoe Cabinet, to act as a national union of patriotic organizations and traditional political parties all of which were merged into a single organization. This transcendental organization was to replace the weak political parties with strong centralized leadership and bring everyone solidly behind wartime policies.

you investigate their thought, he said, it was like opening a piece of candy; the wrapper was rightist thought and the candy leftist.[111] Hiranuma felt the same way; some of the reform bureaucrats were inspired by communist ideas, and a victory for them would lead to a Bolshevik reorganization of the entire society. Conservatives in the army, Home Ministry, and business world shared his concern.[112]

Once the Hiranuma group had identified its opponents as "Reds," or, as they had in the case of the liberals, identified them as the "seedbed of communism," the Peace Preservation Law could be used against them. Prime Minister Konoe, after discovering that he was unable to control the radical faction within the reform movement, invited Hiranuma to enter the Cabinet as State Minister (*Kokumu Daijin*), a position especially created for him by the Privy Council at Konoe's request, with a mandate to restrain the radical reformers. The following month (January 1940) Konoe dismissed his ministers of Home and Justice, replacing them with Hiranuma and Lt. General Yanagawa Heisuke, one of Hiranuma's long-time associates. The key posts in the Home Ministry also were quickly filled with Hiranuma's men. Hiranuma announced first that the government would not allow the Imperial Rule Assistance Association to conduct politics; the new Association, in his view, was not transcendental but was merely a subsidiary organ. Next, Hiranuma moved against individual reformers, accusing them of being communists. Seventeen members of the Association's planning board were arrested and charged with supporting the Comintern's popular front policies. Hiranuma mobilized conservative support in other parts of the bureaucracy, Privy Council, House of Peers, and Cabinet to force the resignation of the planning board's Executive Director Arima Yoriyasu, whom Hiranuma had suspected of being "Red" for some years. A general housecleaning followed, with some of Hiranuma's closest followers moving in as replacements. Within a week of Arima's resignation the conservatives had taken over the Imperial Rule Assistance Association.[113]

It seems that many radical rightists were slow to realize that Hiranuma was essentially a conservative. When they finally understood

111. SKST, LXXXVIII, October, 1941, 143.
112. Yasko, 162–164. Arthur E. Tiedemann, "Big Business and Politics in Prewar Japan," in James W. Morley (ed.), *Dilemmas of Growth in Prewar Japan*, 311.
113. Yasko, 165–173.

what he was doing, rumors of assassination plots against him began to circulate. But despite police protection, a gunman got to him on August 14, 1941. Nishiyama Naohiko, a member of a small rightist group (Makoto Musubi Kai), and a native of Hiranuma's birthplace, came to Hiranuma's residence with a letter of introduction. As Hiranuma was writing a sample of his calligraphy for Nishiyama, the gunman shot him six times. In spite of his serious wounds, Hiranuma chased Nishiyama out of the house. Although Nishiyama's thinking was representative of Hiranuma's foes, his crime was an individual act.[114]

The Trend of the Times

The government's campaign for public support was a success. There were, of course, flaws in its spiritual mobilization program and other policies, but antiwar ideology and other protests were silenced by what Maruyama Masao terms an "all pervasive psychological coercion."[115] The common people, it appears, mainly sympathized with and even feverently supported the war in China. Liberals and others who might have thought about resisting the current of the times were under intense pressure to abandon their lonely positions. The few who continued to resist were haunted by fear of assassination or social ostracism. To many people, it appeared that "the army was riding a wave of the future which could not be stopped or turned back. One could watch its progress from a safe distance, side with it, or be drowned by it."[116] Most people went along, with few putting up real resistance. Some intellectuals retreated into introspection and noninvolvement, which allowed them to maintain their own stability during the years of the "dark valley," while others became active promoters of national policies. Business leaders went along in order to profit from new markets and to remain influential in government circles. By doing so, they managed not only to survive, but also to prevent bureaucratic or military seizure of their organizations.[117]

The failure of the political parties, which stood out in stark contrast to the earlier successes of the Meiji oligarchs, prompted some politicians

114. *Ibid.*, 177–179.
115. Maruyama, *Thought and Behavior in Modern Japanese Politics*, 2.
116. Robert C. Butow, *Tojo and the Coming of the War*, 90.
117. Tiedemann, 315.

to seek a new approach to national problems. Nagai Ryūtarō is a good example. In the 1920's, he was an enthusiastic supporter of liberalism, but by 1940 he was a foremost advocate of the new political order. What caused him to change? It seems that Nagai did not regard his later actions as a betrayal of earlier ones. Rather, his position in 1940 "grew out of an exasperation at the inability of the existing political system to respond to the need for change." He was making "a last stab at finding a modus vivendi to reform when other avenues of political action had led to dead ends."[118] Nagai, along with others who were frustrated by the contending political parties and anxious to solve pressing national problems, was willing to embrace any program that promised results.[119]

Lack of resistance to increasingly harsh thought-control policies and to the drift into the Pacific war stemmed from the strong control mechanism which threatened protesters with prison and even death, and from the social pressures from which no one was fully immune, since within the soul of the most "progressive" individuals traditional concepts like loyalty and harmony weighed heavily. Robert N. Bellah has shown convincingly that the Japanese were schooled in the discipline of tightly structured groups and were quickly obedient to strong leadership. "There was no significant tradition of organized opposition to political authority. . . . There was no form of alienation from authority other than purely private withdrawal and escape."[120]

The suppression of moderate socialists, liberals, Christians, extreme rightists, and some Buddhists and Shintoists resulted not only from the government's push to rally a society suffering from anomie (see Conclusion), but also from what Kai T. Erikson calls a logistic problem. A community defines deviance "so that it encompasses a range of behavior roughly equivalent to the available space in its control apparatus. . . . That is, when the community calibrates its control machinery to handle a certain volume of deviant behavior, it tends to adjust its legal and psychiatric definitions of the problem in such a way that this volume is in fact realized." When agencies of control manage

118. Peter Duus, "Nagai Ryūtarō: The Tactical Dilemmas of Reform," in Albert M. Craig and Donald H. Shively (eds.), *Personality in Japanese History*, 401.

119. *Ibid.*, 423–424.

120. Robert N. Bellah, "Continuity and Change in Japanese Society," in Bernard Barber and Alex Inkeles (eds.), *Stability and Social Change*, 393.

to suppress certain types of crime, Erikson says, they "turn their attention to other forms of behavior, even to the point of defining as deviant certain styles of conduct which were not regarded so earlier. At any given time, then, the 'worst' people in the community are considered its criminals. . . . In that sense, deviance can be defined as behavior which falls on the outer edge of the group's experience, whether the range of experience is wide or narrow."[121] Therefore, once the efficient state control mechanism had crushed the communists and radical socialists it quite naturally moved on to the others.

121. Kai T. Erikson, *Wayward Puritans*, 25–26.

CHAPTER **7 Conclusion**

After the Meiji Restoration, the government formulated policies to promote national integration and to manipulate thought. The imperial institution was refurbished and used as a tool to reinforce that distinct pattern of unity around the emperor called the *kokutai*. Feudalism was completely abandoned in favor of modern political and economic organization, but the modernization plans depended heavily upon traditional values and the tightly bound structure of group life. Over the years large-scale institutional and organizational forms were introduced which provided the social context within which the leadership could achieve its primary goal of national strength and international prestige.

As Japan entered this century, conservatives became disturbed over the breakdown of traditional morals and the spirit of self-sacrifice. The appearance of anarchists, communists, and other deviants provided conservatives with a clear target, and with an opportunity to make a statement about the limits of socially acceptable activities, limitations which had become hazy during the upsurge of democracy. Professor Morito's conviction warned the scholarly world, and the Peace Preservation Law warned everyone, in a much firmer voice. As Japan's troubles deepened, the conservatives repeated their message by revising the peace law, staging the Tokyo open trial of communists, and widely circulating *tenkō* statements. Besides their obvious function to crush leftists these integrative actions also acted as boundary-maintaining devices by demonstrating to the public where the line was that divided acceptable and unacceptable conduct. If we recall that Hiranuma and other conservatives were deeply worried about the nation's spiritual

183

health before the establishment of a communist party in Japan, and also
reflect on Emile Durkheim's observation in his book called *The Rules of
Sociological Method*, then the double purpose of the thought-control
apparatus is better understood. Durkheim wrote that crime and
deviation cause people in a society to draw together in a common
posture of indignation. Like war or some other national emergency, the
antiemperor stance of leftists forced other people to become more alert
to the interests they had in common and drew attention to traditional
values which constituted the "collective conscience" of the nation.[1]

Reference to *kokutai* in the Peace Preservation Law seems out of
place in an antileftists law. Why were not more specific terms
employed? The answer is that the peace law was aimed not only at
annihilating the pitifully weak leftist thrust, but also at easing political
and social problems. For that purpose, *kokutai* was a very precise term
in that it was a rallying symbol that few could resist. Besides being
criminal legislation, then, the 1925 peace law was a symbolic
integrative device designed to rally a divided leadership and society
around the emperor. It can also be seen as a continuation of the effort
begun in the early Meiji period to strengthen the traditional components
of society. Moreover, since *kokutai* included everything worth
protecting, its use acted as a healing balm on the split between state
(*kokka*) and nation or people (*kokumin*). Although these terms were not
entirely exclusive, they were not identical. Japanese nationalism was
divided into one part that focused on the authority of the state, or
statism (*kokkashugi*), and a second part that focused on cultural or ethnic
nationalism (*kokuminshugi*). Some supporters of the latter were by the
1920's attacking the statist ideas of central authorities.[2] Besides using
kokutai to minimize confrontation and promote integration, authorities
employed this term to offset the opening up of the political structure to
new groups (e.g., in opposition to the new suffrage law).

While the Japanese were prone to use integrative devices like the
term *kokutai*, conflict did remain as an undercurrent which sometimes
surfaced. The government sought to obscure the gulf between national

1. Kai T. Erikson, *Wayward Puritans*, 3–4.
2. Thomas R. H. Havens, "Frontiers of Japanese Social History during World War
II," *Shakai Kagaku Tōkyū*, XVIII (March 1973), 579–580.

loyalty and filial piety by declaring in the 1910 revision of the ethics textbooks that both were the same.[3] Soldiers were told that they would become protective spirits of the fatherland and would be worshiped in Yasukuni Shrine (Tokyo) if they were killed. And since the soldier's family name would be listed among the divine spirits, the act of dying for the emperor reflected honor upon both the nation and the family: a unity of filial piety and loyalty. However, not everyone accepted this view. A thirteen-year-old boy talking with his mother on the eve of the bombing of Hiroshima said: "I wonder why the Japanese have to die for the sake of the Emperor? I for one do not wish to die for the sake of the Emperor. I do wish to live long so that I may fulfill my duties of filial piety. Am I an unpatriotic Japanese to think in this way?"[4]

The Japanese solution to the problem of thought criminals was unique, in that the government deliberately promoted a graduated step-by-step reintegration for each offender. Officials institutionalized the *tenkō* system and certified each person who was "cured." Thus, each graduate of the *tenkō* system was given a diploma which was recognized by society. The ceremony of passing through the conversion process was designed to remove the stigma imposed during arrest, trial, and imprisonment.

One of Japan's most knowledgeable experts on thought control, Ikeda Katsu, wrote in 1939 that the Peace Preservation Law punished actions rising out of the actor's ideological beliefs. The law was not designed to punish thought itself.[5] In a dry legal sense this was correct, but in the real world of thought control the system functioned differently. After his arrest for an illegal action, a suspect was pressured to renounce his subversive ideology, and he was not recognized as fully cured until he did so. Therefore, through this law, and the system built upon it, the state was seeking to reach into each offender's mind, and in many cases it seems to have succeeded. At the same time, the peace-law system reached into everyone's mind, since it promoted the concept of self-policing. Intellectuals and students fearfully turned their backs on

3. Wilbur M. Fridell, "Notes on Japanese Tolerance," *Monumenta Nipponica*, XXVII (Autumn, 1972), 262.
4. Tsurumi Kazuko, *Social Change and the Individual*, 125, 269.
5. Ikeda Katsu, "Chian Ijihō," in *Shin Hōgaku Zenshū*, 23–24.

ideas and books that might bring them into conflict with authorities. This writer has spoken to more than one person who recalls that he discarded books which were considered subversive. Thought police, who were under stern orders to prevent thought crimes, lectured anyone who appeared not to have the proper attitude. While "proper attitude" is not the sort of thing that is easily analyzed, it seems clear that people became accustomed to retreating, if they found themselves heading down a path that might lead to an improper thought.

Laws, police, procurators, and judges were central to the expurgation of dangerous thought and the reintegration of offenders, but another part of that success was psychological and dependent on cultural factors outside the legal domain. Leftist ideology crashed into a high wall, fashioned by state pressure and reinforced by a widespread collectivist ethic, and, during the 1930's, this conservatism thickened, with society increasingly unfriendly to heretical ideology. It is a natural question to ask which was more important. Were the communists who converted responding to special efforts to change their thought or to traditional sociocultural factors which kept a majority of people from joining the Japanese Communist Party in the first place? According to the sociocultural-factor viewpoint, *tenkō* would have occurred without an official policy promoting it. If this was the case, why did communists begin to convert only after they were jailed? Was the social system operative only under the pressure of prison? The contradiction here is obvious. While it is true that the government exploited the sociocultural factors (e.g., the family system and the *oyabun-kobun* concept) to pressure radicals into conversion, it would be a mistake to dismiss the important role of state power and the administrative scheme, especially since the government devised new techniques and created a big bureaucracy for the purpose of suppressing thought criminals and crimes.

Maruyama Masao, a harsh critic of prewar political leadership, wrote that the prewar government was a "massive 'system of irresponsibilities'" in which bureaucrats jealously guarded their ministerial domain, kept secrets from outsiders, and avoided responsibility. With the deaths of the charismatic Meiji Emperor and the politically shrewd men who established the modern state structure, political integration declined and the locus of responsibility became increasingly nebulous.[6] Certainly, suspicion of outsiders (i.e., those not in one's group) and xenophobia seem to be an inherent feature of Japanese organizations, from the village level to the imperial bureaucracy,[7] and there were numerous examples of sectionalism in the thought-control system.

Police sometimes withheld information from procurators (whom they were legally bound to follow in an investigation), submitted incomplete reports (why share "secret" Home Ministry material with outsiders?), and failed to notify procurators of arrests.[8] Justice Police who were legally under the thumb of procurators were not always fully loyal, and were influenced by Home Ministry views. Police sometimes engaged in a tug-of-war with thought procurators who were legally in charge of Protection and Supervision Centers, since they felt that what was rightfully police business was being usurped.[9] Sectionalism and the concept of professional secrecy were carried to such extremes that the Home Ministry officially refused to give to justice men the highly valued *Tokkō Geppō*. Of course, this roadblock was bypassed by thought procurators in many district courts who simply asked their police friends to loan their copies.[10] And naturally, within the interministry thought-control apparatus there were many "gray" areas in which responsibility passed to those who sought it most energetically; these rivalries were masked by formal restraints, but sometimes they burst into the open.

Such conflicts, however, are only part of the reality, since many examples of harmony and cooperation can be cited. Joint conferences on thought problems were common; thought procurators held frequent meetings with thought-police chiefs, military police, directors of Protection and Supervision Centers, and others. Police responded by

6. Maruyama Masao, *Thought and Behaviour in Modern Japanese Politics*, 120–128.

7. Robert N. Bellah, "Continuity and Change in Japanese Society," in Barber and Inkeles (eds.), *Stability and Social Change*, 386.

8. SKST, XLV, August, 1938, 86, 224–225. SKST, LXIV, September, 1939, 225. SKST, LXXIX, August, 1940, 195–196. SKST, LXXXVI, May, 1941, 364. SKST, XC, January, 1942, 220, 222, 239, 240.

9. SKST, LXXXVIII, October, 1941, 154.

10. SKST, XVI, October, 1934, 141–142. SKST, XXXVII, July, 1937, 142. SKST, LXIV, September, 1939, 266. SKST, LXXVIII, July, 1940, 127. SKST, LXXXVI, May, 1941, 141.

sending monthly reports to procurators.[11] Procurators also plugged into informal channels of communication: friends in thought-police units, contacts in prefectural offices, and acquaintances in civilian groups. Thus, by combining skillful manipulation of people with police cooperation, thought procurators were usually able to perform their duties.[12]

When applied to the Justice Ministry and the interministry thought-control system, Maruyama's point of view seems slightly out of focus. The following comments, however, are not based on absolute conviction, since concrete material on attitudes such as "irresponsibility" and "responsibility" are difficult to discover and evaluate. Nonetheless, many of the justice officials who led the war on dangerous thought were members of the Hiranuma faction; a majority of the ministers during the 1930's were influenced by him, as were more than half of the justice officials who were involved in major thought cases.[13] And Hiranuma was a strong-willed person devoted to the emperor and the nation. Perhaps Hiranuma's comment as an old man should be accepted at face value: "I have never worked for personal fame or profit."[14] At any rate, all records indicate that he and his clique energetically sought responsibility in their campaign to suppress dangerous thought and to clean up society in general. Finally, despite the flaws within the Japanese bureaucratic structure, which Maruyama may be magnifying, the thought-control apparatus functioned surprisingly well for an institution resting on so many bureaucratic pillars.

While the government effectively suppressed freedom of speech and thought, scholars are in disagreement over a political label. Was it a brand of "totalitarianism," a special kind of "fascism'" or was it neither?

Modern totalitarian states possess a single mass party, a maximum

11. SKST, XXII, September, 1935, Preface, 204–209. SKST, LXXXVI, May, 1941, 344. LXXXVIII, October, 1941, 37. SKST, XC, January, 1942, Preface, 217–218, 222, 239. SKST, XCI, June, 1942, 1–2.

12. SKST, XXXVII, July, 1937, 142. SKST, LXIV, September, 1939, 183. SKST, LXXIX, August, 1940. SKST, LXXXVI, May, 1941, 335–344. SKST, XC, January, 1942, 220.

13. Kawahara Hiroshi, "'Chian Ijihō' no Suishinshatachi," *Shakai Kagaku Tōkyū*, XXXVIII (August, 1968), 6–7.

14. Hiranuma Kiichirō Kaikoroku Hensan Iinkai, *Hiranuma Kiichirō Kaikoroku*, 41.

leader; they employ terror tactics on a wide scale, and aim at totally reshaping society. The ideas and actions of Japan's major interwar leaders do not fit this mold. A leading proponent of the concept of a fascism peculiar to Japan is Maruyama Masao who argues that while fascism did not come from below, as in Italy and Germany, it was imposed from above. Alarmed by the revolutionary situation, the ruling elite gradually created a "totalitarian system . . . within the framework of the State structure determined by the Meiji constitution."[15] While we must respect Maruyama's brilliantly argued analysis, we must also consider the overwhelming weight of more recent reflection: "There has been reluctance to use this label, with its deep roots in the complexities of modern European history, to characterize an era in Japan so obviously fraught with the distinctiveness of indigenous culture."[16] A more satisfying description is the term "highly authoritarian." It is most "useful to view interwar Japan as proceeding developmentally from the political stage represented by the precursory Meiji nationalist 'movement-regime' to a point where the 'extinction' of that regime's original dynamism, coupled however, with the tenacity of its institutions and the onset of total war, brought a reassertion of authoritarian tendencies and a corollary restraint on the exercise of liberalism and individual freedoms."[17] While these developments are distressing, they do not add up to "fascism" from either below or above.

Authoritarianism had deep roots in political tradition, since tight social control, supported by restrictive laws and police, can be traced back to the Tokugawa era (1600–1867). The Meiji government (1868–1912) built on this old platform and expanded the control mechanism, especially the police power. The 1925 peace law added new control institutions. This law, which functioned as the control

15. Maruyama, 80.
16. Havens, 1–2. Morley "Introduction: Choice and Consequence," in Morley, *Dilemmas of Growth in Prewar Japan,* 14, 21. In a 1968 article Michael Hurst lumped Japan together with Germany and Italy as a fascist state. Hurst, "What is Fascism?" *The Historical Journal,* XI (1968), 183. Hurst has since changed his mind, and no longer regards interwar Japan as fascist. Interview with Hurst in St. Louis, October 19, 1973.
17. George M. Wilson, "A New Look at the Problem of 'Japanese Fascism,'" *Comparative Studies in Society and History: An International Quarterly,* X (July, 1968), 411–412.

system's legal nucleus, integrated and systematized what came to be known as the "Peace Preservation Law System."

Comparison of institutions set in different cultures is a stimulating exercise, but it is also a risky one, if each example occurs in a very different social and political atmosphere. This is a major problem when Japan's thought-control system is measured against that of other modernizing nations which exist under highly authoritarian governments. Despite this limitation, comparison of Japanese methods with those of Nazi Germany, Stalinist Russia, and Maoist China bring the degree of repressiveness in Japan into sharper focus. Also, comparison should put to rest any idea that, although they are both East Asian, Chinese and Japanese methods and solutions for the problem were the same, or that there is a peculiarly East Asian mode of thought control.

Hitler's treatment of thought offenders is well known; they were executed, put into forced labor brigades where they often died, or were jailed. Little effort was expended to convert offenders and bring them back into society. Russia, too, used mass terror, executions, and deportations. Aleksandr I. Solzhenitsyn, in *The Gulag Archipelago*, and others have documented the widespread application of terror that began with Lenin, and that Stalin continued. Finally, there is the Chinese Communist program for reforming the thinking of hostile intellectuals by what is popularly known as "brainwashing."

Brainwashing means to indoctrinate so thoroughly as to effect a radical transformation of beliefs. Robert Lifton writes that Chinese Communist brainwashing consisted of two basic elements: confession and re-education which "aimed at social control and individual change." Mao Tse-tung said that the old society was corrupt, but that the people must be saved by expelling dangerous ideology and instilling one supporting the state.[18] Thought reform got its emotional scope and power through a combination of coercion with evangelistic exhortation aimed at the victim.[19] Since confession and education

18. Robert J. Lifton, *Thought Reform and the Psychology of Totalism*, 5, 13–14. Also see Robert J. Lifton, "Thought Reform of Chinese Intellectuals; A Psychiatric Evaluation," *The Journal of Asian Studies*, XVI (November, 1956), 75–88.

19. Lifton, *Thought Reform and the Psychology of Totalism*, 13.

played an important role in the thought-control programs of both China and Japan, the similarity is all too obvious. However, the social and political conditions under which each nation carried out its policies were quite different, as were their goals. Moreover, looking a bit harder at the Chinese program, we discover that they have used terror on a wide scale (like Lenin and Stalin, they killed many who got in their way) and they have deported huge numbers to frontier areas for forced labor (for which the Russian use of Siberia is an obvious parallel). Furthermore, the Chinese have drawn a sharp line between those who have rights and those who are "nonpeople;" the latter are put to death.[20] The similarity with post-1917 Russia is evident. Thus, the Chinese approach to the problem is closer to the Russian than to the Japanese.

Thought control in Japan was different; one might even say unique. No mass application of terror, no Japanese executed in Japan under the provisions of the Peace Preservation Law (prior to the single exception in 1944), no deportations or use of forced labor, and no category of nonpersons. If executions and prison terms are chosen as the yardstick by which to measure repressiveness, then Japanese thought-control policies appear mild. The reasons for this softer Japanese approach have been explored earlier (see Chap. 5), but they may be summarized as a feeling that all Japanese were brothers under the emperor, and that no thought offender was beyond salvation. This is an excellent illustration of Robert N. Bellah's thesis that the Japanese have traditionally taken in new institutional forms but have retained great continuity in their system of values. Thus, the officials who studied foreign ways of dealing with leftist radicals and examined foreign antisubversive laws, as well as the thought procurators who dealt directly with thought offenders, were drawn to a solution based on their cultural heritage. Bellah's analysis of the leader-follower relationship within a group casts additional light on the reason Japan's approach to thought control was unique: "The leadership that excites the strongest emotion and the greatest devotion is more passive and even feminine. Symbolically this more emotionally positive leadership focuses on the mother . . . and the emperor. . . . Both stand for nurturance and benevolence rather than domination and control. . . . Instead of being crushed by despotic

20. *Ibid.*, 433.

patriarchal authority the individual is encouraged to work hard to gain material favor. He is manipulated more by rewards than by threats and punishments."[21] The most natural solution to the thought-control problem was the one which fitted in neatly with traditional values, and because this was so, it was the most effective, and also unique. Finally, it should be noted that no Japanese came forth after 1945 to write a history of the "Japanese Gulag Archipelago," because there was nothing comparable in the Japanese experience to Solzhenitsyn's Russian nightmare.

The reasons for thought control in Japan were complex and not confined to flaws in the Meiji Constitution, a tradition of authoritarianism, and the weakness of liberalism. Other factors less subject to direct manipulation by Japan's leaders must be considered: the rapidity with which the whole world's economic system collapsed and the more and more uncompromising attitudes of China and the United States. These problems, together with the rise of communism, signified the weakening of the old economic and political order. Japan was hit hard by one shock after another at a time when the Japanese political world was floundering for lack of leadership; an appealing new political synthesis had not yet formed to replace the burnt-out dynamism of the Meiji era. Therefore, the collapse of parliamentary democracy and the resurgence of authoritarianism were due as much to foreign events as to domestic happenings. It was, then, in a time of crisis that the thought-control system coalesced. That it eventually expanded into every corner of society was a result of the external and internal pressures which plunged the nation into an era of semiwar after 1931 and full warfare after 1937.

Value judgments on who was responsible for thought control must include consideration of this crisis background. It has been well illustrated that justice officials were mainly responsible for the 1925 peace law, and were deeply involved in creating the Peace Preservation Law System. How culpable were they? Even harsh critics usually concede that they could not have foreseen the uses to which the law would be put in later years. Given this point, how guilty were they for actions taken during the 1930's, the so-called emergency period, when

21. Bellah, "Continuity and Change," 388–389.

many Japanese felt that their national existence was at stake? Could a loyal justice official or thought policeman have done otherwise than carry out policies to rid the nation of those who sapped the will to fight? In a time of crisis, other more democratic states have responded in a manner not totally dissimilar to that of Japan. The civil liberties of Japanese-Americans were forgotten in 1941, and the anti-Red witch hunt of the early 1950's hardly reflect credit on some United States government officials. On balance, then, Japanese thought-control officials were "guilty," but there were mitigating circumstances.

Were the educated elite also guilty, since a majority went along with government policies? If Bellah is correct, that "there was no form of alienation from authority other than by purely private withdrawal and escape," then a strong protest was impossible.[22]

Japanese Marxist scholars leave no doubt about their condemnation of prewar leaders and institutions. As one of the chief symbols of suppression, the Peace Preservation Law has been roundly attacked; it is rare, indeed, to find a publication in which this law is not automatically preceded by the word "notorious." This attitude is hardly surprising, since not a few Marxist scholars were victims. For Marxists, the leaders were bad and the people were good, and the liberalism of the 1920's inevitably led to suppression and warfare. While this approach is a clear-cut statement about the guilt of the men who stamped out unhealthy thought, it is only one small slice of a very big historical pie.

Since the reasons for establishing thought control were complex, and since the Marxist condemnation approach is of limited usefulness, an attempt has been made in this study to be very objective. Value judgments about the morality of government actions were eschewed, but official policies were exposed to the harsh light of history, with no effort to whitewash them. While this method of handling a sensitive subject may not be emotionally satisfying to some, it is hoped that all will recognize that a balanced evaluation has merit.

22. *Ibid.*, 393.

APPENDIX I Special Higher Police Sections

Chart 1. Special Higher Police Section in 1912*

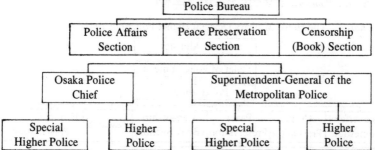

*Source: Ōkasumikai (ed.) *Naimushōshi,* Vol. IV, 734–735, 744–747.
Communication between the Special Higher Police and the Police Bureau could be either direct or through the office of the Superintendent-General of the Metropolitan Police. This double route permitted the flow of secret reports and orders between the thought police and the Peace Preservation Section. Tōyama Shigeki and Adachi Toshiko, *Kindai Nihon Seijishi Hikkei,* 97.

Chart 2. Special Higher Police Section in 1925*

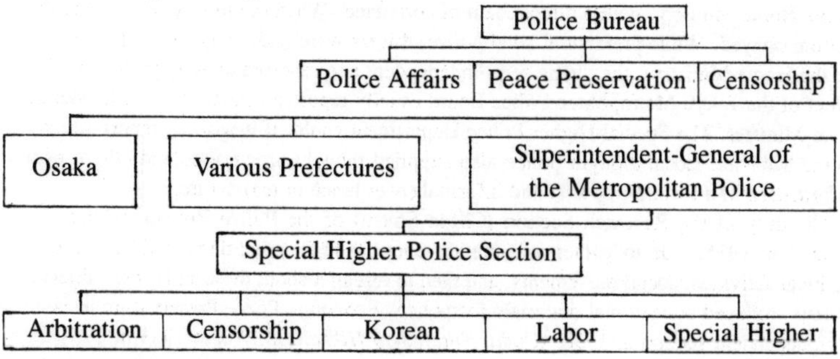

Police Bureau

| Police Affairs | Peace Preservation | Censorship |

| Osaka | Various Prefectures | Superintendent-General of the Metropolitan Police |

Special Higher Police Section

| Arbitration | Censorship | Korean | Labor | Special Higher |

*Source: *Naimushōshi,* Vol. IV, 734–735, 744–747.

195

Chart 3. Special Higher Police Department in 1932*

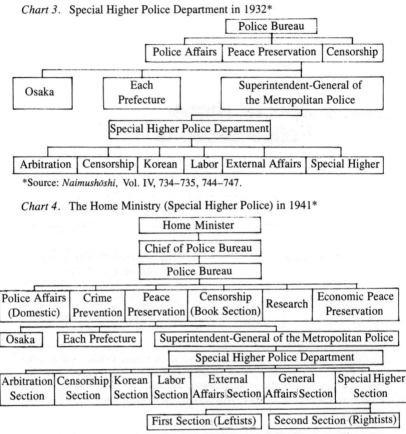

Source: Naimushōshi, Vol. IV, 734–735, 744–747.

Chart 4. The Home Ministry (Special Higher Police) in 1941*

Source: Naimushōshi, Vol. IV, 734–735, 744–747. The Police Bureau was the center of the Home Ministry, with a direct chain of command. When the top gave an order, the bottom obeyed. While prefectural level police officers were under a governor (appointed by the Home Ministry), they were semi-independent and reported directly to Tokyo. The Chief of the Tokyo Metropolitan Police Board usually reported directly to the Minister or Vice-Minister. The Special Higher Police Department could, if it wished, report directly to the Minister. Local thought police also supplied thought procurators and others with information of a formal (reports) and informal (over lunch or tea) nature.

The duty of the Research Section (Chōsa Shitsu) of the Police Bureau, which was created in 1935, was to gather information about thought conditions, public opinion, political activities, social movements, and then to research about these and other subjects. It also produced educational materials for police. Economic Peace Preservation became an independent section in 1938. *Kindai Nihon Seiji Hikkei,* 98. About 1933 or 1934 the Special Higher Section was expanded into two parts: one concentrated on leftists and the other on rightists, with about ten people working in each one. After the attempted army coup of February 26, 1936, the total number of employees jumped to about 100. Okudaira Yasuhiro (ed.), *Gendaishi Shiryō,* XLV, 323.

APPENDIX II Justice Ministry

Chart 1. Justice Ministry Thought Section in 1926*

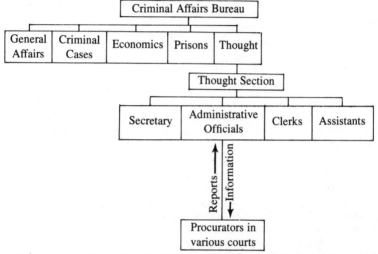

*Information on the number of people working in the Thought Section from 1926 onward is sparse and vague. Matsuzaka Hiromasa recalled in 1938 that Ikeda Katsu was the secretary in charge of the Thought Section at the time of the March 15 arrests, and that he was shorthanded. Matsuzaka, 43. Justice publications like *Shihō Enkakushi* are useful in only a general way, since budget and personnel statistics are lumped together under broad categories. For instance, in 1925 the number of secretaries jumped from six to eleven, but the reader is left to guess in which bureaus and sections the extra personnel were placed. Another big jump in secretaries occurred in 1931, from twelve to seventeen. Moreover, for the first time officials in the Thought Section are clearly identified, but unfortunately, only staff provided by a supplementary budget: one additional secretary and two clerks. In 1938, the supplementary funds provided two extra secretaries and eight clerks. Thus, we can roughly see that the Thought Section expanded in personnel (expansion in duties is outlined in various chapters of this book), especially after 1932. See *Shihō Enkakushi,* 541–542. Budget information for the Thought Section, if it exists, is secreted someplace in the Justice Ministry Library, and is forbidden to scholars. Indeed, if present justice bureaucrats had their way, all prewar secret justice information would remain highly classified and denied to the public.

Chart 2. Justice Ministry Protection and Supervision System in 1936*

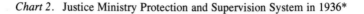

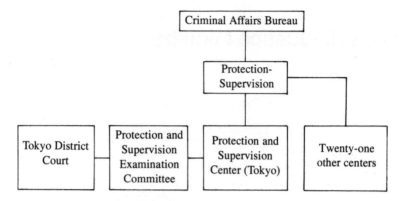

*Source: Hasebe Kingo, "Shisōhan no Hogo ni Tsuite" in Shihōshō Chōsaka, *Shihō Kenkyū,* XXI (10), 77–78. Location and jurisdiction of each Protection and Supervision Center are as follows:

1. Tokyo: Tokyo City, Chiba, Saitama, and Yamanashi Prefectures
2. Yokohama: Yokohama City and Kanagawa Prefectures
3. Mito: Mito City and Ibaragi Prefecture
4. Maebashi: Maebashi City, Gumma and Tochigi Prefectures
5. Shizuoka: Shizuoka City and Shizuoka Prefecture
6. Nagano: Nagano City and Nagano Prefecture
7. Niigata: Niigata City and Niigata Prefecture
8. Osaka: Osaka City, Nara and Wakayama Prefectures
9. Kyoto: Kyoto City and Shiga Prefecture
10. Kobe: Kobe City, and Hyōgo Prefecture
11. Takamatsu: Takamatsu City, Kagawa, Tokushima, Kōchi, and Ehime Prefectures
12. Nagoya: Nagoya City, Aichi, Gifu, and Mie Prefectures
13. Kanazawa: Kanazawa City, Ishikawa, Toyama, and Fukui Prefectures
14. Hiroshima: Hiroshima City, Hiroshima, Shimane, and Yamaguchi Prefectures
15. Okayama: Okayama City, Okayama and Tottori Prefectures
16. Fukuoka: Fukuoka City, Fukuoka, Oita, Saga, and Nagasaki Prefectures
17. Kumamoto: Kumamoto City, Kumamoto, Kagoshima, Miyazaki, and Okinawa Prefectures
18. Sendai: Sendai City, Miyagi and Fukushima Prefectures
19. Akita: Akita City, Akita and Yamagata Prefectures
20. Aomori: Aomori City, Aomori and Iwate Prefectures
21. Sapporo: Sapporo City and rest of Hokkaido except for Hakodate
22. Hakodate: Hakodate City and fifteen surrounding gun (districts).

Chart 3. Justice Ministry Thought Section in 1938*

Criminal Affairs Bureau		
Other parts of Bureau	Thought Fifth Section (Leftists)	Thought Sixth Section (Rightists)

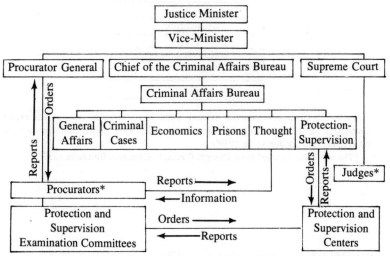

*Procurator Sano Shigeki (Yokohama District Court — later head of the Sixth Section) said in June 1937 that shortly before the attempted army coup (February 1936) the "section" doing research on rightists was abolished. This was done for budgetary reasons. The ministry, however, was still concerned about rightists, and personnel continued to write reports on their activities. It appears that the Justice Ministry formally established the Sixth Section in early 1938. As in other cases, the delay was due to a shortage of funds rather than a lack of concern on the part of justice bureaucrats. See *Shisō Kenkyū Shiryō Tokushū*, LVII, 90, and Okudaira Yasuhiro (ed.), *Gendaishi Shiryō*, XLV, 323.

Chart 4. The Justice Ministry in 1941

*Procurators were directly controlled by the Justice Minister, acting through the Procurator-General; judges were semi-independent under the Meiji Constitution, but were subject to manipulation by the Minister and his administrators.

APPENDIX III Education Ministry

Chart 1. Education Ministry in 1941*

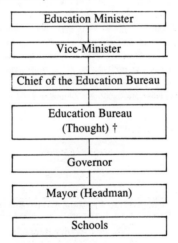

| Education Minister |
| Vice-Minister |
| Chief of the Education Bureau |
| Education Bureau (Thought) † |
| Governor |
| Mayor (Headman) |
| Schools |

*A direct chain of command existed. Japan's educational system was highly centralized. Even the semi-independent universities were pulled into the thought-supervision network during the 1930's.

†The name was changed from Thought Bureau to Education Bureau in 1937.

APPENDIX IV Peace Preservation Law, 1941, Articles 1–16

(Domei Tsushin Sha, *Wartime Legislation in Japan*, 1941, 70–77.)

Art. 1 A person who has organized an association with the object of changing the national polity or a person who has performed the work of an officer or other leader of such an association shall be condemned to death or punished with penal servitude for life or not less than seven years, and a person who knowingly has joined such an association or a person who has committed an act contributing to the accomplishment of its object shall be punished with penal servitude for a limited period not less than seven years.

Art. 2 A person who has organized an association with the object of aiding an association specified in the preceding Article or a person who has performed work of an officer or other leader of such an association shall be condemned to death or punished with penal servitude for life or not less than five years, and a person who knowingly has joined such an association or a person who has committed an act contributing to the accomplishment of its object shall be punished with penal servitude for a limited period not less than two years.

Art. 3 A person who has organized an association with the object of preparing for the organization of an association specified in Article 1 or a person who has performed the work of an officer or other leader of such an association shall be condemned to death or punished with penal servitude for life or not less than five years, and a person who knowingly has joined such an association or who has committed an act contributing to the accomplishment of its object shall be punished with penal servitude for a limited period not less than two years.

Art. 4 A person who has organized a group with the objects stipulated in the preceding three Articles or a person who has directed such a group shall be punished with penal servitude for life or not less than three years, and a person who has joined such a group with the objects stipulated in the foregoing three Articles or a person who has committed an act contributing to the realization of the objects stipulated in the foregoing three Articles in relation to said group shall be punished with penal servitude for a limited period not less than one year.

Art. 5 A person who has conferred with others [sic] person or instigated other [sic] person with the objects mentioned in Article 1 to 3 and regarding the execution of objective matters or propagated such objective matters or committed other acts contributing to the accomplishment of the objects, shall be punished with penal servitude not less than one year and not exceeding ten years.

Art. 6 A person who has instigated sedition, violent act [sic] or other crime injurious to life, body and property of a person, with the objects stipulated in Articles 1 to 3, shall be punished with penal servitude for a limited period not less than two years.

Art. 7 (See Chapter VI)

Art. 8 (See Chapter VI)

Art. 9 A person who has given or offered or promised to give money or other articles or property interests to another person with the object of causing him to commit either of the crimes stipulated in the preceding eight Articles, shall be punished with penal servitude not exceeding 10 years. This provision shall also apply to a person who knowingly has accepted or demanded or promised to accept said offering.

Art. 10 A person who has organized an association with the object of disavowing the system of private ownership or a person who knowingly has joined such an association or a person who has committed an act contributing to the accomplishment of the object of said association, shall be punished with penal servitude or imprisonment not exceeding 10 years.

Art. 11 A person who, with the object stipulated in the preceding Article, has conferred with other [sic] person regarding the execution of the objective matters or a person who has instigated the execution of the objective matters, shall be punished with penal servitude or imprisonment not exceeding seven years.

Art. 12 A person who, with the object stipulated in Article 10, has instigated sedition, violent act [sic] or other crime injurious to life, body or property of a person, shall be punished with penal servitude or imprisonment not exceeding 10 years.

Art. 13 A person who has given or offered or promised to give money or other articles or property interests to other [sic] person with the object of causing him to commit crimes stipulated in the preceding three Articles, shall be punished with penal servitude or imprisonment not exceeding five years. This provision shall apply also to a person who knowingly has accepted or demanded or promised to accept said offering.

Art. 14 Attempts of the crimes stipulated in Articles 1 to 4, Article 7, Article 8 and Article 10 of the present law shall be punished.

Art. 15 When a person, who has committed any of the crimes stipulated in this Chapter, has surrendered himself to justice, punishment on his [*sic*] shall be mitigated or remitted.

Art. 16 Provisions of this Chapter shall also be applied to any person, who has committed either of the crimes under this law outside the territories where this law is in force.

Bibliography

OFFICIAL PUBLICATIONS AND DOCUMENTS

Domei Tsushin Sha (Press Alliance) (Trans. and Comp.) *Wartime Legislation in Japan: A Selection of Important Laws Enacted or Revised in 1941*. Tokyo: Nippon Shogyo Tsushin Sha, 1941.

Hasebe, Kingo. *Shisōhan no Hogo ni Tsuite* (On the Protection of Thought Offenders) in Shihōshō Chōsaka (Justice Ministry, Research Section) *Shihō Kenkyū* (Hōkoku Shoshū) (Justice Research, Collection of Reports). XXI, (10). March, 1937.

Higuchi, Masaru. "Sayoku Zenrekisha no Tenkō Mondai ni Tsuite" (On the Conversion of Individuals with Leftist Records) in Shihōshō Keijikyoku (Justice Ministry, Bureau of Criminal Affairs). *Shisō Kenkyū Shiryō Tokushū* (Thought Research Materials, Special Number). XCV. August, 1943.

Hiranuma, Kiichirō. "Showa Ishin" (Showa Restoration) in Monbushō (Education Ministry). *Kyōka no Shiryō* (Education Materials). 1929.

Itō, Miyoji. "Himitsu Kessha Nihon Kyōsantō Jiken no Gaiyō" (A Summary of a Secret Society: The Communist Party Incident) in Yamabe Kentarō (ed.). *Gendaishi Shiryō* (Materials on Contemporary History). XVI. Tokyo: Misuzu Shobō, 1965.

Japan. Hyōgo Ken Tokkōka (Hyōgo Prefecture, Special Higher Police Section). *Tokkō Keisatsu Reikishū* (A Collection of Special Higher Police Regulations). December, 1935.

———. Keisatsu Kenkyūkai (Police Research Institute). *Shakai Undō ni Chokumen Shite* (Confronted by the Social Movement). Tokyo: Shōkadō, 1932.

———. "Keishi Sōkan no Kenkyo ni Kansuru Tsūhō (August, 1928)" (Report on the Arrest in August, 1928, by the Superintendent-General of the Metropolitan Police) in Yamabe Kentarō (ed.), *Gendaishi Shiryō* (Materials on Contemporary History). XVI. Tokyo: Misuzu Shobō, 1965.

———. Kōan Chōsachō (Public Security Investigation Agency) (ed.). *Senzen ni Okeru Uyoku Dantai no Jōkyō* (Condition of Rightist Groups before the War). I. Tokyo: Kōan Chōsachō, 1964.

———. Kōchi Ken Tokubesu Kōtōka (Kōchi Prefecture, Special Higher Section). *Tokubetsu Kōtō Keisatsu Kankei Hōki Kaigi Shūroku* (A Collection of Laws and Regulations, with Explanations, in Connection with the Special Higher Police). *Tokkō Kyōyō Shiryō 9 gō* (Special Higher Educational Materials Number Nine). March, 1929.

———. Monbushō Gakuseibu (Education Ministry, Student Department). *Shisō Mondai ni*

205

Kansuru Ryōsho Senshō (Valuable Books in Connection with the Thought Problem: A Selected List to Encourage Reading). March, 1933.

———. Naimushō Keihokyoku (Home Ministry, Police Bureau). *Dai 50-kai Oyobi Dai 56-kai Teikoku Gikai Chian Ijihō ni Kansuru Sokkiroku* (Stenographic Record on the Peace Preservation Law at the Fiftieth and Fifty-Sixth Imperial Diets). 1929.

———. ———. *Dai 65-kai Teikoku Gikai Chian Ijihō Kaisei Hōritsuan* (Bill for the Revision of the Peace Preservation Law at the Sixty-Fifth Diet). 1934.

———. ———. *Kyōsanshugisha no Tenkō Hōsaku-Miteikō* (Policy for Converted Communists: A Rough Draft). 1935 (?).

———. ———. *Tokkō Geppō* (Monthly Special Higher Police Report). March, 1936.

———, ———. *Tokkō Keisatsu Reikishū* (Collection of Regulations for the Special Higher Police). 1939.

———. Shihōshō (Justice Ministry). Shihō Daijin Kanbō Hishoka (The Justice Minister's Secretariate). *Kunji Enjutsu Shū* (Collection of Oral Instructions). May, 1909–May, 1933.

———. ———. *Shihō Enkakushi* (Historical Records of the Justice [Ministry]). Tokyo: Hōsōkai, 1939.

———. ———. Chōsaka (Research Section). *Shihō Kenkyū* (Justice Research). IV. May, 1927. *Dai San-kai Jitsumuka Kaidō* (The Third Conference of Administrators).

———, ———. ———. *Shihō Kenkyū* (Justice Research). XVI. August, 1932. *Dai io-kai Jitsumuka Kaidō* (The Tenth Conference of Administrators).

———. ———. Keijikyoku (Bureau of Criminal Affairs). *Shisō Geppō* (Monthly Report on Thought). XXIII. May, 1936.

———. ———. ———. *Shisō Kenkyū Shiryō Tokushū* (Thought Research Materials, Special Number). XII. May, 1934. *Showa 8 nen 10 gatsu Shisō Jitsumuka Kaidō ni Okeru Kōenshū* (Collection of Lectures Given at the October, 1933 Conference of Thought Administrators).

———. ———. ———. *Shisō Kenkyū Shiryō Tokushū* (Thought Research Materials, Special Number). XVI. October, 1934. *Showa 9 nen 5 gatsu Shisō Jimu Kaidō Gijiroku* (Record of the Proceedings at the May, 1934, Conference on Thought Affairs).

———. ———. ———. *Shisō Kenkyū Shiryō Tokushū* (Thought Research Materials, Special Number). XXI. May, 1935. *Shisō Jimu ni Kansuru Kunrei Tsūchō Shū* (Collected Orders and Directives Concerning Thought Administration).

———. ———. ———. *Shisō Kenkyū Shiryō Tokushū* (Thought Research Materials, Special Number). XXII. September, 1935. *Showa 10 nen 6 gatsu Shisō Jitsumuka Kaidō Narabi ni Shihō Kenkyū Jitsumuka Kaidō Giji Sokkiroku* (Stenographic Record of the Proceedings at the Thought Administrators' Conference and the Justice Research Administrators' Conference in June, 1935).

———. ———. ———. *Shisō Kenkyū Shiryō Tokushū* (Thought Research Materials, Special Number). XXXIV. December, 1936. *Showa 11 nen 11 gatsu Shisō Jitsumuka Kaidō Giji Sokkiroku* (Stenographic Record of the Proceedings at the November, 1936, Conference of Thought Administrators).

———. ———. ———. *Shisō Kenkyū Shiryō Tokushū* (Thought Research Materials, Special Number). XXXVII. July, 1937. *Showa 12 nen 6 gatsu Shisō Jitsumuka Kaidō Giji Sokkiroku* (Stenographic Record of the Proceedings at the June, 1937, Conference of Thought Administrators).

———. ———. ———. *Shisō Kenkyū Shiryō Tokushū* (Thought Research Materials, Special

Number). XXXIX. October, 1937. *Showa 12 nen 9 gatsu Shisō Jitsumuka Kaidō Giji Sokkiroku* (Stenographic Record of the Proceedings at the September, 1937, Conference of Thought Administrators).

——. ——. ——. *Shisō Kenkyū Shiryō Tokushū* (Thought Research Materials, Special Number). XLV. August, 1938. *Showa 13 nendo 6 gatsu Shisō Jitsumuka Kaidō Giji Sokkiroku* (Stenographic Record of the Proceedings at the June, 1938, Conference of Thought Administrators).

——. ——. ——. *Shisō Kenkyū Shiryō Tokushū* (Thought Research Materials, Special Number). XLVII. January, 1939. *Showa 13 nendo Kōsoin Kannai Shisō Jitsumuka Kaidō Gijiroku* (Record of the Proceedings at the 1938 Conference of Thought Administrators within the Jursidiction of Appeals Courts).

——. ——. ——. *Shisō Kenkyū Shiryō Tokushū* (Thought Research Materials, Special Number). XLVIII. January, 1939. *Showa 13 nendo Kōsoin Kannai Shisō Jitsumuka Kaidō Gijiroku* (Record of the Proceedings at the 1938 Conference of Thought Administrators within the Jurisdiction of Appeals Courts).

——. ——. ——. *Shisō Kenkyū Shiryō Tokushū* (Thought Research Materials, Special Number). LVII. February, 1939. *Showa 13 nen 10 gatsu Shisō Jitsumuka Kaidō Kōenshū* (Sono I) (Collection of Lectures at the October, 1938, Conference of Thought Administrators, Part I).

——. ——. ——. *Shisō Kenkyū Shiryō Tokushū* (Thought Research Materials, Special Number). LIX. March, 1939. *Showa 13 nen 10 gatsu Shisō Jitsumuka Kaidō Kōenshū* (Sono II) (Collection of Lectures at the October, 1938, Conference of Thought Administrators, Part II).

——. ——. ——. *Shisō Kenkyū Shiryō Tokushū* (Thought Research Materials, Special Number). LXIV. September, 1939. *Showa 14 nen 6 gatsu Shisō Jitsumuka Kaidō Giji Sokkiroku* (Stenographic Record of the Proceedings at the June, 1939, Conference of Thought Administrators).

——. ——. ——. *Shisō Kenkyū Shiryō Tokushū* (Thought Research Materials, Special Number). LXXVIII. July, 1940. *Showa 14 nendo Kōsoin Kannai Shisō Jitsumuka Kaidō Gijiroku* (Record of the Proceedings at the 1939 Conference of Thought Administrators within the Jurisdiction of Appeals Courts).

——. ——. ——. *Shisō Kenkyū Shiryō Tokushū* (Thought Research Materials, Special Number). LXXIX. August, 1940. *Showa 15 nen 5 gatsu Shisō Jitsumuka Kaidō Gijiroku* (Record of the Proceedings at the May, 1940, Conference of Thought Administrators).

——. ——. ——. *Shisō Kenkyū Shiryō Tokushū* (Thought Research Materials, Special Number). LXXXVI. May, 1941. *Showa 15 nendo Kōsoin Kannai Shisō Jitsumuka Kaidō Gijiroku* (Record of the Proceedings at the 1940 Conference of Thought administrators within the Jurisdiction of Appeals Courts).

——. ——. ——. *Shisō Kenkyū Shiryō Tokushū* (Thought Research Materials, Special Number). LXXXVIII. October, 1941. *Showa 16 nen 4 gatsu Rinji Shisō Jitsumuka Kaidō Gijiroku* (Record of the Proceedings at the April, 1941, Extraordinary Conference of Thought Administrators).

——. ——. ——. *Shisō Kenkyū Shiryō Tokushū* (Thought Research Materials, Special Number). XC. January, 1942. *Showa 16 nen 7 gatsu Shisō Jitsumuka Kaidō Gijiroku* (Record of the Proceedings at the July, 1941, Conference of Thought Administrators).

———. ———. ———. *Shisō Kenkyū Shiryō Tokushū* (Thought Research Materials, Special Number) XCI. June, 1942. *Showa 16 nendo Kōsoin Kannai Shisō Kensatsu Kaidō Gijiroku* (Record of the Proceedings at the 1941 Conference on Thought Prosecution within the Jurisdiction of Appeals Courts).

Kawahara, Kenzō. "Gakusei Shisō Mondai" (Student Thought Problem) in Shihōshō Keijikyoku (Justice Ministry, Bureau of Criminal Affairs). *Shisō Kenkyū Shiryō Tokushū* (Thought Research Materials, Special Number). XII. May, 1934.

"Kōhan Hōdō ni Kansuru Shimbun Taisaku (1931)" (Countermeasures for Newspapers in Connection with Reporting on the Public Trial, 1931) in Yamabe Kentarō (ed.). *Gendaishi Shiryō* (Materials on Contemporary History). XVI. Tokyo: Misuzu Shobō, 1965.

Koyama, Matsukichi. "Meiji Jidai no Shakaishugi Undō ni Tsuite" (Socialism and Its Movement during the Meiji Period) in Shihōshō Keijikyoku (Justice Ministry, Bureau of Criminal Affairs). *Shisō Kenkyū Shiryō Tokushū* (Thought Research Materials, Special Number). LIX. March, 1939. *Showa 13 nen 10 gatsu Shisō Jitsumuka Kaidō Kōenshū* (Sono II) (Collection of Lecturers at the October, 1938, Conference of Thought Administrators, Part II).

Matsuzaka, Hiromasa. "San'ichigo, Yon'ichiroku Jiken Kaiko" (Recollection of the March 15 and April 16 Incidents) in Yamabe Kentarō (ed.). *Gendaishi Shiryō* (Materials on Contemporary History). XVI. Tokyo: Misuzu Shobō, 1965.

McLaren, W. W. "Government Documents, First Half of the Meiji Era, *"Transactions, Asiatic Society of Japan*, XLII, Part I (1914).

Miyagi, Minoru. "Watakushi no Keiken Yori Mitaru Kyōsantō Jiken no Shinri ni Tsuite" (On the Communist Party Incident Trial, from the Standpoint of My Experience) in Yamabe Kentarō (ed.). *Gendaishi Shiryō* (Materials on Contemporary History). XVI. Tokyo: Misuzu Shobō, 1965.

Nihon Kindai Shiryō Kenkyūkai (Association for Research on Modern Japanese Historical Materials) (ed.). *Taisho Kōki Keihokyoku Kankō Shakai Undō Shiryō* (Social Movement Materials Published by the Police Bureau during the Late Taisho Period). Tokyo: Nihon Kindai Shiryō Kenkyūkai, 1968.

"Nihon Kyōsantō Jiken ni Kanshi, Shiono Kenjisei Yori Chihō Kenjisei e no Tsūchō (Fu, Angō Tōin Meibo)" (Instructions to the District Chief Procurators from Chief Procurator Shiono in Connection with the Japanese Communist Party Incident, Party Membership List in Code Is Attached) in Yamabe Kentarō (ed.). *Gendaishi Shiryō* (Materials on Contemporary History). XVI. Tokyo: Misuzu Shobō, 1965.

Nitobe, Inazō. "Kokui wa Uchi yori Soto e" (National Prestige Moves Outward) in Monbushō (Education Ministry). *Kyōka no Shiryō* (Cultural Materials). 1929.

Okudaira, Yasuhiro (ed.). *Gendaishi Shiryō* (Materials on Contemporary History). XLV. Tokyo: Misuzu Shobō, 1973.

Omori, Megumu (ed.). *Tokkō Geppō: Sō Mokujishū* (Monthly Special Higher Police Report: Collection of the Entire Table of Contents). Tokyo: Sankō Bunken Kondankai, 1963.

Sakamoto, Hideo. "Shisōteki Hanzai ni Taisuru Kenkyū" (Research on Thought Crimes) in Shihōshō Chōsaka (Justice Ministry, Investigation Section). *Shihō Kenkyū* (Justice Research). VIII (6). December, 1928.

Shakai Bunkohen. *Showaki Kanken Shisō Chōsa Hōkoku* (Reports by the Authorities on Thought Investigation during the Showa Period). Tokyo: Kashiwa Shobō, 1965.

_____. *Taishoki Shisōdan Shisatsunin Hōkoku* (Reports on Thought Organizations and People under Surveillance during the Taisho Period). Tokyo: Kashiwa Shobō, 1965.

"Shihō Keisatsukan Oyobi Kenji no Torishirabe Kiroku (1928)" (Judicial Police and Procurators' Investigation Record, 1928) in Yamabe Kentarō (ed.). *Gendaishi Shiryō* (Materials on Contemporary History). XVI. Tokyo: Misuzu Shobō, 1965.

Tozawa, Shigeo. "Shisō Hanzai no Kensatsu Jitsumu ni Tsuite" (About the Business of Investigating Thought Crimes) in Yamabe Kentarō (ed.). *Gendaishi Shiryō* (Materials on Contemporary History). XVI. Tokyo: Misuzu Shobō, 1965.

Uchikawa, Yoshimi (ed.). *Gendaishi Shiryō* (Materials on Contemporary History). XL. Tokyo: Misuzu Shobō, 1973.

Wagatsuma, Sakae (ed.). *Kyū Hōreishū* (Collection of Former Laws and Regulations). Tokyo: Yūhikaku, 1968.

Yamabe, Kentarō (ed.). *Gendaishi Shiryō* (Materials on Contemporary History). XV–XVII, XIX–XX. Tokyo: Misuzu Shobō, 1965–1968.

BOOKS

Akita, George. "The Other Itō: A Political Failure," in Albert M. Craig and Donald H. Shively (eds.). *Personality in Japanese History.* Berkeley, Calif., University of California Press, 1970.

Akita, Ujaku. *Gojūnen Seikatsu Nenpu* (A Fifty-Year History of My Life). Tokyo: Naukasha, 1936.

Aoki, Kōji. *Nihon Rōdō Undō Shi Nenpyō* (A Chronology of the History of the Japanese Labor Movement). I. Tokyo: Shinseisha, 1968.

Aoki, Sadao. *Tokkō Kyōtei* (A Textbook for the Special Higher Police). Tokyo: Shinkōkaku, 1937.

Arima, Tatsuo. *The Failure of Freedom: A Portrait of Modern Japanese Intellectuals.* Cambridge, Mass.: Harvard University Press, 1969.

Asahi Jānaru. *Showashi no Shunkan* (Historical Moments during Showa). I. Tokyo: Asahi Shimbunsha, 1966.

Association for the Study of International Socialistic Ideas and Movements (ed.). *Japan's Conflict with the Evil of Bolshevism in the Far East.* Tokyo: Kokusai Shisō Kenkyūkai, 1937.

Ayakawa, Takeji. *Fuon Shisō no Shinsō to Sono Taisaku* (The Truth about Seditious Ideology and Countermeasures). Tokyo: Heisho Shuppansha, 1933.

Bamba, Nobuya. *Japanese Diplomacy in a Dilemma: New Light on Japan's China Policy, 1924–1929.* Vancouver, B. C.: University of British Columbia Press, 1972.

Beckmann, George M. "The Radical Left and the Failure of Communism," in James W. Morley (ed.). *Dilemmas of Growth in Prewar Japan.* Princeton, N.J.: Princeton University Press, 1971.

Beckmann, George M., and Okubo Genji. *The Japanese Communist Party, 1922–1945.* Stanford, Calif.: Stanford University Press, 1969

Bellah, Robert N. "Continuity and Change in Japanese Society," in Bernard Barber and Alex Inkeles (eds.). *Stability and Social Change.* Boston, Mass.: Little, Brown and Company, 1971.

_____. "Ienaga Saburō and the Search for Meaning in Modern Japan," in Marius B. Jansen (ed.). *Changing Japanese Attitudes Toward Modernization.* Princeton, N.J.: Princeton University Press, 1965.

Borg, Dorothy, and Shumpei Okamoto. *Pearl Harbor as History.* New York, N.Y.: Columbia University Press, 1974.

Blacker, Carmen. "Millenarian Aspects of the New Religions in Japan," in Donald H. Shively (ed.). *Tradition and Modernization in Japanese Culture.* Princeton, N.J.: Princeton University Press, 1971.

Butow, Robert C. *Tojo and the Coming of the War.* Princeton, N.J.: Princeton University Press, 1961.

Crowley, James B. "Intellectuals as Visionaries of the New Asian Order," in James W. Morley (ed.). *Dilemmas of Growth in Prewar Japan.* Princeton, N.J.: Princeton University Press, 1971.

―――. *Japan's Quest for Autonomy: National Security and Foreign Policy, 1930–1938.* Princeton, N.J.: Princeton University Press, 1966.

Dawson, William. *The German Empire, 1867–1914: And the Unity Movement.* I. Hamden, Conn.: Archon Books, 1966.

deBary, Wm. Theodore (ed). *Sources of Japanese Tradition.* II. New York, N.Y.: Columbia University Press, 1964.

Dore, R. P. "Education–Japan," in Robert E. Ward and Dankwart A. Rustow. *Political Modernization in Japan and Turkey.* Princeton, N.J.: Princeton University Press, 1964.

―――, and Ōuchi Tsutomu. "Rural Origins of Japanese Fascism," in James W. Morley (ed.). *Dilemmas of Growth in Prewar Japan.* Princeton, N.J.: Princeton University Press, 1971.

Dōshisha Daigaku Jinbun Kagaku Kenkyūjo (Doshisha University Social Science Research Center) (ed.). *Senjika Teikō Kenkyū: Kirisutosha Jiyūshugisha no Baai* (Research on Resistance during Wartime: The Case of the Christians and Liberals). 2 Vols. Tokyo: Misuzu Shobō, 1968–1969.

Duus, Peter. "Nagai Ryūtarō: The Tactical Dilemmas of Reform," in Albert M. Craig and Donald H. Shively (eds.). *Personality in Japanese History.* Berkeley, Calif.: University of California Press, 1970.

―――. *Party Rivalry and Political Change in Taishō Japan.* Cambridge, Mass.: Harvard University Press, 1968.

Egi Tasuku Kun Denki Hensankai (Society for the Compilation of the Biography of Egi Tasuku). *Egi Tasuku Den* (Biography of Egi Tasuku). Tokyo: Egi Tasuku Kun Denki Hensankai, 1939.

Erikson, Kai T. *Wayward Puritans: A Study in the Sociology of Deviance.* New York, N.Y.: John Wiley & Sons, Inc., 1966.

Fridell, Wilbur M. *Japanese Shrine Mergers, 1906–1912: State Shinto Moves to the Grassroots.* Tokyo: Sophia University, 1973.

Friedrich, Carl J., and Zbigniew K. Brzezinski. *Totalitarian Dictatorship and Autocracy.* New York, N.Y.: Frederick A. Praeger, 1965.

Fujita, Shōzō. "Showa Hachinen o Chūshin to suru Tenkō no Jōkyō" (Conversion Conditions around the Middle of 1933), in Shisō no Kagaku Kenkyūkai (Association for Scientific Research on Thought) (ed.). *Tenkō* (Conversion). I. Tokyo: Heibonsha, 1959.

Hackett, Roger F. "The Meiji Leaders and Modernization: The Case of Yamagata Aritomo," in Marius B. Jansen (ed.). *Changing Japanese Attitudes Toward Modernization.* Princeton, N. J.: Princeton University Press, 1965.

_____. *Yamagata Aritomo in the Rise of Modern Japan, 1838–1922*. Cambridge, Mass.: Harvard University Press, 1971.

Hall, John W. "A Monarch for Modern Japan," in Robert E. Ward (ed.). *Political Development in Modern Japan*. Princeton, N.J.: Princeton University Press, 1968.

Hall, Robert K. (ed.), and John O. Gauntlett (tran.). *Kokutai no Hongi: Cardinal Principles of the National Entity of Japan*. Cambridge, Mass.: Harvard University Press, 1949.

Hara, Keiichirō (ed.). *Hara Kei Nikki* (The Diary of Hara Kei). IX. Tokyo: Kangensha, 1950.

Hattori, Takaaki. "The Legal Profession in Japan: Its Historical Development and Present State," in Arthur T. von Mehren (ed.). *Law in Japan: The Legal Order in a Changing Society*. Cambridge, Mass.: Harvard University Press, 1963.

Henderson, Dan. F. "Law and Political Modernization in Japan," in Robert E. Ward (ed.). *Political Development in Modern Japan*. Princeton, N.J.: Princeton University Press, 1968.

Hiranuma Kiichirō Kaikoroku Hensan Iinkai (Committee for the Compilation of the Memoirs of Hiranuma Kiichirō). *Hiranuma Kiichirō Kaikoroku* (The Memoirs of Hiranuma Kiichirō). Tokyo: Gakuyō Shobō, 1955.

Hosono, Nagamori. *Shisō Akka no Moto* (The Causes for the Deterioration in Thought). Tokyo: Ganshōdō, 1930.

Ikeda, Katsu. "Chian Ijihō" (The Peace Preservation Law) in *Shin Hōgaku Zenshū* (A New Complete Collection of Jurisprudence). XIX. Tokyo: Nihon Hyōronsha, 1939.

Imai, Seiichi. *Taisho Demokurashī* (Taisho Democracy). *Nihon no Rekishi* (A History of Japan). XXIII. Tokyo: Chūō Kōronsha, 1966.

Inoue, Kiyoshi (ed.). *Taishoki no Seiji to Shakai* (Politics and Society during the Taisho Period). Tokyo: Iwanami Shoten, 1969.

Ishida, Takeshi. "The Development of Interest Groups and the Pattern of Political Modernization in Japan," in Robert E. Ward (ed.). *Political Development in Modern Japan*. Princeton, N.J.: Princeton University Press, 1968.

Ishihara, Masajirō. *Shisō Keisatsu Gairon* (An Introduction to the Thought Police). Tokyo: Shōkadō, 1930.

Ishii, Ryōsuke. *Japanese Legislation in the Meiji Era*. William J. Chambliss (trans. and ed.). Tokyo: Pan-Pacific, 1958.

Itō, Takashi. "Conflicts and Coalitions in Japan, 1930: Political Groups The London Naval Disarmament Conference," in Sven Groennings, E. W. Kelley, and Michael Leiserson (eds.). *The Study of Coalition Behavior: Theoretical Perspectives and Cases from Four Continents*. New York, N.Y.: Holt, Rinehart and Winston, Inc., 1970.

_____. "The Role of Right-wing Organizations in Japan," in Dorothy Borg and Shumpei Okamoto (eds.). *Pearl Harbor as History: Japanese-American Relations, 1931–1941)*. New York, N.Y.: Columbia University Press, 1974.

_____. *Showa Shoki Seijishi Kenkyū* (Research in the Political History of Early Showa). Tokyo: Tokyo Daigaku Shuppankai, 1969.

Iwamoto, Yoshio. "Aspects of the Proletarian Literary Movement in Japan," in Bernard S. Silberman and H. D. Harootunian (eds.). *Japan in Crisis: Essays on Taishō Democrary*. Princeton, N.J.: Princeton University Press, 1974.

Jansen, Marius B. "Changing Japanese Attitudes Toward Modernization," in Marius B.

Jansen (ed.). *Changing Japanese Attitudes Toward Modernization*. Princeton, N.J.: Princeton University Press, 1965.

Johnson, Chalmers. *Conspiracy at Matsukawa*. Berkeley, Calif.: University of California Press, 1972.

———. *An Instance of Treason: Ozaki Hotsumi and the Sorge Spy Ring*. Berkeley, Calif.: University of California Press, 1964.

Kakegawa, Tomiko. "The Press and Public Opinion in Japan, 1931–1941," in Dorothy Borg and Shumpei Okamoto (eds.). *Pearl Harbor as History: Japanese-American Relations, 1931–1941*. New York, N.Y.: Columbia University Press, 1974.

"Kanketsu ni Atatte (Zadankai)" (Toward a Conclusion, A Round-Table Talk), in Wagatsuma Sakae (ed.). *Nihon Seiji Saiban Shiroku, Showakō* (A History of Political Trials in Japan, Latter Showa). Tokyo: Daiichi Hōki Shuppan Kabushikikaisha, 1970.

Kawakami, Hajime. *Gokuchū Nikki* (Prison Diary). Tokyo: Sekai Hyōronsha, 1949.

Kawasaki Takukichi Denki Hensankai. *Kawasaki Takukichi*. Tokyo: Kawasaki Takukichi Denki Hensankai, 1961.

Kazahaya, Yasoji. *Seiji Hanzai no Shomondai* (Various Problems in Connection with Political Crimes). Tokyo: Kenshinsha, 1948.

Kikukawa, Tadao. *Gakusei Shakai Undōshi* (A History of the Student Social Movement). Tokyo: Chūō Kōronsha, 1931.

Kimbara, Samon. *Taishoki no Seitō to Kokumin* (Political Parties and the People during the Taisho Era). Tokyo: Hanawa Shobō, 1973.

Kita, Kazuo. *Nihon Kyōsantō Shimatsuki* (Account of the Disposal of the Japanese Communist Party). Tokyo: Shiokawa Shobō, 1929.

Kobayashi, Gorō. *Tokkō Keisatsu Hiroku* (A Secret Memoir on the Special Higher Police). Tokyo: Seikatsu Shinsha, 1952.

Kobayashi, Takiji. *Senkyūhyakunijūhachinen Sangatsu Jūgonichi, Kanikōsen, Tō Seikatsusha* (The Fifteenth of March, 1928, The Crab Cannery Boat, Party Life). Tokyo: Shin Nihon Shuppansha, 1963.

Kublin, Hyman. *Asian Revolutionary: The Life of Sen Katayama*. Princeton, N.J.: Princeton University Press, 1964.

Kubota, Akira. *Higher Civil Servants in Postwar Japan: Their Social Origins, Educational Backgrounds, and Career Patterns*. Princeton, N.J.: Princeton University Press, 1969.

Large, Stephen S. *The Rise of Labor in Japan: The Yūaikai, 1912–1919*. Tokyo: Sophia University, 1972.

Lensen, George A. *Japanese Recognition of the U.S.S.R.: Soviet-Japanese Relations, 1921–1930*. Tallahassee, Fla.: The Diplomatic Press, 1970.

Lifton, Robert J. *Thought Reform and the Psycology of Totalism: A Study of "Brainwashing" in China*. New York, N.Y.: W. W. Norton & Co., Inc., 1961.

Maezawa, Hiroaki (ed.). *Nihon Kokkai Nanajūnen Shi* (A Seventy-Year History of Japan's Diet). Tokyo: Shimbun Gōdō Tsūshinsha, 1953.

Maruyama, Masao. "Patterns of Individuation and the Case of Japan: A Conceptual Scheme," in Marius B. Jansen (ed.). *Changing Japanese Attitudes Toward Modernization*. Princeton, N.J.: Princeton University Press, 1965.

———. *Thought and Behaviour in Modern Japanese Politics*. Ivan Morris (ed.). London: Oxford University, 1963.

Masaki, Akira. *Reminiscences of a Japanese Penologist.* Tokyo: Japanese Criminal Policy Association, 1964.

Matsuo, Hiroya. "Kyoto Gakuren Jiken: Hatsudō Sareta Chian Ijihō" (The Kyoto Gakuren Incident: Putting the Peace Preservation Law into Motion) in Wagatsuma Sakae (ed.). *Nihon Seiji Saiban Shiroku, Showazen* (A History of Political Trials in Japan, Early Showa). Tokyo: Daiichi Hōki Shuppan Kabushikikaisha, 1970.

Miller, Frank O. *Minobe Tatsukichi: Interpreter of Constitutionalism in Japan.* Berkeley, Calif.: University of California Press, 1965.

Minear, Richard H. *Japanese Tradition and Western Law: Emperor, State, and Law in the Thought of Hozumi Yatsuka.* Cambridge, Mass.: Harvard University Press, 1970.

Mitchell, Richard H. *The Korean Minority in Japan.* Berkeley, Calif.: University of California Press, 1967.

Miyaji, Masato. "Morito Tatsuo Jiken: Gakumon no Jiyū no Hajime no Shiren" (The Morito Tatsuo Incident: The Beginning of Academic Freedom's Ordeal), in Wagatsuma Sakae (ed.). *Nihon Seiji Saiban Shiroku, Taisho* (A History of Political Trials in Japan, Taisho). Tokyo: Daiichi Hōki Shuppan Kabushikikaisha, 1969.

Miyazawa, Toshiyoshi. *Tennō Kikansetsu Jiken* (The Emperor as an Organ Theory Incident). Two Vols. Tokyo: Yūhikaku, 1970.

Moriyama, Takeichirō. *Shisōhan Hogo Kansatsuhō Kaisetsu* (An Explanation of the Thought Criminals' Protection and Supervision Law). Tokyo: Shōtokukai, 1937.

Morley, James W. "Introduction: Choice and Consequence," in James W. Morley (ed.). *Dilemmas of Growth in Prewar Japan.* Princeton, N.J.; Princeton University Press, 1971.

Morris, Ivan I. *Nationalism and the Right Wing in Japan: A Study of Post-war Trends.* London: Oxford University, 1960.

Nabeyama, Sadachika. *Watakushi wa Kyōsantō o Suteta Jiyū to Sokoku o Motomete* (I Discarded the Communist Party in My Search for Freedom and My Homeland). Tokyo: Daitō Shuppansha, 1950.

———, and Sano Manabu. *Tenkō Jūgonen* (Fifteen Years since Our Conversion). Tokyo: Rōdō Shuppanbu, 1949.

Nakamura, Hajime, "Basic Features of the Legal, Political, and Economic Thought of Japan," in Charles A. Moore (ed.). *The Japanese Mind.* Honolulu, Hawaii: University Press of Hawaii, 1967.

Najita, Tetsuo. *Hara Kei in the Politics of Compromise.* Cambridge, Mass.: Harvard University Press, 1967.

Nihon Bengoshi Rengōkai (ed.). *Nihon Bengoshi Enkakushi* (A History of the Development of Japanese Lawyers). Tokyo: Nihon Bengoshi Rengōkai, 1959.

Nihon Jānarisuto Remmei (League of Japanese Journalists). *Genron Dan'atsu Shi* (A History of the Suppression of Speech). Tokyo: Ichō Shobō, 1949.

Notehelfer, F. G. *Kōtoku Shūsui: Portrait of a Japanese Radical.* Cambridge, England: Cambridge University Press, 1971.

Odanaka, Toshiki. "Daiichiji Kyōsantō Jiken: Nihon Kyōsantō Sōritsu to Chian Ijihō Jidai Zenya no Saiban" (The First Communist Party Incident: The Establishment of the Communist Party and the Trial on the Eve of the Peace Preservation Law Era), in Wagatsuma Sakae (ed.). *Nihon Seiji Saiban Shiroku, Taisho* (A History of Political Trials in Japan, Taisho). Tokyo: Daiichi Hōki Shuppan Kabushikikaisha, 1969.

_____. "San'ichigo Yon'ichiroku Jiken: Chian Ijihō Saiban to Hōtei Tōsō" (The March 15 and April 16 Incidents: The Peace Preservation Law Trial and the Court Struggle), in Wagatsuma Sakae (ed.). *Nihon Seiji Saiban Shiroku, Showazen* (A History of Political Trials in Japan, Early Showa). Tokyo: Daiichi Hōki Shuppan Kabushikikaisha, 1970.

Ogawa Heikichi Bunsho Kenkyūkai Hen (Society for Researching and Compiling the Archives of Ogawa Heikichi). *Ogawa Heikichi Kankei Bunsho* (The Archives of Ogawa Heikichi). I. Tokyo: Misuzu Shobō, 1973.

Ohara Naoshi Kaikoroku Hensankai (Society for the Compilation of the Memoirs of Ohara Naoshi). *Ohara Naoshi Kaikoroku* (The Memoirs of Ohara Naoshi). Tokyo: Ohara Naoshi Kaikoroku Hensankai, 1966.

Ōkasumikai (Great Mist Society) (ed.). *Naimushōshi* (A History of the Home Ministry). I, IV. Tokyo: Zaidan Hōjin Chihō Zaimu Kyōkai, 1971.

Okudaira, Yasuhiro. *Political Censorship in Japan from 1931 to 1945.* Institute of Legal Research (Mimeographed). Philadelphia, Pa.: University of Pennsylvaina, 1962.

Ōtani, Keijirō. *Showa Kenpei Shi* (A History of the Military Police during Showa). Tokyo: Misuzu Shobō, 1966.

Ōuchi, Tsutomu. *Fashizumu e no Michi* (The Road to Fascism). *Nihon no Rekishi* (A History of Japan). XXIV. Tokyo: Chūō Kōransha, 1967.

Parsons, Talcott. *Politics and Social Structure.* New York, N.Y.: The Free Press, 1969.

Pittau, Joseph. *Political Thought in Early Meiji Japan.* Cambridge, Mass.: Harvard University Press, 1967.

Reed, John P. *Kokutai: A Study of Certain Sacred and Secular Aspects of Japanese Nationalism.* Chicago: The University of Chicago Libraries (Private Edition), 1940.

Reischauer, Edwin O. "What Went Wrong? in James W. Morley (ed.). *Dilemmas of Growth in Prewar Japan.* Princeton, N.J.: Princeton University Press, 1971.

Sasaki, Yoshizō. *Tokkō Zensho* (A Complete Book on the Special Higher Police). Tokyo: Shōkadō, 1933.

Sase, Shōzō. *Seiji Hanzairon* (An Essay on Political Crimes). Kyoto: Seikei Shoin, 1936.

Scalapino, Robert A. *Democracy and the Party Movement in Prewar Japan: The Failure of the First Attempt.* Berkeley, Calif.: University of California Press, 1962.

Shibata, Yoshihiko. *Shisō Torishimari Kankei Hōrei Hanrei Gakusetsu Sōran* (An Outline of Legal Precedents and Academic Theories in Connection with Thought Control). Tokyo: Ganshōdō Shoten, 1932.

Shinobu, Seizaburō. *Taisho Seijishi* (A Political History of the Taisho Period). Tokyo: Keisō Shobō, 1968.

Shiono Suehiko Kaikoroku Kankōkai (Society for the Publication of the Memoirs of Shiono Suehiko). *Shiono Suehiko Kaikoroku* (The Memoirs of Shiono Suehiko). Tokyo: Shiono Suehiko Kaikoroku Kankōkai, 1958.

Shisō no Kagaku Kenkyūkai (Association for the Scientific Study of Thought) (ed.). *Tenkō* (Conversion). Three Vols. Tokyo: Heibonsha, 1959–1961.

Smethurst, Richard J. *A Social Basis for Prewar Japanese Militarism: The Army and the Rural Community.* Berkeley, California: University of California Press, 1974.

_____. "The Military Reserve Association and the Minobe Crisis of 1935," in George M. Wilson (ed.). *Crisis Politics in Prewar Japan: Institutional and Ideological Problems of the 1930's.* Tokyo: Sophia University, 1970.

Smith, Henry D. *Japan's First Student Radicals,* Cambridge, Mass.: Harvard University

Press, 1972.

Solzhenitsyn, Aleksandr I. *The Gulag Archipelago, 1918–1956; An Experiment in Literary Investigation*. New York: Harper & Row, Pub., 1973.

Sone, Chūichi. *Tokkō Keisatsu to Shakai Undō no Gaisetsu* (An Outline of the Special Higher Police and the Social Movement). Yamagata: Yamagata Ken Keisatsubu Tokubetsu Kōtōka, 1930.

Spaulding, Robert M., Jr. "The Bureaucracy as a Political Force, 1920–1945," in James W. Morley (ed.). *Dilemmas of Growth in Prewar Japan*. Princeton, N. J.: Princeton University Press, 1971.

Steiner, Kurt. *Local Government in Japan*. Stanford, Calif.: Stanford University Press, 1965.

Storry, Richard. *The Double Patriots: A Study of Japanese Nationalism*. London: Chatto and Windus, 1957.

Suzuki Kisaburō Sensei Denki Hensankai (Society for the Compilation of the Biography of Suzuki Kisaburō). *Suzuki Kisaburō*. Tokyo: Suzuki Kisaburō Sensei Hensankai, 1945.

Takai, Kenzō. *Shihō Keisatsu Ron* (On Justice Police). Tokyo: Ganshōdō, 1924.

Takeuchi Kakuji Den Kankōkai (Association to Publish a Biography of Takeuchi Kakuji). *Takeuchi Kakuji Den* (A Biography of Takeuchi Kakuji). Tokyo: Sakai Shobō, 1960.

Tanaka, Tokihiko. "Toranomon Jiken: Kōtaishi o Sogeki Shita Namba Daisuke" (The Toranomon Incident: Namba Daisuke's Shot at the Crown Prince), in Wagatsuma Sakae (ed.). *Nihon Seiji Saiban Shiroku, Taisho* (A History of Political Trials in Japan, Taisho). Tokyo: Daiichi Hōki Shuppan Kabushikikaisha, 1969.

Tiedemann, Arthur E. "Big Business and Politics in Prewar Japan," in James W. Morley (ed.). *Dilemmas of Growth in Prewar Japan*. Princeton, N.J.: Princeton University Press, 1971.

Tokuda, Kyūichi, and Shiga Yoshio. *Gokuchū Jūhachinen* (Eighteen Years in Prison). Tokyo: Jiji Tsūshinsha, 1947.

Totten, George O. *The Social Democratic Movement in Prewar Japan*. New Haven, Conn.: Yale University Press, 1966.

Tōyama, Shigeki, and Adachi Toshiko. *Kindai Nihon Seijishi Hikkei* (A Handbook of Modern Japanese Political History). Tokyo: Iwanami Shoten, 1969.

Tsurumi, Kazuko. *Social Change and the Individual: Japan Before and After Defeat in World War II*. Princeton, N.J.: Princeton University Press, 1970.

Ushiomi, Toshitaka (ed.). *Gendai no Hōritsuka* (Modern Jurists). Tokyo: Iwanami Shoten, 1966.

Watanabe, Sōzō. *Hokkaido Shakai Undō Shi* (A History of the Social Movement in Hokkaido). Sapporo: Repōtosha, 1966.

Wilson, George M. *Radical Nationalist in Japan: Kita Ikki, 1883–1937*. Cambridge, Mass.: Harvard University Press, 1969.

Yamada, Yoshio. *Kokumin Seishin Sakkō ni Kansuru Shōsho Gikai* (Commentary on the Imperial Rescript in connection with the Prosperity of the People's Spirit). Tokyo: Tokyo Hōbunkan, 1923.

Yoshino, Sakuzō. *Nihon Musan Seitōron* (Comments on the Japanese Proletarian Political Parties). Tokyo: Ichigensha, 1929.

Young, A. M. *Japan in Recent Times, 1912–1926*. New York, N.Y.: William Morrow & Company, Inc., 1929.

ARTICLES

Altman, Albert A. "A Recently Discovered Document on Early Meiji Press Censorship Legislation," *Gazette,* XVII (Number 4, 1971), 217–223.

Bellah, Robert N. "Japan's Cultural Identity: Some Reflections on the Work of Watsuji Tetsurō," *The Journal of Asian Studies,* XXIV (August, 1965), 573–594.

Colegrove, Kenneth. "The Japanese Privy Council," *The American Political Science Review,* XXV (August, November, 1931), 589–614, 881–905.

Fisher, Galen M. "Revisiting Japan," *Amerasia,* I (July, 1937), 219–224.

Fridell, Wilbur M. "Government Ethics Textbooks in Late Meiji Japan," *The Journal of Asian Studies,* XXIX (August, 1970), 823–833.

Fridell, Wilbur M. "Notes on Japanese Tolerance," *Monumenta Nipponica,* XXVII (Autumn, 1972), 253–271.

Griffin, Edward G. "The Universal Suffrage Issue in Japanese Politics, 1918–25," *The Journal of Asian Studies,* XXXI (February, 1972), 275–290.

Havens, Thomas R. H. "Frontiers of Japanese Social History during World War II," *Shakai Kagaku Tōkyū* (Social Science Review), Waseda University, XVIII (March, 1973), 1–45.

Hurst, Michael. "What is Fascism?" *The Historical Journal,* XI (Cambridge, 1968), 165–185.

Ishida, Takeshi. "Urbanization and Its Impact on Japanese Politics—A Case of a Late and Rapidly Developed Country," *Annals of the Institute of Social Science,* Tokyo University, No. 8 (March, 1967), 1–11.

Kawahara, Hiroshi. " 'Chian Ijihō' no Suishinshatachi—'Chian Ijihō no Seiji Katei' " (Promoters of the Peace Preservation Law—the Political Process of the Peace Preservation Law), *Shakai Kagaku Tōkyū* (Social Science Review), XXXVIII (August, 1968), 1–25.

Lee, Edwin B. "Nichiren and Nationalism: The Religious Patriotism of Tanaka Chigaku," *Monumenta Nipponica,* XXX (Spring, 1975), 19–35.

Lifton, Robert J. "Thought Reform of Chinese Intellectuals; A Psychiatric Evaluation," *The Journal of Asian Studies,* XVI (November, 1956), 75–88.

Maruyama, Masao. "Japanese Thought," *Journal of Social and Political Ideas in Japan,* II (April, 1964), 41–48.

Matsumoto, Sannosuke. "The Significance of Nationalism in Modern Japanese Thought: Some Theoretical Problems," *The Journal of Asian Studies,* XXXI (November, 1971), 49–56.

Metheson, Walker G. "Japan Dams 'Dangerous Thoughts,'" *The Nation,* CXXVII (November 7, 1928), 504–505.

Mitchell, Richard H. "Japan's Peace Preservation Law of 1925: Its Origins and Significance," *Monumenta Nipponica,* XXVIII (Autumn, 1973), 317–345.

Okudaira, Yasuhiro. "Some Preparatory Notes for the Study of the Peace Preservation Law in Pre-war Japan," *Annals of the Institute of Social Science,* Tokyo University, No. 14 (1973), 49–69.

Pyle, Kenneth B. "The Technology of Japanese Nationalism: The Local Improvement

Movement 1900–1918," *The Journal of Asian Studies,* XXXIII (November, 1973), 51–65.

Rickett, W. Allyn. "Voluntary Surrender and Confession in Chinese Law: The Problem of Continuity," *The Journal of Asian Studies,* XXX (August, 1971), 797–814.

Seidensticker, Edward. "The Japanese Novel and Disengagement," *The Journal of Contemporary History,* II (April, 1967), 177–178.

Shiota, Shōbee. "Kazoku Kokka no Omomi" (The Weight of the Family Nation), *Asahi Jānaru* (Asahi Journal), VII (June 20, 1965), 74–78.

Spinks, Charles N. "Indoctrination and Re-education of Japan's Youth," *Pacific Affairs,* XVII (March, 1944), 56–70.

Stein, Guenther. "Through the Eyes of a Japanese Newspaper Reader," *Pacific Affairs,* IX (June, 1936), 177–190.

Thomas, A. F. "Japan's National Education," *Transactions and Proceedings of the Japan Society London,* XXXVI (1938–1939), 29–52.

Tsurumi, Shunsuke. "Cooperative Research on Ideological Transformation," *Journal of Social and Political Ideas in Japan,* II (April, 1964), 54–58.

Wildes, Harry E. "Japan Returns to Feudalism," *The Nation,* CXXIII (October 27, 1926), 436–438.

―――. "Press Freedom in Japan," *The American Journal of Sociology,* XXXII (January, 1927), 601–614.

Wilson, George M. "A New Look at the Problem of 'Japanese Fascism,'" *Comparative Studies in Society and History: An International Quarterly,* X (July, 1968), 401–412.

Young, A. Morgan. "Religious Revival in Japan, How It Serves the Purposes of Nationalism," *Asia,* XXXV (September, 1935), 542–545.

PERIODICALS

The Foreign Affairs Association of Japan (ed.). *The Japan Year Book, 1940–1941.* Tokyo: The Japan Times, 1940.

Shisō Tōsei (Thought Control), Tokyo, December, 1931.

BIBLIOGRAPHIES AND DICTIONARIES

Omori, Megumu (ed.). *Teikoku Kenpōka ni Okeru Shakai, Shisō Kankei Shiryō* (Materials in Connection With Society and Thought Under the Imperial Constitution). This is a compilation of articles originally published in *Misuzu,* November, 1960–July, 1961. Privately published in Tokyo. No date.

Kyoto Daigaku Bungakubu Kokushi Kenkyūshitsu (National History Research Division, Department of Literature, Kyoto University) (ed.). *Nihon Kindaishi Jiten* (A Dictionary of Modern Japanese History). Tokyo: Tōyō Keizai Shinpōsha, 1958.

Uyehara, Cecil H. *Leftwing Social Movements in Japan: An Annotated Bibliography.* Tokyo: The Charles E. Tuttle Co., 1959.

UNPUBLISHED MATERIAL

Durkee, Travers E. "The Communist International and Japan, 1919–1932." Unpublished Doctoral Dissertation, Stanford University, 1953.

Griffin, Edward G. "The Adoption of Universal Manhood Suffrage in Japan."
    Unpublished Doctoral Dissertation, Columbia University, 1965.
Nadolski, Thomas P. "The 1921 and 1935 Suppression of the Ōmoto Religious
    Movement, *Abstracts of the Papers to be Read at 19th International Conference of
    Orientalists in Japan* (May 24, 1974).
Steinhoff, Patricia G. "Tenkō: Ideology and Social Integration in Prewar Japan."
    Unpublished Doctoral Dissertation, Harvard University, 1969.
Yang, Eun Sik. "Katō Kōmei (1860–1926): Ethics Vs. Power in Political Leadership."
    Unpublished Doctoral Dissertation, Claremont Graduate School, 1971.
Yasko, Richard. "Hiranuma Kiichirō and Conservative Politics in Pre-war Japan."
    Unpublished Doctoral Dissertation, University of Chicago, 1973.

Index

Police: brutality (cont.)
tions of, 29; reports of, 24, 160;
Research Institute, 120–121; work of,
29; *see also* Higher Police, Justice
Police, Special Higher Police, *and*
Thought Police
Preliminary Examination Record, 35
Preventive detention, 122–123, 168–169;
see also Toyotama Prison
Prison System Research Committee, 98
Privy Council, 36; and peace law bills,
58–62, 89; role of, 60
Procurators, 35–37; powers of, 36; *see
also* Thought procurators
Propaganda, 50
Protection and Supervision Centers:
122–123, 135–136, 139, 187; Exam-
ination Commission of, 135–136; *see
also* Thought Criminals' Protection and
Supervision Law
Public Peace Police Law (Chian
Keisatsuhō), 45–47, 51, 51n, 88, 94;
legal loophole in, 45; main purpose of,
23
Public trial: of communists in Tokyo, 86,
104–109, 165; sentences at, 109; *see
also* Miyagi Minoru
Publication Law, 45–46, 73–74, 94; *see
also* Newspapers

Radicals (leftists), 30, 97; need for new
control methods, 33; a new breed, 97;
purge of professors, 93; *see also*
Anarchists, Japanese Communist Party,
Kawai Eijirō, Kōtoku Shūsui, Morito
Tatsuo, Ōsugi Sakae, *and* Ōuchi Hyōe
Red Flag, 82, 100, 157
Rehabilitation groups, 129–130; *see also*
Meitoku Kai, *and* Thought criminals
Revisionist bureaucrats, 174–175
Rice Riots (1918), 27, 31n
Rightists: criticism of, by justice officials,
113; number arrested and prosecuted
from 1935 to 1943, 160; outrageous
actions of, 124; special section for, in
Justice Ministry, 165; close watch set
on, after 1932, 159
Rōdō Zasshi (Labor Magazine), 156
Rōnōha (Labor-Farmer faction), 158
The Rules of Sociological Method, 184
Russia: Eastern Workers Communist

University, 100; restoration of
diplomatic relations with Japan, 58;
Revolution, 31n, 53
Russo-Japanese War (1904–1905), 26
Ryūho Shobun (charges withheld), 36

Saigō Takamori, 145
Saionji Kimmochi, 152
Saitō Makoto: Cabinet (1932–1934), 123
Sakai Toshihiko, 51n
Sakamoto Hideo, 94, 98
Sano Manabu, 103–104, 106, 109, 113,
122–123, 128, 141, 146; and *tenkō*,
109–111
Sano Shigeki, 172, 178
Sasaki Shōichi, 42, 75
Sase Shōzō, 121–122, 158
Satsuma-Chōshū, 27
Sedition: Morito Tatsuo case, 42
Seiyūkai party, 27, 49, 57–59, 81–82,
153, 176
Seitai (form of government), 50, 65
Shakaishugi Undō Geppō (Monthly Report
on the Socialism Movement), 29
Shiga Yoshio, 103, 105–106
Shihō Kenkyū (Justice Research), 78
Shimizu Heikurō, 76
Shinobu Seizaburō, 69–70
Shin'yūkai, 44, 44n
Shiono Suehiko, 37, 44, 80, 82–86, 98,
104, 112; as justice minister
(1937–1939), 164
Shisō Buhō (Thought Section Report), 78
Shisō Chōsa (Thought Investigation), 79,
94
Shisō Dantai Jōkyō (The Condition of
Thought Groups), 29
Shisō Hogo Geppō (Thought Protection
Monthly), 140n
Shisō Kenkyū Shiryō (Thought Research
Materials), 94
Shisō Tōsei (Thought Control), 150
Shisōhan Hogo Kansatsuhō, *see* Thought
Criminals' Protection and Supervision
Law
Showa regime (1912——), 19; Restor-
ation, 38, 175
Shrine merger movement, 26
Sino-Japanese conflict (July 1937), 161
Social Democratic Party, 127n
Social Masses' Party (Shakai Taishūtō),

**Thought Control in
Prewar Japan**

Designed by R. E. Rosenbaum.
Composed by Utica Typesetting Co., Inc.
in 10 point VIP Times Roman, 3 points leaded,
with display lines in Helvetica Bold.
Printed offset by LithoCrafters, Inc.
on Warren's Number 66 text, 50 pound basis.
Bound by LithoCrafters
in Columbia book cloth
and stamped in All Purpose foil.

Library of Congress Cataloging in Publication Data
(For library cataloging purposes only)

Mitchell, Richard H.
  Thought Control in Prewar Japan.

  Bibliography: p.
  Includes index.
  1. Internal security — Japan — History.   2. Political crimes and offenses — Japan —
History.   3. Japan — Politics and government — 1912–1945.   I. Title.
Law   345'.52'023   75-39566
ISBN 0-8014-1002-9